Rising Sea Levels

Rising Sea Levels

An Introduction to Cause and Impact

HUNT JANIN
and SCOTT A. MANDIA

McFarland & Company, Inc., Publishers
Jefferson, North Carolina, and London

Hunt Janin has written or cowritten nine other books for McFarland: *Trails of Historic New Mexico* (and Ursula Carlson, 2010), *Medieval Justice* (2009), *The University in Medieval Life* (2008), *Islamic Law* (and André Kahlmeyer, 2007), *The Pursuit of Learning in the Islamic World, 610–2003* (2006), *Four Paths to Jerusalem* (2006), *Fort Bridger, Wyoming* (2006), *Claiming the American Wilderness* (2006), *The India-China Opium Trade in the Nineteenth Century* (1999)

LIBRARY OF CONGRESS CATALOGUING-IN-PUBLICATION DATA

Hunt, Janin, 1940–
  Rising sea levels : an introduction to cause and impact /
Hunt Janin and Scott A. Mandia.
      p.   cm.
  Includes bibliographical references and index.

  ISBN 978-0-7864-5956-8
  softcover : acid free paper ∞

  1. Sea level — Climatic factors.   2. Coast changes.
3. Floods.   4. Climatic changes.   I. Mandia, Scott A., 1965–
II. Title.
GC89.J355 2012
551.45'8 — dc23   2012037149

BRITISH LIBRARY CATALOGUING DATA ARE AVAILABLE

On the cover: The Maeslant, the world's largest moveable storm surge barrier, is shown closed during a test. To protect the 1.5 million inhabitants of the Rotterdam area, the automated gates shut when storm surges cause the water level to reach 3 meters or higher over mean sea level (courtesy Rijkswaterstaat, part of the Dutch Ministry of Infrastructure and Environment)

Manufactured in the United States of America

McFarland & Company, Inc., Publishers
  Box 611, Jefferson, North Carolina 28640
  www.mcfarlandpub.com

Table of Contents

Appendices

Acknowledgments

We hereby extend our sincere thanks to all the men and women, living and working in many different parts of the world, who have *personally* helped us, by email or other means, as we have thought about, researched, wrote, and edited this introductory survey on rising sea levels. Listed in alphabetical order, these kind people include:

Richard Alley, David Anderson, Bilal Ayyub, Daniel Bailey, Bob Bindschadler, Mary Jean Buerer, Michael Blum, Ken Caldeira, Josh Carmichael, Ursula Carlson, Anny Cazenave, John Church, Robert Collier, John Cook, Piet Dircke, Pete Dunkelberg, Job Dronkers, Kerry Emanuel, Matthew England, Richard Edwing, Aslak Grinsted, Vivien Gornitz, Jonathan Gregory, William Hansen, Regine Hock, Simon Holgate, John Hunter, Pave Karat, Caroline Katsman, Richard Katz, Bob Kopp, Krishna Krishnamurthy, Manfred Lange, Robert Larter, Anders Leverman, John Marra, Michael Mastrandrea, Glenn Milne, David Miller, R.J. Nicholls, Jessica O'Reilly, Henry Pollack, Philippe Pypaert, Stefan Rahmstorf, John Reilly, Stefan Rimkus, Marci Robinson, Vladimir Ryabinin, Brent Saddler, Ted Scambos, the late Stephen Schneider, Konrad Steffen, Ken Sullivan, Claudia Tebaldi, Jim Titus, Kevin Trenberth, Emma van den Bosch, David Vaughan, Rob Verchick, Martin Vermeer, Peter Wadhams, Grace Wahlbrink, Harold Wanless, Phil Woodworth, Carl Wunsch, Jianjung Yin, Gary Yohe, and Jay Zwally.

Preface

This book is designed to be a clear, broadly-based, wide-ranging, introductory survey written for the educated general reader, that is, for someone who has only a limited knowledge of sea level rise — or perhaps none at all. Our fundamental point is easily stated. To quote Dr. John Church, one of the world's leading experts on sea level rise, it is this:

> It is obvious that there are clear policy and planning implications from present and rising sea levels. Much of society's past development has occurred in a period of relatively stable sea level. *The world is now moving out of this period and future coastal planning and development must consider the inevitable increase of regional sea level.*[1]

When technical terms are used for the first time in this book, they will be defined unless their meaning is self-evident. Endnotes are used here very generously, both for attribution and to provide additional information on points which are too detailed to be discussed in the text itself. To keep the text flowing along as briskly as possible, six "lesser issues" which are relevant to our story but not perhaps of cardinal importance have been relegated to the appendices. Readers who want more information on most of the subjects mentioned in the text will find excellent sources awaiting them in the extensive bibliography.

For the benefit of non–American readers, non-metric measurements (that is, imperial measurements used in the United States) in inches, feet, etc., will generally be given first, followed by their metric equivalents. If, however, we are quoting a source that gives only metric measurements, or one that gives them before imperial measurements, we will usually follow that format.

To prevent the text from getting bogged down in complicated explanations, some technical issues will be mentioned only in passing, if at all. In Chapter I, we offer a short primer on global warming. It is critically important for us to discuss global warming because this is a well-documented subject that lies at the very heart of debates over sea level rise, now and in the future. Indeed, one of the most important impacts of global warming will be the progressive rise in sea level throughout the 21st century — and well beyond.

Much like Blanche DuBois (the memorable character in Tennessee Williams's 1947 play *A Streetcar Named Desire*), during the long process of researching, writing, and editing this book we have always "depended on the kindness of strangers." By this we mean that many climate scientists and researchers have kindly given us their views in private communications, e.g., by email and by referring us to articles which they have written or have found useful. In some cases, they have also diligently read and commented on draft portions of this book. These very courteous and helpful men and women are listed in the Acknowledgments.

Some experts who read sections of this book in draft suggested numerous small changes in the text. Most of these changes we readily accepted. We want to stress here, however, that while we have profited mightily from the comments of others, any errors or omissions in this book are our responsibility alone.

To this we must add that some of the future-based analyses presented in this book are, necessarily, highly speculative. In the area of ice-sheet projections, for example, there is a good deal of disagreement today among well-informed experts on the most probable sea levels of the future. One of the greatest unknowns in projections for sea level rise in the future is what can best be described as "the potential for rapid dynamic collapse of ice sheets."[2] In less technical terms, this means that whereas it was previously believed that the thick ice sheets covering Greenland and Antarctica would take thousands of years to respond to global warming, it is now thought that they might possibly do so much more rapidly, e.g., conceivably even within decades rather than millennia.

It must be stressed here that although human-caused global warming is now considered "settled science," i.e., now considered a fact, by every international academy of sciences, the jury is still out on how much sea levels will rise in the future. What is a reasonable guess right now, however, is that many and — indeed, perhaps *most of*— the political, economic, and social impacts of rising seas will turn out, in the long term, be very detrimental to human societies as these societies are constituted. For the sake of the future generations who will be living in the coastal countries of the world, it is time to give careful thought to these matters right now.

Introduction

In the 1120s, the medieval scholar Bernard of Chartres told his students:

> We are like dwarfs standing on the shoulders of giants. We see better and further than they could, not because our perception is better or our learning more advanced, but because only we are borne aloft by their gigantic stature.[1]

In terms of the book you now hold, the biggest "giant" is surely the Intergovernmental Panel on Climate Change (hereafter cited in this book simply as the IPCC). This is an international scientific body, under the auspices of the World Meteorological Organization (WMO) and the United Nations Environment Programme (UNEP), and headquartered in Geneva, Switzerland. However, most of its work is done by researchers working in universities, data centers, and national laboratories scattered around the world.[2] Founded in 1988, the IPCC evaluates the scientific consensus on climate change, the likely effects of such change, and possible ways to deal with it.

(The terms "climate change" and "global warming" are often used interchangeably in the popular press. Technically and more accurately, however, climate change refers to change in any direction, and from all causes—both natural and man-made. Global warming, on the other hand, refers only to warming and is usually associated with the man-made component, not with natural changes.)

The "giant" analogy is colorful and is accurate enough in broad terms for the IPCC but it is also a bit imprecise: in fact, the IPCC is not *one*, but *many*. For example, its current Assessment Report (the Fourth Assessment Report, published in 2007) included contributions from more than 450 Lead Authors (i.e., the scientists in charge of one or more chapters of an Assessment Report), as well as from more than 800 contributing authors (i.e., the writers who produce text, graphs or data for inclusion by the lead authors).[3] The Fourth Assessment Report, along with numerous other IPCC publications, can be found on the IPCC's website: www.ipcc.ch.

The IPCC Fourth Assessment Workgroup I (WGI) leaves little doubt that the planet is rapidly warming and that humans are the primary cause.

A few of the WGI findings are as follows (the italicized phases were italicized by the IPCC)[4]:

- Global atmospheric concentrations of carbon dioxide, methane, and nitrous oxide have increased markedly as a result of human activities since 1750 and now far exceed pre-industrial values, as determined from ice cores spanning many thousands of years. The global increases in carbon dioxide concentration are primarily due to fossil fuel use and land-use change, while those of methane and nitrous oxide are primarily due to agriculture.
- Warming of the climate system is unequivocal, as is now evident from observations of increases in global average air and ocean temperatures, widespread melting of snow and ice, and rising global sea level.
- Most of the observed increase in globally averaged temperatures is *very likely* due to the observed increase in anthropogenic (man-made) greenhouse gas concentrations. Discernible human influences now extend to other aspects of climate, including ocean warming, continental-average temperatures, temperature extremes, and wind patterns.
- Even if greenhouse gas concentrations are somehow stabilized, additional sea rise totaling several meters will continue for centuries due to the long, slow time scales associated with climate processes and feedbacks.

The bottom line is that no international body of science holds a dissenting viewpoint. In fact, in 2010, after reviewing more current climate research, the United States National Academy of Sciences issued this strong statement:

> A strong, credible body of scientific evidence shows that climate change is occurring, is caused largely by human activities, and poses significant risks for a broad range of human and natural systems.... Some scientific conclusions or theories have been so thoroughly examined and tested, and supported by so many independent observations and results, that their likelihood of subsequently being found to be wrong is vanishingly small. Such conclusions and theories are then regarded as settled facts. This is the case for conclusions that the Earth system is warming and that much of this warming is very likely due to human activities.[5]

The IPCC's Fifth Assessment Report is due in 2013–2014. It will be released in four distinct sections[6]:

- Working Group I: The Physical Science Basis (this will include a chapter on sea level change)
- Working Group II: Impacts, Adaptation, and Vulnerability
- Working Group III: Mitigation of Climate Change
- Synthesis Report (this will integrate and compact the findings of the Working Groups into a readable and concise document for use by policymakers)[7]

Since the founding of the IPCC, many interested parties have been "borne aloft" by it. Indeed, the IPCC's work was so impressive that in 2007 the men and women who produced the Fourth Assessment Report were collectively awarded the Nobel Peace Prize. This award was also jointly given to Al Gore, the former vice president of the United States who became a climate-awareness activist. All this was, so to speak, the good news.

As might be expected, any document as large and as complex as the Fourth Assessment Report, which was nearly 3,000 pages long, was bound to contain a few errors. In 2009, glaciologists noticed that a serious mistake had crept into the text of the Working Group II report: namely, an erroneous claim that the Himalayan glaciers could disappear by 2035. (Glaciers are slow-moving rivers of ice, formed from compacted snow, that slowly deform and flow in response to gravity. Glacier ice is the largest reservoir of the world's supply of fresh water.) A network of well-funded and highly vocal individuals and organizations who refuse to accept the findings of the IPCC quickly seized upon this mistake on and a few other real or purported errors and demanded that the IPCC itself either be completely restructured or be abolished entirely. It should be noted here that no errors have been found in the Working Group I report, which focuses on the underlying science, i.e., climate change. As an analogy, one would not throw away an entire encyclopedia set if a few random errors were found within.

On the other hand, the IPCC has also been criticized for being far too cautious—for example, by underestimating the prospects for sea level rise.[8] In 2007, the IPCC projected that by 2100 sea level would only rise between 0.59–1.93 feet (0.18–0.59 meters), depending on which of six possible climate model scenarios turns out to be the most realistic one.[9] These IPCC figures, however, *purposefully* did not include an estimate for ice sheet dynamics. This term refers to accelerated ice flow toward the edges of the ice sheets, which can be continent-sized glaciers up to several miles thick.

Ice sheets are not static slabs of ice: on the contrary, they are always in motion. In a never-ending ballet, snow is constantly added to the top and is eventually compressed into ice, while ice is constantly lost at the margins, thanks to the huge glaciers flowing from the interior out towards the edges of Greenland and into the sea. Ice sheets are expected to shrink in size as the world continues to warm; this melting will contribute to sea level rise.[10] Ice is also lost due to calving (the breaking-off of big blocks of ice at the face of a glacier) and to the disintegration of ice shelves themselves. (An ice shelf is a thick, floating platform of ice that forms where a glacier or ice sheet flows down to a coastline and thence out onto the ocean surface.)

We must note in this context that in 2002 the Larsen B Ice Shelf in Antarctica — a 2,018-mile-long (3,250 kilometer) section of ice estimated to be over 10,000 years old and 650 feet (198 meters) thick — disintegrated completely within six weeks.[11] Prior to its breakup, local air temperatures had increased by more than 2.7 degrees Fahrenheit (1.5 degrees Celsius) over the previous 50 years. The melting or breakup of ice shelves, however, does not change the sea level significantly[12] because the ice shelves are floating and are already in hydrostatic equilibrium with the underlying sea — much like melting ice cubes in a glass of water do not cause the water to rise and overflow the glass. The ice at the other end of the world — the North Pole — is not nearly as thick as the ice around the South Pole and it floats on the Arctic Ocean. If it melted, sea levels would not be significantly affected, either.

The IPCC was of course aware of ice sheet dynamics but since there were no agreed-upon published studies of them, it did not feel free to address them in its own report. As a result, its sea level rise estimates were clearly too conservative. The upshot of these and other related climate-change controversies was that the Secretary-General of the United Nations and the Chairman of the IPCC jointly asked the Amsterdam–based InterAcademy Council to review the IPCC's procedures for writing its reports. The essence of this review, completed in August 2010, was that the IPCC had earned good marks on substantive matters but not on management issues:

> The process used by the Intergovernmental Panel on Climate Change to produce its periodic assessment reports has been successful overall, but IPCC needs to fundamentally reform its management structure and strengthen its procedures to handle ever larger and increasingly complex climate assessments as well as the more intense public scrutiny coming from a world grappling how best to respond to climate change.[13]

Global warming remains a complex and controversial subject. As Denmark's Ministry of Energy and Climate has put it,

> Predicting the consequences of global warming is one of the really difficult tasks for the world's climate researchers.... Many of the effects of global warming have been well-documented, and observations from real life are very much consistent with earlier predictions. It is the precise extent [and the rate of change] that is difficult to quantify."[14]

These processes are under continual study and computer modeling. In 2011, Dr. Gavin Schmidt, a climate modeler at the NASA Goddard Institute for Space Studies, had this to say about the Greenland and Antarctic ice sheets:

> The ice sheets themselves are the biggest challenge for climate modeling since we don't have direct evidence for many of the key processes that occur at the ice sheet base (for obvious reasons), nor even of what the topography or conditions are at the base itself. And, of course, the future fate of the ice sheets and how they will respond dynamically to climate warming is hugely important for pro-

jections of sea level rise and polar hydrology. The fact that the ice sheets will respond to warming is not in doubt (note the 4–6 m [13.1–19.6 feet] sea level rise during the last interglacial [a warmer era 125,000 years ago]), but the speed at which that might happen is highly uncertain...[15]

If both these sheets melted completely, the Antarctic ice sheet, which covers about 5.4 million square miles (14 million square kilometers) and is the largest in the world, would add — very roughly — 190 feet (52.8 meters) to the level of the sea. The Greenland ice sheet (the second largest in the world — it covers 80 percent of the surface of Greenland — would add, again very roughly, an additional 21.6 feet (6.6 meters).[16]

In this worst case and highly unlikely (in the short term) "total melt" scenario, the concomitant melting of all the other ice caps (masses of ice that cover highland areas), ice fields, and valley glaciers in the world might contribute an additional 1.4 feet (0.45 meters) to the overall rise. If so, the total rise would then peak at more than 196 feet (60 meters) above today's level. Needless to say, the impact of such a rise on the coastal societies of the world would be devastating. Chapter I will have much more to say about global warming.

I

A Short Primer on Global Warming

Our planet is now well into a new geologic epoch, which can justly be called the "Anthropocene" (*anthropo* = human; *cene* = new), during which the human activities that give rise to global warming will be responsible for many of the changes in the Earth's environment.[1] As used here, global warming refers to (1) the increase in the average temperatures of the near-surface air and oceans of the Earth which has been observed since the early part of the 20th century, and (2) the expected continuation of these increases during the decades to come.

The global sea level rose gradually during the 20th century and is now rising at an even faster rate.[2] As a general statement, sea levels are rising worldwide, with a few local exceptions; by this same token, they are of course rising along much of the coast of the United States.[3] To understand this important and potentially threatening process, we first need to come to grips with global warming itself, if only in the most general terms. This concept deserves center-stage here because current sea level rise is primarily due to global warming. Unfortunately, global warming is both a scientifically complex and a politically controversial subject. Indeed, it is one of the most complicated and difficult issues facing world leaders today. This, in a nutshell, is the problem:

- The dangers posed by global warming, especially by rising levels of greenhouse gases, are becoming more evident every year. After an exhaustive review of the science, the U.S. Environmental Protection Agency officially concluded in 2009 that greenhouse gases threaten the public health and welfare of the American people.[4] Legally, this finding opens the door for a more active regulatory role by the U.S. Government. Moreover, rapidly rising greenhouse gas concentrations may lead to fundamental and irreversible ecological changes. Impacts of man-made climate change now include decreasing ocean productivity, altered food web dynamics, reduced abundance of habitat-forming species, and changing species distribution.[5]

• Nevertheless, despite the health, welfare and other dangers posed by green-house gases, no *legally-binding*, effective, international correctional measures are likely in the foreseeable future. (See Appendix 1 for brief discussions of Climate Change Conferences: the 2009 Copenhagen Conference, the 2010 Cancun Conference, and the 2011 Durban Conference.) The fundamental reasons for this inaction are that most world leaders believe — incorrectly, in our view — that the political, economic, and social costs involved are simply too great. Furthermore, it is difficult to activate citizens on an issue that appears to be very far removed from their more pressing personal and financial concerns.

Some technical definitions and explanations are necessary at this point. Global surface temperature is based on air temperature data over land and sea-surface temperatures observed from land stations, ships, buoys, and satellites. The global temperature record is one of the most-cited indicators of global climate change and it shows an increase of approximately 1.4 degrees Fahrenheit (0.8 degrees Celsius) since the early twentieth century. Over the last 30 years, the warming trend has been much more dramatic, with about 0.3 degrees Fahrenheit (0.17 degrees Celsius) per decade and, according to the IPCC, is likely to continue.

Despite the unmistakable evidence of a long-term warming trend, a given year does not always show a temperature increase relative to the previous year, and some years show greater changes than others. These year-to-year fluctuations in temperature are due to natural processes, such as (among others) the effects of the El Niño/La Niña Southern Oscillation (a quasi-periodic climate pattern that occurs across the tropical Pacific) and the eruption of enough volcanoes capable of injecting large amounts of aerosol particles into stratosphere. Notably, the 20 warmest years have all occurred since 1981, and the ten warmest years have all occurred since 1998. Each of the three previous decades has set a record as the warmest decade in the instrumental period. This decade is already beginning at a record pace because 2010 was tied with 2005 as the warmest year on record.

"Anthropogenic global warming" (often abbreviated in climate literature as "AGW") refers to that portion of present warming which can be attributed to human activities, primarily the addition of greenhouse gases from fossil fuel burning and, to a lesser, extent from emissions from land-use changes. In less technical terms, this is to say that human beings are responsible for overloading the air with heat-trapping greenhouse gases, such as carbon dioxide, methane, and others.

If current levels of greenhouse gas emissions *simply remain constant*, rather than increase (as they are very likely to do), there will certainly be

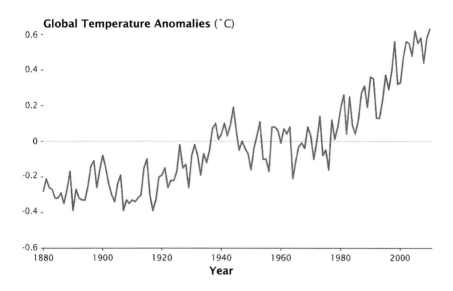

Global Temperature Anomalies (˚C)

Global air temperature anomalies (deviation from the 1960–1990 average). In 2010, global temperatures continued to rise. 2010 tied with 2005 as the warmest year on record and was part of the warmest decade on record. Note that 0.6 degrees C equals 1.04 degrees F (NASA/Earth Observatory/Robert Simmon).

additional global warming throughout the 21st century and beyond — because the climate system has not yet caught up with the heat imbalance caused by humans. With increasing concentrations of these gases, warming on the Earth can only be greater in this century than it has been over recent decades.

Climatologists refer to the factors that initiate the process of climate change as "forcings." These forcings hasten the rate of progress or growth and include changes in atmospheric composition (chiefly greenhouse gas concentrations), changes in solar luminosity, products of volcanic eruptions, and changes in the Earth's orbit around the sun. "Responses" are the effects that occur as a result of forcings. Some of these responses can act themselves like forcings; when they do, they are known as "feedbacks."

At the top of the Earth's atmosphere, there is normally a balance between the incoming radiation from the sun and the outgoing infrared radiation from the Earth. Radiative forcing refers to the difference in incoming vs. outgoing radiation. Such forcing causes climate to change until the forcing becomes zero once again and a new climate is established. Radiative forcing can result from changes in the composition of the atmosphere, in addition to the presence of heat-trapping gases or volcanic materials that reflect sunlight; changes at the Earth's surface, such as the amount of snow or vegetation, which can alter the reflectivity of the surface; or by changes in solar output.

While the amount of radiative forcing from the sun itself has probably changed only slightly in the last several hundred years (it is customary to use the year 1750 as the starting point for this estimate), greenhouse gases have increased radiative forcing since then.[6] The IPCC has concluded that only 0.18 degrees Fahrenheit (0.1 degrees Celsius) of the 1.44 degrees Fahrenheit (0.8 degrees Celsius) warming since the Industrial Revolution has been caused by the sun, and that since 1980 changes in solar intensity have been negligible. The IPCC also judged, in its Fourth Assessment Report (2007), that it is "very likely"—i.e., there is a greater than 90 percent probability—that global warming since 1950 has been forced, i.e., driven, mainly by the buildup of carbon dioxide and other heat-trapping greenhouse gases. Such gases are often generated by human activities, e.g., burning fossil fuels (petroleum, coal, and natural gas), deforestation, and other land-use changes.

Today, responsible people who study global warming carefully do not dispute the IPCC's judgment on the effects of greenhouse gases. This finding has been endorsed by all major national academies of science and by every significant international scientific society. While there is still a good deal of intellectual room to discuss details and to learn more, today there is little substantive basis to challenge the concept itself. It is simply too heavily supported by observational and experimental evidence to be dismissed. Indeed, it seems likely that global warming is now the most carefully and most fully studied scientific topic in human history. As a result, most of the responsible debate now going on is about *regional changes*, which usually are different from (i.e., larger or smaller) the global average. These regional changes are much more affected by local natural variability and are difficult to predict.

Nevertheless, there is a small fringe of highly vocal—indeed, often *strident*—"global warming critics" scattered throughout the scientific, financial, political, and media communities.[7] These individuals dispute some or all of the international scientific findings on global warming. They ask whether other environmental effects (e.g., solar activity, natural climate cycles, divine intervention, etc.) could be the causes of warming temperatures. They also question both the dangers to the human community posed by global warming and the costs of remedial efforts (e.g., limits on carbon dioxide emissions).

There is still much responsible debate about the maximum warming that might occur. For our purposes here, it will be accepted that further global warming and—as an inevitable result, higher sea levels—can be expected in the years, decades, and centuries ahead. As the U.S. Climate Change Science Program[8] puts it, in conservative and understated terms:

> Understanding of the magnitude and timing [of the processes responsible for sea level rise] is limited and, thus, there is currently no consensus on the upper bound of sea level rise. Recent studies suggest the potential for a meter [3.2 feet]

or more of global sea level rise by the year 2100, and possibly several meters within the next several centuries.[9]

It is not impossible that the rise by 2100 may be appreciably higher than expected. A 2009 semi-empirical study (e.g., a study using observed sea level data and their link to temperature) by sea level rise experts Drs. Stefan Rahmstorf and Martin Vermeer forecast a rise of 3.7 feet (114 centimeters) by 2095 and of 4.0 feet (124 centimeters) by 2100. This study was based on the concept that the rate of sea level rise is proportional to the amount of global warming, i.e., the warmer it gets, the faster the ice melts and the higher the sea rises.[10]

In 2011, an updated assessment of the net mass balance of Antarctica and Greenland (i.e., how much ice is there) showed that the downward trend in ice mass is continuing. Extrapolating these melt rates forward to 2050, the results are very close to the best estimate of Rahmstorf and Vermeer for that year. If this melt rate continues, ice sheets will be the dominant contributor to sea level rise in the 21st century.[11]

A "high-risk, low-probability" scenario for the United Kingdom has forecast a maximum sea level rise there of up to 6.2 feet (1.9 meters) by 2100.[12] A Stanford University study in 2010 predicted that a 6.5 feet (2 meters) sea level rise was "a conservative scenario" for a 100-year time frame.[13] (A "100-year flood" is the standard used in the U.S. by the National Flood Insurance Program for floodplain management and to determine the need for flood insurance.) A 2011 study by Dr. Robert J. Nicholls et al. also put the credible upper boundary of such a rise at 6.5 feet (2 meters), while warning that while there is a only a low probability of such a rise, this probability cannot be quantified now.[14] Looking much further ahead, a 2011 study by S. Jevrejeva and others forecast a rise of 18 feet (5.49 meters) by 2500.[15]

It is very difficult to estimate future sea level rise accurately because it is an enormous challenge to get a better estimate of dynamic ice sheet processes, e.g., the likely contributions from the melting of the Greenland Ice Sheet and the West Antarctic Ice Sheets (the latter is often abbreviated in climate-change literature as "WAIS).[16]

Because the WAIS itself has been nicknamed "the 800-pound gorilla" of sea level rise, we will devote a separate chapter to it later in this book. Perhaps we should explain here that the phrase "800-pound gorilla" is a humorous expression in English.[17] It refers to a creature that is so big, so powerful, and so uncontrollable when aroused that it can do precisely what it wants to do, without any regard for the needs or feelings of others. Indeed, it is up to others to take full account of the potential dangers posed by this "gorilla."

Let us now consider some of the historical background of our present understanding of global warming, beginning in the early decades of the 19th century.[18]

In 1827, Joseph Fourier, once a mathematician in Napoleon's army, hit upon the concept of the greenhouse effect. Scientists had discovered in 1800 that energy is transmitted by infrared radiation, which is invisible to the naked eye. Fourier perceived that, if this energy is blocked by atmospheric gases, the temperature of the Earth will rise as these gases absorb and redirect the outgoing infrared radiation, causing a portion of the energy to build up in the atmosphere and warm the Earth.

This is similar to what happens in a greenhouse. A greenhouse is an enclosed structure with a glass or plastic roof and frequently with glass or plastic walls as well. It heats up because incoming solar radiation (e.g., heat) from the sun warms the plants and soil in the building. Although solar radiation enters the greenhouse, the heat from within the greenhouse cannot escape through the glass. (Technically speaking, the greenhouse effect is a misnomer: a greenhouse suppresses convection, i.e., the circulation of hot air, and not radiation.)

It is worth stressing here that the impact of the greenhouse effect on the world today is not disputed by responsible scientists. It is widely understood that, in general terms, incoming short wave radiation, much of which goes through the atmosphere, is converted to long wave radiation when it is re-radiated from the ground into wavelengths partially blocked by the atmosphere. Here is a more technical explanation of this phenomenon, kindly provided by Dr. Kevin Trenberth, head of the National Center for Atmospheric Research (NCAR):

> Radiant solar or shortwave energy is transformed into sensible heat, latent energy (involving different water states), potential energy (involving gravity and height above the surface) (or in the oceans, depth below) and kinetic energy (involving motions) before being emitted back to space as longwave radiant energy.[19]

The Earth's climate depends on this fact: if our atmosphere had no greenhouse gases at all, the average global temperature of the Earth would be about 1.4 degrees Fahrenheit (-17 degrees Celsius).

In 1859, John Tyndall identified carbon dioxide, "olefiant gas" (that is, ethylene), several other organic compounds, and water vapor (the gas phase of water) as greenhouse gases. In 1862, he described, in a graceful metaphor, how they function. Tyndall wrote:

> As a dam built across a river causes a local deepening of the stream, so our atmosphere, thrown as a barrier across the terrestrial rays, produces a local heightening of the temperature of the earth's surface.[20]

When humans add greenhouse gases to the atmosphere, the level where outgoing radiation can escape to space moves to a higher and colder location. Cold air does not emit as much outgoing radiation. Because the incoming solar radiation is unchanged, there will be less heat leaving the planet than coming in. The result will be a warmer lower atmosphere. This is known as the enhanced greenhouse effect.

In terms of the total greenhouse effect, water vapor is by far the most important greenhouse gas, accounting for about 60 percent of the greenhouse effect under clear skies. Under typical atmospheric conditions, water vapor is continuously generated by evaporation and is removed by condensation. The amount of water vapor the air can have present is a function of the temperature of the air itself. Thus, as concentrations of carbon dioxide warm the atmosphere, more water vapor can be present in the air. This is known as the "water vapor positive feedback" effect — a process that is sufficient to roughly double the amount of warming which occurs with increasing carbon dioxide alone.[21]

Although water vapor is such a powerful greenhouse gas, it has only a short atmospheric lifetime. Water vapor in the atmosphere is part of an active climate system, and any excess will rain out in days. On the other hand, the lifetime of an excess carbon dioxide concentration in equilibrium in the atmosphere runs into decades, so it has a persistent forcing on climate.

Carbon dioxide is the second most important greenhouse gas, accounting for about 26 percent of the greenhouse effect. It lasts longer in the atmosphere than many of the other greenhouse gases released by human beings, and is relatively inert. The processes that remove it permanently act only slowly. Sources of carbon dioxide include the burning of coal, oil, and natural gas. If we are serious about limiting climate change, we must limit the emission of carbon dioxide. The rate of emission, however, has soared in recent decades.

Methane is another greenhouse gas. Unlike carbon dioxide, however, it does not persist in the atmosphere for an exceptionally long period of time. A molecule of methane survives on average for approximately nine years. There are present and potential natural sources of methane: for example, swamps and — if the Earth warms sufficiently — the vast permafrost regions of the Arctic as well. There are also numerous man-made sources. These include the artificial wetlands established for rice farming, the fossil fuel industry, waste natural gas emissions, landfills, livestock production, and biomass decomposition.

Halocarbons are man-made gases used in refrigerators and air conditioners. They are very powerful greenhouse gases because they absorb a wide range of radiation. Another greenhouse gas is ozone. In the lower atmosphere, it is an air pollutant with harmful effects on the respiratory systems of animals and will burn sensitive plants. In the upper atmosphere, however, the ozone layer is beneficial: it prevents potentially damaging ultraviolet light from reaching the Earth's surface.

Still another greenhouse gas is nitrous oxide, which is also known as "laughing gas" or "happy gas" because, beginning in about 1835, it was used to dull pain during medical and dental procedures and it created euphoria in otherwise healthy people. It is now used in rocket motors and in high-performance internal combustion engines. Any discussion of global warming must necessarily involve ice, which will be discussed repeatedly in this book. It is estimated that today about 10 percent of the Earth's surface is covered by ice.[22] Three general categories of ice are contributors to global sea level rise:

- The continent-size ice sheets of Antarctica and Greenland, which drain into the seas via ice streams (relatively faster-moving "rivers" of ice bounded by walls of slower ice) or via outlet glaciers.
- The mountain glaciers and ice caps which are located elsewhere. Their mass balance (the difference between the amount of snow accumulated during the winter and the amount of snow and ice removed by melting during the summer) was slightly below zero around 1970 and has been growing more negative since then.[23] In short, they are melting. Indeed, during the last decade, they have been melting at about twice the rate of the previous several decades.[24]
- The third category is snow, which has a very large seasonal component.

There are now, very roughly, between 6.2 and 7.2 million cubic miles (26 to 30 million cubic kilometers) of ice in all the world's ice sheets, ice caps, and mountain glaciers. Ice plays a pivotal role in the climate of the Earth and especially in sea level rise. Indeed, if all the land ice in the world were to melt, this would cause a sea-level rise of more than 196 feet (60 meters).[25]

Because ice and snow reflect sunlight, when present they tend to cool the Earth. When ice melts due to atmospheric or hydrospheric warming, however, the darker ground or darker water underneath it absorbs more energy from sunlight, so the initial warming is amplified. This process is known as the "ice albedo feedback" (after "albedo," the Latin word for "whiteness").

The ice albedo feedback can now be seen in the Arctic. With the rapid loss of Arctic Ocean sea ice during the summer months, the albedo of this ocean is changing: the balance between the white ice and the dark water of the ocean is shifting toward more darkness. Thus, gradually, the albedo is falling. Less sunshine is being reflected; more is being absorbed. In climate terms, this means that the Arctic is rapidly becoming warmer because it is retaining more solar energy.[26]

In recent decades, the rise in Arctic near-surface air temperatures has been almost twice as large as the global average. This has been demonstrated by a disturbing trend in the reduction of Arctic sea ice during the boreal summer. (There has been speculation that Arctic summers may be completely ice-free as early as 2030.) The reasons for this striking trend, which is known as "Arctic amplification," are not yet fully understood. Possible explanations include changes in cloud cover, increases in atmospheric water vapor, more atmospheric and oceanic heat transport from lower latitudes, and declining sea ice.[27]

Although all of the information presented above is freely available to the public, climate change has long been a controversial subject. This is still true today, even though between 97 percent and 98 percent of the 1,372 climate researchers whose work was reviewed in one study in 2010 supported the tenets of anthropogenic climate change. Moreover, this study also concluded that the level of climate expertise and the scientific prominence of the researchers who were not convinced by the reality of anthropogenic climate change was *substantially below* that of the convinced researchers.[28]

Nevertheless, for variety of reasons (most of them based on non-scientific criteria), a sizeable minority of citizens remains unconvinced about the nature of climate change. For example, the Yale Project on Climate Change Communication found that one of the groups it polled — which it identified as the "Dismissive," i.e., those who believe that global warming is not happening and is probably a hoax — more than doubled in size since 2008. In 2009 this group included 16 percent of the American public.[29]

In an October 2010 poll conducted in the United States by the well-respected Pew Research Center, 59 percent of those interviewed agreed that there is solid evidence the earth is warming, while 32 percent disagreed. The public was evenly divided over the answer to a follow-up question: "Do scientists agree the earth is getting warmer because of human activity?" The replies: 44 percent said "yes" and 44 percent said "no."[30]

According to a Gallup poll in 2011,

> The plurality of Americans continue to believe that the seriousness of global warming is generally exaggerated in the news (43 percent of the respondents believed this) rather than generally correct (26%) or generally underestimated (29%). This is the third year in a row that a substantial plurality has believed global warming's effects are not as bad as they are portrayed, a departure from previous years, when Americans were about evenly split between the three points of view. The percentage who think global warming's effects are exaggerated is down a bit from last year.[31]

Although some Americans may still harbor doubts about the reality and causes of global warming, the same cannot be said of major reinsurance companies, such as the Munich Reinsurance Company, known in the trade as "Munich Re." Reinsurance is insurance that is purchased by an insurance company (the insurer) from another insurance company (the reinsurer) as a means of risk management, i.e., to transfer risk from the insurer to the reinsurer.

Munich Re, one of the world's largest insurance companies, is a German firm that has about 5,000 insurance companies as its clients, located in some 150 countries. With 50 offices around the world, it assumes part of the risk covered by these insurance companies. In addition, Munich Re also provides reinsurance cover for life, health, casualty, transport, aviation, space, fire, and engineering businesses. It deals with climate *facts*, not with climate *feelings*.

For all these reasons, it is useful to understand what Prof. Dr. Peter Hoeppe, chief of Munich Re's Geo Risk Research Department, has to say about "Trends in Natural Disasters—The Role of Global Warming."[32] Lightly edited, this Munich Re document makes a number of important points. They include the following:

> Recent years have set "natural disaster" records in terms of intensities, frequencies, damages, and losses. For example, the heat wave of 2003 was the largest humanitarian natural catastrophe in Europe for centuries: there were approximately 34,000 "excess deaths," i.e., over and above the normal mortality, due to heat stress.
>
> In 2004, the first hurricane in the South Atlantic (Hurricane Catarina, off the coast of Brazil) occurred. In 2005, there was severe flooding in India: 37.1 inches (944 millimeters) of rain fell within 24 hours, the highest ever in India. Hurricane Katrina (2005) was the sixth strongest hurricane on record and generated the largest losses of a single natural event.
>
> The trendline of "Great Natural Disasters"—defined by Munich Re as earthquakes, tsunamis, volcanic eruptions, storms, floods, and temperature extremes—has been upward since the early 1950s. Munich Re gives three technically "problematic" (but, in fact, highly likely) reasons for globally increasing losses due to natural disasters: concentration of people and assets in large conurbations; settlement in and industrialization of very exposed regions; and changes in environmental conditions, i.e., due to global warming.
>
> Of all the factors that drive a major storm at sea, only the steady increase of sea surface temperatures over the last 35 years can account for the rising strength of storms in six ocean basins around the world.
>
> Wealthy countries may be better able to cope with financial losses from increasing disasters by means of insurance solutions and state funding, but the poorest countries will suffer the most. [According to the IPCC, "greater access to wealth and technology generally increases adaptive capacity, while poverty limits adaptation options."[33]] The increasing natural catastrophe damages in poor

countries will consume more and more of the funds they get as foreign aid, thus delaying their economic development — and, we may speculate, their political development as well.

Munich Re judges that natural catastrophes, especially weather-related events, are increasing dramatically in number and magnitude. Loss potentials have reached new dimensions. Climate change is already happening — it can no longer be stopped, just attenuated. There is more and more scientific evidence for causal links between global warming and increasing frequencies and intensities of natural catastrophes. We have to mitigate global warming and adapt to the changing risks with respect to regionally-specific risk patterns. And, finally, insurance mechanisms are part of the adaptation process— they must be designed with attention to regional characteristics.

While we ourselves are not at all optimistic that global warming will rise high in the American public's pecking order of important issues any time soon, we do hope that the background information summarized in this Introduction will help readers to arrive at a better understanding of sea level rise itself.

We must stress here, in closing, that the information sketched out in this chapter could easily be expanded to fill a bookshelf of scientific volumes. It is now time for us, however, to consider why the rise of the oceans is so important. As a first step, we must look, very briefly, at the intertwined concepts of the World Ocean and the hydrologic cycle.

II

The World Ocean and the Hydrologic Cycle

The World Ocean is the interconnected system of the Earth's marine waters. Its evocative name, which dates from classical antiquity where it referred to Oceanus, "the great Sea–god who girdles the world," was revived by the Russian oceanographer Yuly Shokalsky in the early 20th century.[1] The World Ocean forms the bulk of the hydrosphere (i.e., all the water on, or close to, the surface of the earth) and covers almost 71 percent of the Earth's surface. It is estimated that of the 332,500,000 cubic miles (1,386,000,000 cubic kilometers) of the world's water supply, about 321,000,000 cubic miles (1,338,000,000 cubic kilometers) is stored in the oceans, i.e., 95 percent.[2] The unity and continuity of the World Ocean, coupled with relatively free interchange among its component parts, is a fundamental fact of oceanography.

The World Ocean embraces the Atlantic Ocean, the Arctic Ocean (sometimes considered to be a sea of the Atlantic Ocean), the Indian Ocean, the Pacific Ocean (the largest of the oceans), and the Southern Ocean (a term often used to refer, collectively, to the southern portions of the Atlantic, Indian, and Pacific Oceans). For most purposes, the shape of the World Ocean can be treated as constant and unchanging, although in fact the slow but big-shouldered process of continental drift is always modifying its structure.

The hydrologic cycle, also known as the water cycle, is the never-ending movement of water on, above, and below the surface of the Earth.[3] Sketched out briefly, the cycle can be summarized as follows:

> The hydrologic cycle starts with the evaporation of water from the surface of the oceans. As this moist air rises, it cools and water vapor condenses to form clouds. This moisture eventually returns to the surface as precipitation. Once it reaches the surface, one of two things may happen: (1) some of the water may evaporate back into the atmosphere, or (2) the water may penetrate into the ground and become groundwater. (Groundwater is not an "underground lake." Rather, it is the water which is found in the pore spaces between the grains of rock and sediment that constitute the structure of the Earth.) Eventually, groundwater either seeps its way into streams, rivers, and oceans, or is released

back into the atmosphere through transpiration. The balance of water that remains on the surface of the Earth is known as runoff. It empties into streams, rivers, and lakes, finally ending up in the oceans. There the water cycle begins anew.[4]

The U.S. Geological Survey (USGS) has identified 16 components of this cycle. Many of these are self-explanatory but in the interests of clarity a few words of explanation have been added in each case.[5] The components are:

1. Water storage in oceans (saline water existing in oceans and inland seas)
2. Evaporation (the process by which water is changed from liquid to a gas or vapor)
3. Sublimation (the changing of snow or ice to water vapor without melting)
4. Evapotranspiration (the process by which water vapor is discharged to the atmosphere as a result of evaporation from the soil and transpiration by plants)
5. Water in the atmosphere (water stored in the atmosphere as clouds and humidity)
6. Condensation (the process by which water is changed from vapor to liquid)
7. Precipitation (the discharge of water, in liquid or solid state, out of the atmosphere, generally upon a land or a water surface)
8. Water storage in ice and snow (freshwater stored in frozen form, generally in glaciers, icefields, and snowfields)
9. Snowmelt runoff to streams (the movement of water as surface runoff from snow and ice to surface water)
10. Surface runoff (precipitation runoff which travels over the soil surface to the nearest stream channel)
11. Streamflow (the movement of water in a natural channel, such as a river)
12. Freshwater storage (freshwater existing on the Earth's surface)
13. Infiltration (the downward movement of water from the land surface into soil or porous rock)
14. Groundwater storage (water existing for long periods below the Earth's surface)
15. Ground water discharge (the movement of water out of the ground)
16. Spring (a place where a concentrated discharge of ground water flows at the ground surface)

Water can change states at various places in the cycle: sometimes it is liquid, at other times vapor, and at still other times ice. The balance of water on Earth is more or less constant, although individual water molecules can move in and out of the atmosphere. Water is transported from one reservoir

The global hydrologic (water) cycle (NOAA).

to another—from rivers to oceans, from oceans to atmosphere—by means of evaporation, condensation, precipitation, infiltration, runoff, and subsurface flow.

Because the hydrologic cycle involves the exchange of heat energy, it also warms and cools the environment. During cold climatic periods, more ice caps and glaciers form, and enough of the global water supply is stored as ice to decrease the amounts in other parts of the water cycle, thus lowering the sea level. The opposite is true during warm periods. About three million years ago, for example, the oceans might have been up to 165 feet (50 meters) higher than they are today.[6]

The continual excess of evaporation versus precipitation in the hydrologic cycle would eventually leave the oceans empty if they were not being constantly replenished by additional means, e.g., through runoff from the land areas. Not only are they still being replenished but they are now being *over*-replenished: sea level around the globe rose approximately 6.7 inches (17 centimeters) over the course of the last century.[7] There are two main reasons for this rise, which is continuing and which will probably accelerate in the years ahead: thermal expansion, and the calving or melting of land ice. These processes will be discussed later.

Evaporation from the oceans is the primary process driving the surface-to-atmosphere portion of the hydrologic cycle, but transpiration is also important. For example, a field of corn (maize) only 1 acre (4,048.8 square meters) in size can transpire as much as 4,000 gallons (15,141.6 liters) per day.[8] One consequence of a warmer ocean surface (due to global warming) is a large vapor-pressure difference between the sea surface and the adjacent atmosphere. This will enhance the evaporation rate and thus increase the other components of the hydrologic cycle, too.[9]

The water cycle, which is powered by energy from the sun, plays a crucial role in maintaining life and ecosystems on our planet and, of course, in the rise and fall of the seas themselves. NASA has summed up the path of a hypothetical water molecule in these felicitous sentences:

> Throughout the hydrologic cycle, there are many paths that a water molecule might follow. Water at the bottom of Lake Superior may eventually rise into the atmosphere and fall as rain in Massachusetts. Runoff from the Massachusetts rain may drain into the Atlantic Ocean and circulate northeastward toward Iceland, destined to become part of a floe of sea ice, or, after evaporation into the atmosphere and precipitation as snow, part of a glacier ... the water molecules that once fell 100 years ago as rain on your great-grandparents' farmhouse in Iowa might now be falling as snow on your driveway in California.[10]

III

Why Should We Care About the Rise of the Oceans?

Seen from space, the Earth is dominated by its oceans—a fact demonstrated by "The Blue Marble," a remarkable photograph of the Earth taken on 7 December 1972 by the crew of the Apollo 17 spacecraft at a distance of about 18,000 miles (29,000 kilometers). This image, taken on the last Apollo lunar mission, is one of the few to show a fully illuminated Earth: the astronauts had the sun behind them when they took the picture. To them, the Earth looked just like a big, blue, glass marble. Since then, no humans have been at a range where taking another whole–Earth photograph would be possible.[1] This is rather a shame: we need to be reminded more frequently that the Earth should really be called "the Water Planet."

Oceans cover nearly 71 percent of its surface, i.e., about 139 million square miles (361 million square kilometers, and, according to the World Resources Institute, "wash approximately 1,015,755 miles (1,634,700 kilometers) of coastlines around the world."[2] The United States itself has 12,380 miles (19,924 kilometers) of coastline. These coastlines now provide a wide range of essential goods and services to society, but today many of them are at increasing risk. The areas most affected by sea level change will be those which are already experiencing rapid erosion rates—for example, the Southeast and the Gulf Coasts of the United States. These are low-relief coasts, which leaves them especially vulnerable to flooding and storm surges.[3]

A storm surge can be defined as the temporary increase, at a particular locality, in the height of the sea due to extreme meteorological conditions, e.g., low atmospheric pressure and/or strong winds.[4] Because of the enormous threat which storm surges can pose to life, property, and the environment, these events will be mentioned frequently in this book. We shall discuss them and other extreme events at some length in the next chapter.

Here we must remember that a storm surge must not be confused with a tsunami, which is a series of water waves caused by the displacement of a large volume of water, usually in an ocean. Earthquakes, volcanic eruptions and other underwater explosions (including detonations of underwater nuclear devices), landslides and other mass movements, meteorite ocean impacts or similar impact events, and other disturbances above or below the waterline all have the potential to generate a tsunami.[5]

As far as sea level rise itself is concerned, the foundation of Stockholm, Sweden in the middle of the 13th century was mainly a result of the post-glacial uplift of the land around it. In the Stockholm area, a bay of the Baltic Sea was gradually cut off by this uplift and became a lake known as the Mälaren, the narrow outlets of which became bottlenecks for the shipping industry. In 1642, the Swedes had to call in Dutch experts to build a lock with sluice gates. This lock was replaced in 1755 by a bigger and deeper one.

At the 1772 session of the Swedish parliament, however, there were complaints that the level of the lake was now too high and was flooding neighboring fields. By order of King Gustaf III, a hydrographic survey of the lake's outlets was therefore undertaken in 1773. The next year, in 1774, systematic observations of the water levels began on both sides of the lock, i.e., of the lake itself and of the sea.

The measurements thus obtained were carefully recorded in water level books and other documents which are now preserved in Stockholm's City Archives. This process marks the beginning of longest sea level record in the world. A page from the 1787 record of water level observations at the Stockholm lock, for example, contains columns of figures giving in feet and inches, on specific dates, both the lake level and the sea level.[6]

Now, jumping ahead 220 years to our own time, we can note that a 2007 study estimated the likely impact of future sea level rise on 31 coastal cities, towns, and areas in the United States itself. These are located in Massachusetts, New York, New Jersey, Virginia, Georgia, Florida, Louisiana, Texas, California, Washington, and Hawaii. The study warned:

> Beginning with just one meter [3.2 feet] of sea level rise, the impact on the US would be calamitous, having the potential to destabilize many areas of the country.... The US is vulnerable at very small increments of sea level rise. Starting in East Boston and moving down the East Coast, around Florida and over to the Gulf of Mexico, then up along the West Coast and ending with the city of Honolulu, Hawaii, a picture of inundation, population displacement and catastrophic property loss develops.[7]

Projections made in 2009 give us some interesting insights into the likely spatial extent of two different sea rise scenarios—one of 3.2 feet (1 meter), the other of 19.6 feet (6 meters)—along the East and Gulf Coasts of the United States. The former rise quite possible by 2100; the latter could take centuries, although its rate will depend on the speed and extent of global warming.

The first category given below is the name of the municipality being studied. The second is the percentage of its area which is affected by a 1 meter rise. The third is the percentage of its area which is susceptible to a 6 meter rise[8]:

Municipality	1 meter rise	6 meter rise
Boston	3%	35%
New York	7%	34%
Washington, D.C.	1%	13%
Norfolk	9%	98%
Savannah	11%	75%
Jacksonville	7%	48%
Miami	18%	98%
Tampa	15%	43%
New Orleans	91%	99%
Houston	1%	3%

Perhaps the best way to understand sea level change is, first, to master a few technical concepts and terms; then to consider sea level rise itself; and, finally, to mention the likely impacts of sea level rise on the coasts of the world. The technical concepts and terms can be stated very briefly but the most important thing for us to recognize here is that, *once set in motion, sea level rise cannot possibly be stopped.*

Sea level varies naturally, e.g., due to the continual erosion of coastal regions and the encroachment of the ocean, which can be countered by uplift due to earthquakes and glacial isostatic rebound. "Isostatic rebound" means changes in the Earth's mantle as the ice sheets melt.[9] The weight of the ice depresses the bedrock beneath it. As the ice melts, the bedrock rebounds very slowly — on the order of 15,000 years. In fact, parts of Canada (Hudson Bay) and Scandinavia (the Baltic Sea) are still rising due to ice that melted over 7,000 years ago.[10]

But there are also two underlying reasons why sea level rise is an inevitable consequence of global warming:

1. Water expands when heated: this is the mechanism that causes the mercury in a thermometer to rise as it warms. The ocean is by far the most important heat reservoir in the climate system. As the ocean warms, it expands (its density decreases and its volume increases) — a process known as thermal expansion. Salinity changes within the ocean also have a significant impact on the local density and thus on local sea level, but have little effect on average sea level change.[11]

2. The exact amount of expansion depends on several factors, e.g., the amount of heat absorbed, water temperature (greater expansion in warm water), pressure (greater expansion at depth), and, to a lesser extent, salinity (greater expansion in saltier water). A 3,280-foot (1000-meter) column of

sea water would expand by about 0.4 to 0.8 inches (1 to 2 centimeters) for every 0.18 degree Fahrenheit (0.1 degree Celsius) of warming.[12]

Thermal expansion is estimated to have accounted for about 25 percent of the observed sea level rise between 1960 and 1993, and for about 30 percent from 1993 to 2009.[13] In the future, thermal expansion will contribute significantly to sea level rise. The exact amount of the rise will be a function of whether we can stabilize greenhouse gas emissions or whether they continue to grow. At this writing, the latter seems far more likely than the former.

3. In addition, with higher average global temperatures, some of the water which had previously been locked up on land in glaciers and in ice sheets ends up flowing into the oceans, thus increasing their volume and, at least locally, marginally decreasing their salinity. For the period 1961–2003, shrinking mountain glaciers and ice sheets have contributed about 60 percent to the observed sea level rise.[14] (The melting of floating sea ice, however, does not contribute appreciably to rising sea levels because it already displaces its own weight, just as ice melting in a glass of water does not cause the glass to overflow.) Published measured shrinkage and retreat rates are few,[15] but it is clear that Greenland is now losing hundreds of billions of tons of ice per year and the melt rate is increasing.

There are some other important concepts and terms, too. Since late 1992, absolute sea levels (i.e., geocentric sea levels which are relative to the Earth's center of mass and which are independent of land movements) have been monitored by satellite altimeters, codenamed Topex/Poseidon, Jason-1, and OSTM/Jason-2. Now these altimeters continuously measure the ocean surfaces under their orbits, completing a full measurement every ten days, and are accurate to within a few centimeters. This process has led to advances in physical oceanography and climate studies.

In so doing, they demonstrate the non-uniform nature of the sea level changes which have taken place since 1992. Remarkably, the seas are not in fact completely level. The gravitational pull on sea water varies around the earth due to variations in the diameter and composition of the planet.[16] While the average sea level rise has been 0.11 inches (3 mm) per year, there are regions showing trends of over .39 inches (10 mm) per year. Indeed, there are also areas, e.g., the northeastern Pacific, where sea level has actually fallen over this period.[17] These regional variations are due to numerous factors, e.g., ocean warming and cooling; freshwater exchange with the atmosphere and land via evaporation, precipitation, and runoff; and redistribution of water mass via ocean advection, i.e., the transfer of heat, and changes in air-ocean circulations such as El Niño/La Niña Southern Oscillation.[18] To these events one must also add solid Earth processes, e.g., the planet's elastic responses to changing crust and mantle parameters, and water mass distribution.[19]

Useful ocean readings are also taken both by the Array for Realtime Geostrophic Oceanography (Argo) network, which consists of a series of approximately 3,000 autonomous floats that sink and ascend, monitoring temperature and salinity in the top 0.62 to 1.24 miles (1–2 kilometers) of the ocean, and by the Gravity Recovery and Climate Experiment (GRACE) satellite mission, which measures the global gravity field every month.[20] GRACE can also be used to measure the contributions of glaciers and ice caps to sea level rise. According to a 2012 NASA press release, during the period 2003 to 2010 GRACE measured a total global ice mass lost from Greenland, Antarctica and Earth's glaciers and ice caps of 4.3 trillion tons (1,000 cubic miles), adding about 0.5 inches (12 millimeters) to global sea level. That was enough ice to cover the United States 1.5 feet (0.5 meters) deep.[21]

Mean sea level is one of the most important indicators of climate change because it includes inputs from several different components of the climate system. Between 1902 and 2006, the mean sea level trend as measured at Baltimore, Maryland, was equivalent to a rise of 1.01 feet in 100 years.[22] Precise monitoring of changes in the mean level of the oceans is a key to understanding both the climate and the future socioeconomic impacts of sea level rise. Local mean sea level is the height of the sea, measured with reference to a given point on the land and averaged over a long enough period of time so that the variations caused by wind waves are smoothed out.

Tidal effects, for their part, are typically estimated from the data and are not used in the computations of local mean sea level. Determining this level is not easy: daily, seasonal, annual and even decadal sea levels fluctuate strongly, masking the relatively tiny residual sea level rise contribution which is produced in part by global warming. Surface–based measurements are subject to distortion and misinterpretation due to several factors, e.g., tide gauge movements (see below) and gravitational effects.

The concept of "relative sea level" refers to a change in sea level relative to the local land as measured at a tide gauge.[23] Tide gauges have been used for about 140 years (this was when they first became widely available) to measure the motion of the sea surface relative to the land. Tide gauge data suggest that global sea level has risen approximately 3.9 to 9.8 inches (10–25 centimeters) during the past century.[24] Relative sea level takes vertical land motion into account and is thus more pertinent for our purposes than absolute sea levels. As the climate-change specialist Dr. Robert J. Nicholls tells us,

> When analyzing sea level rise impacts and responses, it is fundamental that impacts are a product of *relative* (or local) sea level rise rather than global

changes alone.... [The underlying drivers of relative sea level rise are] (1) climate change such as melting land-based ice, thermal expansion of ocean waters, and changing ocean dynamics, and (2) non-climate uplift/subsidence processes such as [plate] tectonics [the large scale motions of the Earth's lithosphere, i.e., its crust and outer mantle], glacial isostatic adjustment, and natural and anthropogenic subsidence. Hence relative sea-level rise is a response to both climate change and other factors and varies from place to place.[25]

The concept of eustatic change (as opposed to merely local change) refers to change which results in an alteration to the global sea levels, such as change in the total volume of water held in the world's oceans, or to change in the volume of a given ocean basin. The term "steric," e.g., steric sea level change, refers to global changes in sea level due to thermal expansion and salinity variations.

We must recognize that no measurement of the sea, however, is entirely accurate: a tide gauge may measure sea level changes to 0.39 inches (0.01 meters) but because of inaccurate leveling or poor maintenance, its accuracy relative to a fixed datum may be in error by as much as 1.96 inches (0.05 meters).[26] Tide gauges do record considerable variations in sea levels. The reason for such variations is that some land areas are sinking, while others are rising. Indeed, sea level has increased 5 to 6 inches [12.7 to 15.2 centimeters] more than the global average along the Mid-Atlantic and Gulf coasts because coastal lands there are subsiding.[27] On the other hand, some parts of the Alaskan coast, e.g., Skagway, are now rising. This is due to isostatic rebound of the basement rocks as they respond to glacial mass loss.

Changes in relative sea level can thus differ from place to place, depending on such localized forces as currents, air pressure variations, temperature, and salinity variations. Contrary to what we might intuitively expect, sea level — because of these forces — is not the same over the entire oceanic surface of the Earth. Mean sea level at the Pacific side of the Panama Canal, for example, is about 20 centimeters (7.8 inches) higher than it is at the Atlantic end of the canal. This is due to prevailing weather and ocean conditions, and to the fact that the water is less dense on the Pacific side. In fact, if we resort to a thought-experiment and imagine that this canal had been dug so deeply that it did not need any locks at all, there would then be a current flowing through it —from the Pacific to the Atlantic.[28]

Sea level rise is important to us today because of its grave implications for the future. It cannot be halted and it will, in general, have overwhelmingly negative impacts on many of the coastal countries of the world. (One of the very few *positive* impacts we can think of is that some up-river ports may possibly evolve into shallow seaports.) It bears repeating that even if greenhouse emissions are somehow stabilized—which does not seem at all likely in the foreseeable future—the world climate will continue to warm and sea levels must therefore continue to rise. Sea level rise will thus probably continue for many centuries and will increasingly conflict with human settlement patterns and aspirations.[29]

The Climate Change Research Centre at Australia's University of New South Wales warns that because sea levels will continue to increase, even if global temperature rise is somehow (and unexpectedly) stabilized, several meters of sea level rise must therefore be expected over the next few centuries.[30] Such a rise will pose grave threats to major coastal cities and may well lead to the loss of some small-island nations, such as the Maldives in the Indian Ocean and Vanuatu in the South Pacific.[31]

Dr. John Church of the Centre for Australian Weather and Climate Research made the same basic point when he told the 2009 United Nations Climate Change Conference (commonly known as the Copenhagen Conference):

> The most recent satellite and ground based observations show that sea level is continuing to rise at 3mm/yr [0.11 inches per year] or more since 1993, a rate well above the 20th century average. The oceans are continuing to warm and expand, the melting of mountain glaciers has increased and the ice sheets of Greenland and Antarctica are also contributing to sea level rise.[32]

We believe it now self-evident that we can ignore this rise only at our own peril. During the last interglacial stage, it is very likely that sea levels were about 6 meters (19.6 feet) higher, or even more, than they are today.[33] However, our ancestors then (there may have been a few hundred thousand of them, mostly living in Africa) could have responded to the rising oceans simply by staying on higher ground. Indeed, since the beginnings of recorded history, sea level has risen so slowly that, as a practical matter, it has been constant.[34] The world today is of course a much different and more complex place.

During the last 10,000 years, the amount of water lost by the oceans due to evaporation, on the one hand, and the amount gained by them due to rain, snow, rivers, and glaciers, on the other, was roughly equal. Dr. Henry Pollack, an emeritus professor of geophysics at the University of Michigan, puts it in these terms:

> Over the past several millennia these withdrawals and deposits have continued to take place in the oceanic account, but the balance has remained pretty steady. But the twentieth-century warming of Earth and the loss of ice from the continents is beginning to change the oceanic balance—in the upward direction.[35]

Today, the accelerated increases in average air and ocean temperatures, the widespread melting of snow and ice, and the rising sea levels all offer proof that the world's climate system is warming. It now seems likely that global warming will cause, among other things, more storm surges and more "extreme events." There is no single definition of what constitutes an extreme event. The IPCC bases its own definition on the frequency of the occurrence of a given event, e.g., an event that is as rare as the 10 percent or 90 percent quintile of a particular distribution of an atmospheric variable such as temperature, wind velocity, or precipitation. In terms of sea level rise, for our purposes here we will define an extreme event simply as "a period of much above average sea level."

The long term effects of global warming on sea levels cannot now be predicted with much confidence because these processes are so complex and will stretch out so far into the future. This state of affairs is made even more intractable because of the lack of clarity about some less dramatic issues. For example, a considerable amount of fresh water is now stored on land behind dams.

Nearly 30,000 dams have been built worldwide since 1900. These impoundments are estimated to have prevented about 1.2 inches (3 centimeters) of sea level rise.[36] Water is also stored on land in many other forms, too. Diverse examples include artificial reservoirs, lakes, rivers, wetlands, soil moisture, snow pack, permafrost, and aquifers. What, if anything, will happen to this land-stored water in the years to come is not fully understood now. Some of it may eventually run into the seas; on the other hand, new impoundments may be built in the future.

It is certain that human intervention regarding water storage, e.g., by pumping out and depleting groundwater for agricultural, industrial, domestic, and other purposes, contributes — directly or indirectly — to sea level rise.[37] If so, this process may offset, or even cancel out, the effects of water impoundment through dams. A reasonable guess is that although dam building is decreasing now, ground water pumping will continue at a sustained or probably at an even greater rate, thus marginally contributing to sea level rise in the coming decades.[38]

All that seems certain now is that it is the coastlines of the world that will have to bear the brunt of rising sea levels. For example, at some locations along the coastline of the United States, "average high water" (the higher of the two high waters of any tidal day) has been rising faster than average sea level. The reasons for this are not yet fully understood but this trend obviously increases the risk of extensive coastal flooding even more than the rise in average sea levels would suggest.[39] A global sea level rise of only 14.5 to 14.9 inches (37–38 centimeters) by the 2080s will greatly enhance the occurrence of local flooding and will increase the loss of coastal wetlands. These negative impacts will not be uniform around the globe: some regions will be more affected than others.[40]

It is been estimated that today about 250 million people live within 16.4 feet (5 meters) of high tide, that 600 million people live within 32.8 feet (10 meters) of sea level, and that these populations are growing more rapidly than global trends.[41] Moreover, about 160 million people live in locations of the world that are only 3.2 feet (1 meter) above mean sea level, or even less.[42] Their numbers are growing quite rapidly, too, both due to natural increase and to the fact that the hope of jobs in coastal cities pulls more and more men and women into them. Thus even small changes in sea levels in the future can jeopardize the livelihoods of millions of people. As the National Research Council explains,

> The coastlines of the United States and the world are major centers of economic, social, and cultural developments, and coastal areas are home to critical ecological and environmental resources. Climate change poses a number of risks to coastal environments. Foremost among these is sea level rise, which threatens people, ecosystems, and infrastructure directly and also magnifies the impacts of coastal storms.[43]

In 2007, the IPCC made a number of important points in this regard. Edited and annotated here to soften the IPCC's often-leaden bureaucratic prose, they vividly depict the potential severity of the coastal issues facing the world[44]:

- Very few of the world's coastlines are now immune from human pressures, even though some of them are still uninhabited. During the 20th century, these pressures increased dramatically — a trend that is certain to continue and expand during our present century. The reality of more and more people living and working along the coasts has already led to many far-reaching changes. Chief among them are that low-lying deltas, barrier islands [long, narrow coastal sandy islands that are above high tide and parallel the shore], and estuaries all around the world have been converted to industrial and residential uses. They have been transformed, in many cases quite radically, by intensive human uses — for example, farming, aquaculture, forestry, port facilities, migration, and tourism. Moreover, global mean sea level rise will lead to higher local water levels and greater salinity in estuarine systems, thereby displacing existing coastal plant and animal communities.[45]
- Over 23 percent of the world's population (or more than 1.2 billion people) now live within 62 miles (100 kilometers) of the coasts, at densities of about three times the global average. Twenty of the world's 30 mega-cities are located on the coasts. As a result, the coastal zones (whose responses to sea level rise can be dynamic and more complex than passively submitting to

inundation) and their inhabitants are becoming increasingly vulnerable — especially against the coming and inevitable increase in sea levels — to storm surges and flooding. Indeed, each year about 120 million people are now exposed to tropical cyclones, which killed an estimated 250,000 people between 1980 and 2000.[46]

Throughout the 20th century, the global rise of sea level contributed to increased coastal inundation, erosion and ecosystem losses (but with considerable local and regional variations due to other factors). Coasts will be exposed to increasing risks over the coming decades. Climate changes there will probably include an accelerated rise in sea level, a further rise in sea surface temperatures, an intensification of tropical and extra-tropical cyclones, extreme waves, altered precipitation and run-off, and ocean acidification.

Along many of the coasts and low-lying areas of the world of the world, hurricanes and storm surges occurring on top of a slowly-rising baseline of higher sea levels and higher tides will threaten low-lying cities and farmlands. Moreover, higher sea levels may well destroy biologically-productive wetlands. As the U.S. Environmental Protection Agency notes:

> Coastal wetland ecosystems, such as salt marshes and mangroves[47] [as well as swamps, tidal mud flats, brackish marshes, and bayous] are particularly vulnerable to rising sea level because they are generally within a few feet of sea level. Wetlands provide habitat for many species, play a key role in nutrient uptake, serve as the basis for many communities' economic livelihoods, provide recreational opportunities, and protect local areas from flooding.[48]

The U.S. Environmental Protection Agency has reported that most wetlands along the mid–Atlantic Coast probably will not be able to survive an acceleration in sea level rise by 0.25 inches (7 millimeters) a year.[49] If they do keep pace with sea level rise, the result will be an overall loss of wetland area. In 2010, the Secretariat of the Convention on Biological Diversity added this warning about a possible tipping point for wetlands and beaches:

> A tipping point occurs when the surface elevation of a coastal ecosystem does not keep pace with the rise in sea level, i.e., the balance between sea level rise and sedimentation rates results in flooding. When this tipping point occurs, the coastal ecosystem can be rapidly reduced to a point where it is reduced to a narrow fringe or is lost. Additional non-climate stressors on coastal ecosystems, such as the reduction of sediments reaching coastal zones due to dams, changes in river beds, etc., and pollution increase the vulnerability of coastal ecosystems to sea level rise.[50]

A related problem is known as coastal squeeze. This term refers to what happens to coastal habitats that are trapped between a fixed landward boundary, such as a sea wall, and rising sea levels and/or increased storminess. In this process, the habitat is squeezed between two inexorable forces and thus diminishes in quantity or in quality. A good example here is the arm of the sea known as the Solent, which is located on the south coast of England between the Isle of Wight and the mainland. Salt marshes there are under threat. They cannot respond to sea level rise by migrating inland because the mainland is already heavily used for industry, housing, or recreation; has a very high commercial value; and will not, willingly, ever be surrendered to the sea.[51]

All the above phenomena will vary considerably in different coastal regions, but, taken cumulatively, their impacts will certainly be negative. Increased flooding—coupled with degradation of fresh water, fisheries, and other shore side resources—could easily impact hundreds of millions of people. The socio-economic imposed costs on coasts can only escalate as a result of continuing sea level rise. Many of the world's shorelines have retreated during the last century; sea level rise is an underlying cause. Acceleration of sea level rise can only speed up beach erosion in most parts of the globe. In fact, it has been estimated that for every 0.3 inches (one centimeter) of sea level rise in vertical measurement, a sandy coast will retreat by 50 to 200 times as much in horizontal measurement.[52]

Although the impacts of climate changes on the coasts will be exacerbated by the ever-growing numbers of human beings living there, there do not seem to be many reliable estimates of how many people will be involved in this process. We can note, however, that most of Bangladesh is less than 39.3 feet (12 meters) above the present sea level and that if the sea level rises by only 3.2 feet (1 meter), about 50 percent of the country will be flooded. Bangladesh is very densely populated—the greater Dhaka area is currently home to more than 13 million residents and the country is exceptionally vulnerable to rising waters. It is estimated, for example, that about 300,000 people died there in 1970 during Cyclone Alia and its attendant storm surges.[53]

Densely populated deltas, megadeltas (a generic term given to very large river deltas, often in Asia[54]), low-lying coastal urban areas, and atolls will thus be at great risk in the years to come. Their vulnerability can only increase in the future as the seas rise further and as local subsidence continues. It is estimated that, worldwide, nearly 300 million people now live in about 40 densely-populated deltas.[55]

In its 2007 Assessment Report, the IPCC drew attention, using on an outline map of the world, to all the important deltas and megadeltas which will be affected by sea level rise by the year 2050.[56] This map shows that more than 1 million people may be displaced in each of three megadeltas: the Ganges-Brahmaputra Delta in Bangladesh, the Mekong Delta in Vietnam,

Relative vulnerability of coastal deltas as shown by the indicative population potentially displaced by current sea-level trends to 2050 (Extreme = >1 million; High = 1
million to 50,000; Medium = 50,000 to 5,000; following Ericson et al., 2006) (Fig. 6.6
from Contribution of Working Group II to the Fourth Assessment Report of the Intergovernmental Panel on Climate Change, M.L. Parry, O.F. Canziani, J.P. Palutikof, P.J.
van der Linden and C.E. Hanson, Eds. Cambridge University Press, UK, p. 327).

and the Nile Delta in Egypt, i.e., a total of some 3 million people. (These
megadeltas will be discussed in more detail in later parts of this book.) In
addition to the 3 million megadelta-dwellers likely to be affected by sea level
rise, more than 50,000 people are also likely to be directly impacted in each
of nine additional large deltas, plus more than 5,000 in each of a further 12
smaller deltas. The overall total of those likely to be affected by sea level rise
in the megadeltas and deltas of the world was thus estimated at about 3.51
million people, as of 2007.[57] Due to rapid population growth in these regions,
this figure is certain to rise further in the future.

In that same IPCC report, we find another listing of some of the probable
climate-related impacts on the socio-economic sectors of coastal zones. These
impacts will include temperature rises of both air and seawater; extreme
events, e.g., bigger storms and higher waves; floods; rising water tables; erosion; salt water intrusion; and adverse effects on many living organisms, great
and small. In various ways and to various degrees, such impacts can be
expected to affect, directly or indirectly, freshwater resources, agriculture and
forestry, fisheries and aquaculture, recreation and tourism, biodiversity, and
human settlements and infrastructure.[58]

It can be said that there are four fundamental (but by no means mutually
exclusive) ways for societies to cope with sea level rise[59]:

• *Mitigation.* This includes broadly-based — ideally, *global* — efforts to reduce
the rate and magnitude of climate change, e.g., by reducing the emissions

of heat-trapping greenhouse gases which are primarily responsible for sea level rise. However, because the momentum of sea level is so huge, mitigation can hope to reduce its impacts only over the long term and only to a limited extent.

- *Adaptation.* This focuses on more narrowly-based national, regional, and local efforts to cope with sea level rise, e.g., via protective storm surge barriers, salt water intrusion barriers, dikes and polders. (Dikes hold back salt water, brackish water, or fresh water. Polders are low-lying tracts of land, enclosed by dikes, which are artificial hydrological entities, that is to say, they have no natural connections with outside water except through such man-made devices as drainage ditches, canals, and pumping stations.)

  Given the enormous difficulty of negotiating legally-binding international climate-change agreements, adaptation appears to offer a simpler and quicker — but inherently limited — way to cope with sea level rise. A concept closely related to adaptation is "accommodation to natural systems." This means adjusting human use of the coastal zone by means of flood resilience, warning systems, insurance, etc.

- *Retreat.* This means a conscious decision to pull back from the coast (via land use planning and legal controls) and to surrender land to the sea.

- *Lots of talk, no action.* Given the intractable political, economic, and social problems conjured up by sea level rise, it is much easier for legislators in democratic societies to make speeches and to commission studies rather than to vote for very expensive and often controversial remedial measures. Sea level rise may be a very important problem in the very long run but in terms of local politics it is not a problem which *simply must be addressed this week.*

The IPCC warns that neither mitigation nor adaptation alone will be able to solve all the likely climate change impacts, including sea level rise.[60] The most effective response to sea level rise in coastal areas will ideally be some combination of the two. In case of dire need, the third and less palatable choice — a planned retreat from the shoreline — is available. The fourth option — lots of talk and no action — is always an attractive option for legislators and governments.

Compared to the rich countries, the poor countries will find it quite difficult — and perhaps quite impossible — to shoulder the political, economic and social burdens of sea level rise. Its impacts of may well be catastrophic for some developing countries. The World Bank has estimated that even a 3.2 feet (1 meter) rise in sea level in the coastal counties of the developing world might flood about 74,903 square miles (194,000 square kilometers) of land area and displace at least 56 million people.[61]

The actual impacts of climate changes will depend on countries' abilities to adapt to sea level rise in the future, but, if the past and the present are any prologues, a reasonable guess is that most of the developing nations will be unable to generate the financial resources and the political will needed to relocate the people who live in their low-lying coastal zones. These coastal peoples, some of whom will be among the poorest of the poor and will lack any political or economic leverage, will have to move on their own, if they are to move at all. Population growth and urbanization in the developing countries will swell any such climate-induced migration streams.

Painful though they will be, over the long run the adaptation costs for vulnerable coasts will much less than the costs of doing nothing at all. Without adaptation, significant sea level rise, combined with other climate changes (e.g., increased storm intensity), is very likely to make some small islands and low-lying areas entirely uninhabitable. The long range outlook, then, is that the irresistible momentum of sea level rise will increasingly conflict with human development patterns and plans for the future. As we said earlier, this rise has great inertia and will continue for hundreds of years.

The IPCC has performed a valuable service for us by drawing up a list of the "Key hotspots of societal vulnerability in coastal zones." These hotspots are as follows[62]:

- Coastal areas where there are substantial economic, institutional, environmental, financial, and/or technical barriers to effective adaptation to sea level rise. Examples: Venice, Asian megadeltas, atolls and small islands, New Orleans.
- Coastal areas subject to multiple natural and human-induced stresses, such as subsidence or declining natural defenses. Examples: Mississippi, Nile and Asian megadeltas, Netherlands, Mediterranean, Maldives.
- Coastal areas already experiencing adverse effects of temperature rise. Examples: coral reefs (although coral reefs can keep pace with sea level rise if they are not at the same time subjected to other environmental or man-made stresses), Arctic coasts (United States, Canada, Russia), Antarctic peninsula.
- Coastal areas with large flood-plain populations that are exposed to significant storm surge hazards. Examples: Bay of Bengal, Gulf of Mexico/Caribbean, Rio de la Plata/Parana delta, the North Sea.
- Coastal areas where freshwater resources are likely to be reduced by climate change. Examples: West Africa, West Australia, atolls and small islands.
- Coastal areas with tourist-based economies where major adverse effects on tourism are likely. Examples: Caribbean, Mediterranean, Florida, Thailand, Maldives.

• Highly sensitive coastal systems where the scope for inland migration is limited. Examples: many developed estuarine coasts, low small islands, Bangladesh.

In summary, it is evident that most of the points touched upon in this chapter will invite further discussion and will readily lend themselves to further studies. In the interests of brevity, however, we shall call a halt here and will now look, very briefly, at storm surges and other extreme events.

IV

Storm Surges and
Other Extreme Events

Sea level rise will probably become most evident to us as an increase in the frequency or likelihood of extreme events (storm surges), rather than simply as a steady increase in otherwise constant conditions.[1] The damage that can be caused by storm surges is potentially so great that this topic must be discussed relatively early in this book. Storm surges must not be confused with storm tides, which are defined as a water level rise due to the *combination* of storm surges plus the astronomical tides. For example, assuming for purposes of illustration that the high tide in a given place is 2 feet (0.6 meter) and that there is a 15 foot (4.5 meter) storm surge coming ashore on top of it, then the storm tide itself will be 17 feet (5.18 meters) high.[2]

As mentioned earlier, a storm surge is an offshore and temporary rise in the height of the sea. This rise is caused by extreme meteorological conditions of low atmospheric pressure and/or strong winds over the sea. High winds produced by hurricanes push the ocean forward in front of them. As this water is forced into shallower zones along the coastline, the local sea level rises. At the same time, sea level also rises, though to a lesser amount, beneath the eye of the storm due to the low barometric pressure that exists in the hurricane eye itself.[3] The combined effects of low pressure and persistent winds over a shallow body of water generally leads to flooding along the adjacent coast.

Some experts believe that the forecast increase in sea surface temperatures may lead to more intense tropical cyclones, which may in turn lead to heightened storm surges. The question of the relationship of global warming to tropical cyclones has not yet been fully understood and is still being studied. However, a paper published in 2010 by Dr. Thomas Knutson and some of the top hurricane researchers in the field concluded that

> ...future projections based on theory and high-resolution dynamical models consistently indicate that greenhouse warming will cause the globally averaged intensity of tropical cyclones to shift toward stronger storms, with intensity

increased of 2–11 percent by 2100. Existing modeling studies also consistently project decreases in the globally averaged frequency of tropical cyclones, by 6–34 percent. Balanced against this, higher resolution modeling studies typically project substantial increases in the frequency of the most intense cyclones, and increases in the order of 20 percent in the precipitation rate within 100 km [62 miles] of the storm centre.[4]

There has been an observed increase in the most intense tropical cyclones since the mid–1990s. Warmer oceans have played a significant role in this increased frequency, because cyclones derive their power from rising moisture, which releases heat during condensation.

By 2100, the climate is expected to warm by 9 degrees Fahrenheit (5 degrees Celsius) or more above pre–Industrial Revolution values unless our current greenhouse emissions decrease considerably. During the Pliocene Epoch (about 2.5 to 5 million years ago), carbon dioxide levels were comparable to today's levels, the climate was appreciably warmer, and sea levels fluctuated dramatically.[5] Geographically, the Earth was then very similar to what it is today, so the Pliocene may offer a glimpse of what the world may be like by 2100. Models suggest that, in this long-passed scenario, tropical cyclone activity and intensity increased dramatically in all ocean basins. This is a sobering look at what may lie ahead for our planet by 2100.

To return to storm surges: the height of the storm surge depends on a wide range of factors, such as the shape of and offshore slope of the coast, the track of the storm, and the details of the storm — e.g., wind speed, size of the storm, forward speed of the storm, exact storm track, etc. The biggest storm surge ever measured in Australia occurred in 1899: it was estimated at about 42 feet (12.8 meters) high, though some of this may have been wave run-up due to the steep coastal topography. The Galveston Hurricane of 1900 drove ashore a devastating storm surge that killed at least 8,000 people — still the greatest loss of life in the United States caused by a natural disaster. Although elevated (e.g., built on stilts), some North Carolina beach houses still could not withstand the 15 foot (4.5 meter) storm tides that accompanied Hurricane Floyd in 1999.[6]

During the past 200 years, some 2.6 million people may have drowned during storm surges.[7] In 2010 a presentation at a meeting of the American Geophysical Union made an important point:

Even now, episodic storm surges may create significant damage, and consideration of their return levels for long periods (50/100 years) have to be taken into account when planning structures or protecting pre-existing valuables, both within artificial and natural systems. When these same return levels are combined with the expected sea level rise in the next few decades, it is very likely that

Abandoned, condemned houses, Nags Head, North Carolina, after severe storm surges (© Gary Braasch/ WorldViewOfGlobalWarming.org).

the risk assessment will have to change, since the return period of damaging events is going to be in cases shortened, and in many cases substantially so.[8]

For example, in a 2011 modeling test case focused on a seawall in Walcott, United Kingdom, where extensive flooding occurred in 2007, it was shown that water level had a more significant impact on overtopping this seawall than near-shore wave height alone. This study concluded that future sea level rise will be the main driver for future coastal flooding. A flood initially likely to occur once every 100 years is likely by 2100 to occur once every five years with a sea level rise of 1.14 feet (0.35 meters) and once every year with a sea level rise of 3.2 feet (1 meter).[9]

A fundamental problem is that we cannot now accurately predict future changes in extreme storm surges and associated wave heights. They will be the indirect and possibly lethal consequences of long-term changes in atmospheric pressure fields, winds, and mean sea level. Despite this frustrating uncertainty, policymakers will be remiss in their duties if they do not try to focus on the future.

It is increasingly important that policymakers take account of probable long-term trends in sea level, extreme surges, and record waves in ensuring the protection of life and property in coastal regions. It is now very likely that long-term trends in sea level and in the frequency and magnitude of extreme waves and storm surges will have a very negative impact on vulnerable coastal facilities such as ports and harbors, coastal process plants, offshore oil- and gas-production platforms, and even coastal waste-disposal sites.

Over the next 50 to 100 years, for example, the 3.2 feet (1 meter) rise in sea level (due to a combination of sea level rise and local subsidence) which has been projected for the Gulf Coast region between Alabama and Houston, where there are a number of major refining installations, would permanently flood nearly a third of the region's existing roads, as well as putting 70 percent of its ports at risk.[10] See Appendix 3 for an account of the impact on ports of a 3.2 foot (1 meter) sea level rise.

According to a 2011 study of wind speeds and wave heights over the world's oceans between 1985 and 2008, wind speeds increased by as much as 10 percent. The study also showed that extreme waves (i.e., the largest 1 percent of the waves) increased by an average of 0.5 percent every year; in some regions, extreme waves increased by up to 1 percent a year.[11] That said, while it is understood that the oceans are warming and that energy can generate storms with much stronger winds and greater wave heights, it is still too early for scientists to determine whether there is in fact a long-term trend. If so, its chief driving force is presently unknown.

In the United States, the National Hurricane Center forecasts storm surges using the SLOSH model. (SLOSH stands for Sea, Lake, and Overland Surges from Hurricanes.) The inputs used in this model include the central pressure of tropical cyclone, storm size, the cyclone's forward motion, its track, and the maximum sustained winds. In addition, the local topography, bay and river orientation, depth of the sea bottom, astronomical tides, and other physical features are taken into account.

Coastal planners need to investigate storm surges and other extreme events with the greatest care, e.g., via SLOSH, before deciding upon which adaptation and coastal protection measures will work best in a given situation. Global warming could very well cause more frequent extreme high sea levels and thus more far-reaching waves. The relationship between sea level rise and the associated waves themselves depends on a large number of factors.

As a general proposition, we can say that a higher sea level will not necessarily result in a higher amplitude of waves: the waves themselves may be much then as they are now. However, as these waves approach the shore, they will be "jumping off" from a higher oceanic platform. As a result, over the long run, the cumulative effects of sea level rise and its accompanying waves will pose greater risks to shoreside structures and will lead to deeper inundations farther inland.

In a 2010 study of the coast of East Anglia, researchers used extreme event analysis to estimate the effect of climate change on inshore waves in that low-lying region of the British Isles. (See Appendix 4 for a brief discussion of extreme event analysis.) Lightly edited to improve readability, this is what the East Anglia researchers found:

> In coastal areas, offshore wave propagation towards the shore is influenced by water depth variations, due to sea bed bathymetry, tides, and storm surges. Considering the implications of climate change both on atmospheric forcing and sea level rise, a simple methodology was used to compute inshore waves from 1960 to 2099. [Computer] simulations took into account five scenarios of linear sea level rise and one climatic scenario for storm surges and offshore waves.
>
> It was found that wave statistics are indeed sensitive to sea level rise. For example, a given climate change scenario leads to a significant increase in extreme wave heights. For nearshore points, the increase in the mean sea level alters not only extreme wave heights but also the frequency of occurrence of extreme wave conditions.[12]

One of the very best reasons to study sea level change is to improve our ability to assess and predict the frequency and severity of coastal flooding in the future. Toward this end, coastal planners seek to master the general concept of risk and how it is calculated for extreme sea levels. The planners' goal is to design appropriate safeguards and protection against extreme sea conditions for the lifetime of any proposed project. High water events along the coasts of the United Kingdom sometimes result from the combination of a spring tide (a higher tide when the moon is either full or new, regardless of season) and a storm surge. Careful study of the probabilities of extreme sea levels is an essential part of the design of coastal structures, since any higher levels will make coastal inundation from naturally-occurring higher seasonal tides a factor to be taken into careful consideration.

Estimating risk should be based on good data and on a full set of analytical techniques. Known risks can be measured from observations using probability theory and can then be included in planning, design, and investment. If potential risks are not known, then there is no way to make intelligent decisions: one must, in effect, simply trust to luck. That approach is simply not good enough when facing the risks of more frequent and higher floods lapping at homes, factories, power stations, and all other natural and human infrastructure along the coasts.

Probabilities of extreme sea levels and coastal flooding can be identified in different ways, e.g., via the still water levels, which include the tide, surges, and mean sea level elements, and via the total levels, which include waves. Although waves are usually treated separately in risk analysis, more sophisticated methods can also take into account the correlation between storm surges and high wave conditions.

To avoid complexity but at the same time to highlight this issue, let us now look briefly at a generalized instruction-level example of how the probabilities of extreme sea levels and coastal flooding along the British coast were studied.[13] This example has been edited in the interests of clarity, e.g., by removing the algebraic symbols in it.

The basic objective of this study was to determine the probability of a certain water level being exceeded in any given year. To calculate this probability, tide gauge data, numerical modeling information, and statistical models—all deployed in varying combinations—were used. Other calculations were used to determine the "return period"—i.e., the average time between which higher-than-average levels would occur.

"Design risk" is the probability that a certain water level will be exceeded during the design life of the structure. Houses along the British coast usually have a relatively short design life. However, if the objective is to accept only a very limited risk that a given spot will be flooded, then the design life must be as long as possible. For this reason, the design life for nuclear power stations may be up to 100,000 years or even longer.

The full impacts of sea level change on the coasts do not result from any single or uniform process. A range of factors is normally involved, including individual extreme sea level or wave events; storm surges; long-term changes in mean sea level; and even the flows of major rivers, which, when flooding, can exacerbate coastal flooding. In most cases, what is usually in play is a potent combination of such processes. Indeed, research has showed that extreme sea levels in the coastal area of the Netherlands may result from the extreme sea storm-surge levels, waves, and river discharges: it is not easy to quantify which one is a major contributor to a particular extreme event.[14]

One example of the power of various combined and mutually reinforcing impacts was the horrendous damage inflicted by Hurricane Katrina on the New Orleans area. Losses there were caused by a combination of storm surges, failures of the coastal defenses, a high rate of local mean sea level rise relative to the low land level of the Mississippi Delta (the portion of New Orleans which suffered the greatest damage was located about 19 feet below sea level), and man-made changes in the delta itself. At least 1,836 people lost their lives in the actual hurricane and in the subsequent floods; total property damage was estimated as high as $100 billion. It will be many years more before the region fully recovers.

It is not certain now to what exact extent climate change can be a contributing factor in unusually high precipitation rates, but it does appear to be playing a role here. Human–generated increases in greenhouse gases have contributed to the observed intensification of heavy precipitation events found over about two-thirds of data-covered parts of Northern Hemisphere land areas.[15] Dr. Kevin Trenberth, whom we quoted earlier in this book, commented in a climate change blog (his remarks have been lightly edited here):

There is a systematic influence of all these weather events nowadays because of the fact that there is this extra water vapor lurking around in the atmosphere — more than there used to be, say, 30 years ago. It's about a 4 percent extra amount. It invigorates the storms. It provides plenty of moisture for these storms and it's unfortunate that the public is not associating these storms with the fact that this is one manifestation of climate change. And the prospects are that these kinds of things will get only bigger and worse in the future.[16]

A series of floods hit the state of Queensland, Australia, in 2010–2011, leaving 35 people dead, 9 missing, and about $30 billion in damages. One theory is that the rise in ocean temperatures around Australia (perhaps due to global warming) produced extra water vapor and thereby intensified the monsoon. Critics of this theory say that it is too early to draw such a dramatic conclusion. Early in 2011, Australia set up a Commission of Inquiry to look into the floods and to issue a report in one year.

Interesting as they are, we should note here that researching extremes is appreciably harder than researching mean sea levels, chiefly due to the difficulty of getting access to comparable hourly values of sea level data. Some countries still restrict outsiders' access to raw sea level data, citing national security concerns or the costs of getting and sharing the data. Although some international programs are now addressing this issue, e.g., the Global Sea Level Observing System and the Global Climate Observing System, there is still a lack of long-term time scale series for study, particularly from the Southern Hemisphere — excluding Australia, New Zealand, and parts of the Pacific, for all of which there are in fact good and readily-available data.

In addition, technical problems of measurement can arise when scientists try to identify extreme sea levels as accurately as possible. For example, before the era of the automatic tide gauge, i.e., for early tidal measurements made during the 18th or early 19th centuries, researchers today are sometimes forced to use approximations rather than historical raw data. The full tidal curve is now an important bit of data, but in the early records only high waters were recorded.

Because extreme events frequently result in flooding and deaths, it is worthwhile to ask whether their amplitudes and frequencies are changing, and whether levels of extreme high waters are changing in a significantly different way from mean sea levels themselves. At this writing, there seem to be no definite answers to these important questions. A quasi-global investigation of this issue, conducted in 2004, concluded that there has indeed been a worldwide increase in extreme high water levels since 1975.

However, it also found that, in most cases, the changes and variability in the extremes were similar to those in mean sea level. Other studies have come to a similar conclusion with regard to the rate of rise in the level of extremes and mean sea level along the U.S. coast. They have judged that there has been no discernible long-term trend in storm-surge activity or severity in that region during the last 100 years.[17]

If we accept the general proposition that there is some evidence now that extreme sea levels are changing by amounts significantly different from mean sea level itself, this tells us something about the future — which is, after all, of the greatest interest to us. It seems inevitable that as mean sea level continues to rise due to global warming, extreme sea levels are likely to rise, too.

What lies ahead for us? Storm surges, generated by low atmospheric pressures and by high winds over the sea, can generate destructive waves along the coast. We do not know now the extent to which, in the decades to come, the continued and internationally-unregulated emission of greenhouse gases may affect the patterns and severity of tropical storms. The bottom line here is that more climate-change research is needed.

In particular, to alert inhabitants to likely adverse impacts on the coastal zone in the future, e.g., inundation and shoreside erosion, more modeling should be done on extreme sea level changes, on waves, and on river flows in coastal areas. What is self-evident is that with rising seas, hurricanes, and other storms, even if they do not rise in strength they will cause more damage in the future than in the present day. If, as expected, these storms also increase in intensity, then the risk to coastal regions can only be compounded.

What can be said now, reasonably and modestly, is that climate change may increase the probability of some ordinary weather events reaching extreme levels, or of some already-extreme events becoming even more extreme.

As an analogy, consider a die (half of a pair of dice), where rolling a "one" represents weak storms with low waves and less surge, while rolling a "six" represents the strongest storms with the greatest waves and surge. Climate change is loading the dice by putting a little more weight, as it were on the "6." On a given roll, any number could be rolled but the "6" will come up a bit more often due to being loaded. It is also possible that climate change may exacerbate an extreme event, either by extending the period during which it lasts or by causing more extreme conditions.

Extreme events and their possible relationships to climate change are thus very complicated issues which cannot accurately be captured in user-friendly sound-bite quotes or snappy Internet headlines. Indications of changes in various kinds of extreme climate events are evident in several regions of the world, e.g., a devastating heat wave in Russia and epic floods in Pakistan and Australia. Further research is now being undertaken to learn just how big a role climate change does play in severe weather events, but much more work remains to be done in this field.

To improve our understanding of sea level rise and variability, and to reduce the associated uncertainties, we will need more observations, as well as an open data policy encouraging timely and unrestricted international access to the data thus generated.[18] A good step in this direction is the work of the Global Earth Observation System of Systems (GEOSS), an international body which seeks to connect the producers of environmental data and decision-making tools with the end users of these products. The ultimate goal of the GEOSS is, over a 10-year implementation plan ending in 2015, to produce comprehensive, near-real-time environmental data, information, and analysis for a wide range of member states and participating organizations.[19]

For the immediate future, it will be very hard for climate scientists to explain the causes of extremes. An educated guess is that some extremes may become more common as time goes on. As a *New York Times* article put it in 2011,

> ... the National Oceanic and Atmospheric Administration said 2010 had tied for the warmest year on record in terms of land and sea surface temperatures. At the simplest level, a warmer ocean surface means more evaporation into the atmosphere — and all that extra water has to come down somewhere, probably accounting for more frequent and more extreme storms. But it is not easy to predict which places will suffer snow or rain and which will experience drought. Munich Re [the German insurance company we have discussed earlier] is already tailoring its offerings to a world of more extreme weather.[20]

In that same article Dr. Peter Hoeppe, the meteorologist who heads Munich Re's Corporate Climate Center, told a *New York Times* interviewer:

> "Your own perception that there are more storms and more flooding causing damage — that is well documented. There is definitely a plausible link to climate change."[21] What is painfully clear is that sea level rise threatens to increase the impacts of future storms and hurricanes on coastal communities in many parts of the world, including the United States. Along the southern shores of Long Island, New York, for example, even a modest and probable rise of only 1.6 feet (0.5 meters) by 2080 will vastly increase the number of people (a 47 percent increase) and property loss (a 73 percent increase) subjected to and resulting from storm surges there.[22]

V

The Changing Seas

Sea levels are never constant or permanent. They have changed greatly in the past, albeit slowly; they are still changing today; and they will continue to change throughout the foreseeable future, imperiously advancing and retreating over the low-lying coastlines of the world. To take but one small example, the Capo Malfatano breakwater and Punic–age dock in Sardinia, Italy, which are about 2,300 years old, now lie under 6.8 feet (2.1 meters) of water.[1]

The Greek philosopher Heraclitus, who died in about 475 B.C., is best known for his doctrine that change is central to the workings of the universe. He famously said: "You cannot step twice into the same river." Perhaps we can modify this by saying: "Nor can you step twice into the same sea level, because it is ever-changing." This chapter offers some thoughts on sea levels' distant past and on their near-term future.

Geologists have outlined for us their estimates of past sea level fluctuations. What follows is only a very rough summary of complex findings but it is enough for our purposes here. The dates cited below reflect the approximate beginnings of different geological epochs:

> During the Cambrian (542 million years ago), the sea level rose. In most of the Ordovician (488 million years ago), sea level was relatively stable but then dropped sharply at the end of the period due to glaciation. It remained relatively stable at this lower level during the Silurian (443 million years ago). Subsequently, it fell gradually through the Devonian (416 million years ago), continuing through the Mississippian (359 million years ago) to a long-term low at the Mississippian-Pennsylvanian boundary (325 million years ago). There was then a gradual rise until the start of the Permian (299 million years ago), followed by a gentle decrease lasting until the Mesozoic (covering the period 251–67 million years ago).[2]

It would be misleading to try to give these sea level changes more specifically, i.e., in meters or in feet. In the graph cited in the endnote above, two different sets of sea level reconstructions were used. These gave significantly different estimates of sea level changes during some of the early geological epochs. Nevertheless, what can safely be said is that, historically, sea level changes have been on the order of several hundred feet.

Specialists in sequence stratigraphy can track, thanks to coastal sediment deposits, dozens of shifts and later recoveries of the shorelines. In 2006, for example, French scientists investigated the paleoshorelines of the Gulf du Lion (Gulf of the Lion). This is a wide embayment of the Mediterranean coastline near the modern ports of Marseilles and Toulon. They found that, at different times over the last 500,000 years, relative sea levels there have been much lower than the present level, ranging from 367 feet (112 meters) to 859 feet (262 meters) below what it is today.[3]

Ice ages have played a major role in sea level changes. For a number of reasons, the volume of glacial ice near the two poles waxes and wanes over time. The result is that water is alternatively taken from or added to the world's oceans—a process which can result in sea level variations of up to 656 feet (200 meters).[4] The causes of the five major ice ages of our planet's past are not fully understood at this point but seem to involve a number of interrelated factors. The most likely among them are the small periodic variations in the Earth's tilt angle and shape of its orbit around the sun. Known as Milankovitch cycles, these set the stage for the buildup of snow at high latitudes (due to decreased summer melting during cooler summer periods) and thus for the start of an ice age by initiating a polar chill.[5] Other possible causes are thought to include the composition of the atmosphere, e.g., concentrations of carbon dioxide and methane; the motion of tectonic plates; variations in the strength of the sun; the impact of big meteorites; and, finally, volcanism.

What is obvious is that during the ice ages, high-latitude continental ice sheets are formed. These ice sheets grow from the top down as evaporated ocean water is deposited as snowfall and is slowly compressed into ice as many layers accumulate, one on top of the other. The result has been that, at various times in the distant past, a large part of the Earth's stock of water has been locked up in the cryosphere. (Derived from the Greek word for "cold," the cryosphere is that portion of the Earth's surface where water exists in solid form, i.e., as ice. Examples of the cryosphere include mountain glaciers, ice caps, and especially the high-latitude continental ice sheets. Such "locked up" water cannot immediately contribute to sea level rise.)

For illustrative purposes, here are a few selected snapshots of the "relatively recent" (in geological terms), incremental, and, above all, *never-ending process* of sea level change.[6]

- About 35 million years ago (in the Eocene), sea level was nearly 229 feet (70 meters) higher than it is today. This was the last era in which there were no permanently-grounded ice sheets anywhere on the Earth. The warmer world of that time was caused by high carbon dioxide concentrations arising from plate tectonics. (Plate tectonics spur the recycling of carbon atoms when the part of the continental crust slides beneath another part, melts, and becomes magma, the material that fuels volcanic eruptions. The process of eruption includes outgassing, in which carbon dioxide is released into the atmosphere.)

- Roughly 32 million years ago, carbon dioxide contributions dropped. The Antarctic ice sheet formed and sea level fell, but remained about 98 feet (30 meters) higher than it is today.

- During the Pliocene (3 million years ago), the average climate was warmer than today by about 5 to 9 degrees Fahrenheit (3 to 5 degrees Celsius), and sea level was about 49 to 114 feet (15 to 35 meters) higher than it is now. It should be noted that the Pliocene may offer us a glimpse of our own future because continents and oceans at that time were similar to what they are today. Carbon dioxide levels were around today's value of nearly 400 ppm (parts per million); and by 2100 it is expected that global temperatures will be comparable to those of the Pliocene. Given this state of affairs, we may well ask: are the oceans now on their way to rising over 50 feet (over 15 meters)?

- During the glacial eras of the last half-million years, sea level has varied by more than 328 feet (100 meters) as the great ice sheets, especially those of Europe and North America, majestically expanded and shrank. These changes in sea level, and the related global average temperature changes, were the Earth's natural response to shifts in solar radiation reaching its surface. Underlying these shifts were a variety of interrelated factors, e.g., variations in the Earth's orbit around the sun, feedbacks associated with changes in the Earth's albedo, and greenhouse gas concentrations that had the effect of trapping an increasing amount of heat.

- About 125,000 years ago, because of differences in the Earth's orbit the polar regions were appreciably warmer than they are today. The resulting retreat of polar ice led to a rise in sea levels of some 13–19 feet (4 to 6 meters).[7]

- During the following 100,000 years, sea level fell to about 426 feet (130 meters) below today's values as the northern European and American ice sheets formed.

- During the Last Glacial Maximum (the most recent ice age), which was at its peak approximately 26,000 years ago, sea level was about 393 feet (120 meters) lower than it is now.[8] During this time, the shallow continental shelves around the world were exposed. As a result, there seems to have been a dry-land connection over the Bering Strait (about 85 kilometers or 53 miles wide), which enabled some of the early hunter-gatherers to

Global Mean Sea Level Change

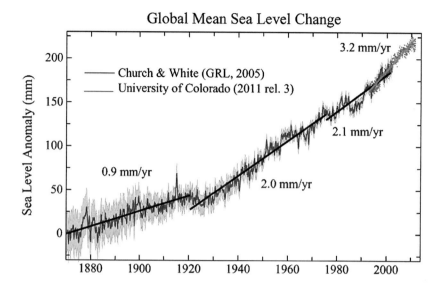

Sea level change for 1870–2001, based on tide gauge measurements, from J.A. Church and N.J. White University of Colorado data are shifted to have the same mean for 1993–2001 as Church and White. The trends were computed for 1870–1920, 1920–1975, 1975–2001 for Church and White data, and 1993 — September 10, 2011 for University of Colorado data. Note that 3.2 mm/yr equals .13 inches/yr and since 1870, sea level has risen about 8.3 inches (Sato, M. and J. Hansen, http://www.columbia.edu/~mhs119/SeaLevel/. Original data: Church, J.A., and N.J. White, "A 20th century acceleration in global sea-level rise" *Geophys. Res. Lett.* 2006; 33: L01602. and University of Colorado).

migrate from Asia into North America and thus begin to populate the Americas.

• By about 6,000 years ago, global average sea level had risen to near its present level. Since then, it has remained relatively constant. Historical records suggest that there was little net change from the first century CE to about 1800.[9]

Today, when used in combination with the global network of tide gauges, satellite altimeter data suggest that global mean sea level rose a total of some 7.6 inches (19.5 centimeters) between 1870 and 2004.[10] Satellite altimetry covering from 1993 to the present shows a recent acceleration.[11]

As a result of climate change, the global mean air temperature is rising now (and has done so for about the last 100 years), the volume of ice on the Earth is shrinking, and the heat content of the ocean is increasing. The net result is that global mean sea level is rising — and at a more rapid pace than it did previously.[12] Satellite altimeter data revealed, between January 1993 and

March 2010, a more-or-less steady increase in global mean sea level. The slope of the curve is 0.12 inches (3.25 millimeters) per year, though this rise is not uniform across all the oceans.[13] If level of change continues at this rate, after 10 years the sea level will have risen another 1.27 inches (32.5 millimeters). Given the impact on coastal regions of storms and wind-driven waves, this rise is significant.

It is now believed that global sea level rise will approach and probably pass 3.2 feet (1 meter) by the end of this century, with important local variations. Other estimates range from about 4 feet (1.24 meters)[14] to 6.2 feet (1.9 meters).[15] Peering much further into the future — all the way to the year 2300 — it has also been estimated that by then the sea may rise by as much as 9.8 to 16.4 feet (3 to 5 meters) above today's level — or even higher.[16]

An educated guess is that if it ever reaches 32.8 feet (10 meters), at least 397 million people will be adversely affected.[17] This estimate was made in 2006. Later and future population increases in the coastal zones of the world will certainly result in many more people being affected. In the very long run — that is, over thousands of years— the sea level could creep higher still, perhaps eventually peaking at about 38 feet (11.5 meters) above today's level.[18] If so, our descendants will probably have adapted to this inexorable and unstoppable rise long before then, but not without exorbitant costs.

VI

At the Edges of the Sea

Because coasts will continue to be mentioned frequently in this book, a quick look at them now, in overview, will pay good dividends later on. As a start, we can do no better than to quote Rachel Carson (1907–1964), the American marine biologist and conservationist whose gentle but lucid writings significantly advanced the global environmental movement in its earliest stages. In *The Edge of the Sea* (1955), the third book in her well-received trilogy on the sea, she writes:

> The edge of the sea is a strange and beautiful place. All through the long history of Earth it has been an area of unrest where waves have broken heavily against the land, where the tides have pressed forward over the continents, receded and then returned. *For no two successive days is the shore line precisely the same. Not only do the tides advance and retreat in their eternal rhythms, but the level of the sea itself is never at rest.* It rises or falls as the glaciers melt or grow, as the floor of the deep ocean basin shifts under its increasing load of sediments, or as the earth's crust along the continental margins warps up and down in adjustment to strain and tension. Today a little more land may belong to the sea, tomorrow a little less. Always the edge of the sea remains an elusive and indefinable boundary.[1]

Whenever we turn our attention to the ocean beaches, the river deltas, the barrier islands, the marshes, or the coral atolls, we shall find that life there is always in a subtle minuet with the level of the sea. In this chapter, we will offer some thoughts on the coasts themselves; on the current impacts of climate change and the human use (and abuse) of them; and on their likely future prospects. Two of the best and most exhaustive sources on these subjects are (1) the IPCC's 2007 report on "Coastal systems and low-lying areas," in which Drs. Robert J. Nicholls and Poh Poh Wong were the Coordinating Lead Authors, and (2) the U.S. Environmental Protection Agency's 2009 study, "Coastal Zones and Sea Level Rise," led by Dr. James G. Titus as the Coordinating Lead Author. We will draw on both of these authoritative works in this chapter.[2]

When all the intricacies of their many indented bays, promontories, and offshore islands are counted, the total length of the coastline of the world is estimated to be approximately 621,371 miles (1 million kilometers).[3] As will become evident, an underlying and fundamental point in this chapter is the *complex interactions* between the seas, the lands, and the many forms of life (including human life) which are dependent upon or are heavily influenced by them.

As the IPCC points out, coasts are constantly seeking a dynamic equilibrium, falling into different "states" in response to changes in wave energy and sediment supply. Such natural variability can make it difficult for scientists to isolate the impacts of climate change, including sea level rise. A major challenge for them is to judge whether observed changes are resulting from external factors, e.g., from sea level rise; from exceeding some kind of internal threshold, such as deltas shifting to new locations; or from short-term disturbances which are part of normal climate variability, such as storms.[4]

Sea level rise is just one of a wide range of factors that can strongly affect shorelines and coastal habitats. Other factors include winds; waves; tidal currents; the geological framework[5]; storms; the sediment budget (the amount of sediment being gained or lost along the shore — a key factor in future shoreline changes); nutrient runoff; biological processes; and, last but certainly not least, human activities.

As a result, coastal landforms and processes are never, ever static. Indeed, they are the crossroads where earth, ocean, and sky meet, mingle, and affect each another over a wide range of time scales. Features that today may seem to us to be fixed in place eternally — for example, spits (fingerlike extensions of beaches formed by longshore sediment transport), barrier islands, bluffs, dunes, wetlands — are in fact only transient phenomena. They have no choice but to respond to the ever-changing seaside forces which ceaselessly erode, rework, winnow, redistribute, and mold them.[6] Sea level rise can only strengthen these forces.

The U.S. Environmental Protection Agency warns us:

> There is some recent scientific opinion that coastal landforms such as barrier islands and wetlands may have threshold or tipping points with sea level rise and storms, leading to rapid and irreversible change.[7]

A study published in 2010 reported that scientists and policymakers may be underestimating the impact of sea level rise because they are focusing on the magnitude of the rise, rather than the relative rate of rise. The study showed that in the Gulf of Mexico region, when the rate of relative rise exceeds sediment accumulation rates, widespread coastal flooding occurs, even when the magnitude of sea level rise is minimal. In the northern Gulf of Mexico, the current rate of sea level rise is about six times the average rate for the past

Exhibit 6-20. Changes in relative sea level along U.S. coasts, 1958-2008[a]

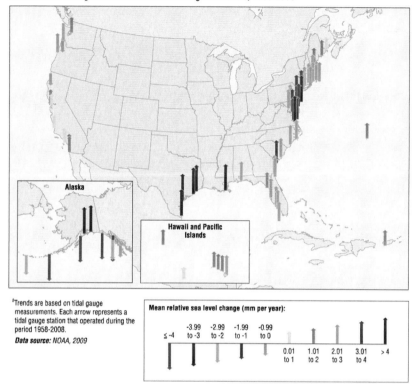

[a]Trends are based on tidal gauge measurements. Each arrow represents a tidal gauge station that operated during the period 1958-2008.

Data source: NOAA, 2009

Mean relative sea level change (mm per year):

| ≤ -4 | -3.99 to -3 | -2.99 to -2 | -1.99 to -1 | -0.99 to 0 | 0.01 to 1 | 1.01 to 2 | 2.01 to 3 | 3.01 to 4 | > 4 |

Changes of relative sea levels along U.S. coasts, 1958–2008. Note that 25.4 mm equals 1 inch (EPA, 2009).

4,000 years. According to model projections, the global rate will at least double by the end of this century, exceeding the highest average rate of rise in the Gulf for the past 7,500 years. The coasts of Louisiana and Texas are now experiencing unprecedented changes in some areas, due to the inability of sedimentation to keep pace with accelerating sea level rise.[8]

The management of most coastal regions is still based on the traditional but now "overtaken by events" assumption that shorelines are more or less static. The traditional school of thought holds that if a shoreline threatens to give us any trouble, e.g., by beginning to move in an unwanted direction, we can make it behave simply by relying more heavily on coastal engineering structures such as seawalls, revetments, groins, jetties, and breakwaters. (See Appendix 4 on Sea Level Rise and Breakwater Damage.) Coastal regions, however, have lives of their own. The U.S. Environmental Protection Agency lists seven ways in which they can respond to sea level rise[9]:

1. Land loss by inundation of low-lying lands.
2. Land loss due to erosion (removal of sediment from beaches, dunes, and cliffs)
3. Barrier island migration, breaching, and segmentation.
4. Wetland drowning (deterioration and conversion to open water).
5. Expansion of estuaries.
6. Saltwater intrusion (into freshwater aquifers and surface waters).
7. Increased frequency of storms (especially their effects on uplands and developed coastal lands).

While it is theoretically possible that a very rapid rate of sea level rise — say, 3.2 feet (1 meter) in just one year — could quickly flood parts of many low-lying coasts, e.g., the mid–Atlantic edge of the United States, which consists of a gradually upward-sloping coastal plain, a much more likely outcome is that higher waves and stronger currents would slowly but inexorably reshape existing shorelines to fit the rising sea level. Here it is worth quoting Rachel Carson again. She tells us:

> During the long ages of geologic time, the sea has ebbed and flowed over the great Atlantic coastal plain. It has crept toward the distant Appalachians, paused for a time, then slowly receded, sometimes far into its basin.... And so the particular place of its sand today is of little moment in the history of the earth or in the nature of the beach — a hundred feet higher, or a hundred feet lower, the seas would still rise and fall unhurried over shining flats of sand, as they do today.[10]

The headlands, barrier islands, and spits of the mid–Atlantic coast (and, by extension, other similar areas) will respond to sea level rise and stronger storms over the next 100 years in various ways. Erosion will change shoreline positions. Landforms will be affected. At much higher sea levels and with bigger storms, some barrier islands will probably migrate toward the shore or will be cut into adjacent but separate pieces.

Tidal salt marshes, flats, and aquatic plant beds will be at risk, too. This is important because they are among the most productive habitats in the world. Salt marshes have one of the highest rates of primary productivity, as measured by the amount of photosynthesis and organic matter they produce. They profit mightily from the continuous influx of nutrients borne on each tidal cycle and are essential spawning, nursery, and shelter areas for many different kinds of fish and shellfish. Some of these species are adapted to life on what has been termed the "coastal conveyer belt," spawning far out on the on the continental shelf and producing estuarine-dependent young that grow up close to the shore in coastal embayments.

Coastal vegetated wetlands are very sensitive to climate change and long-term sea level rise: their survival is closely linked to sea level. As the sea rises, losses of these wetlands would be most pronounced on the Atlantic and Gulf of Mexico coasts of North and Central America, the Caribbean, the Mediterranean, the Baltic, and most small island regions, due to their low tidal range.[11] The U.S. Environmental Protection Agency adds that in tidal salt marshes,

> Protection, rapid growth, and the ability to deposit energy reserves from the rich marsh diet prepare young fish for the rigors of migration and/or overwintering.... [Therefore] loss of tidal salt marshes would significantly affect fish populations, both estuarine and marine....[12]

We must also mention here the abundant but, to the layman, little-known estuarine beach organisms which are much too small to be seen with the naked eye. These are the microscopic invertebrates that live *between the sand grains* in the estuaries, dining on bacteria and single-celled protozoa. Their numbers defy easy computation: it is thought that there are over two billion of them in just 10.7 square feet (1 square meter) of sand. Tiny as they are, they form a vital link in beach food chains, e.g., between bacteria, on the one hand, and larger consumers, on the other — such as sand diggers, fleas, crabs, and little creatures that burrow in sediments or hide themselves under rocks. As the seas rise, estuarine beaches must adjust and must have sufficient sediment to replenish eroded sands.[13]

Let us conclude this chapter by peering into the future to see what probably lies ahead for the shores. The first thing we notice is that many of the megacities of this planet, with populations of many millions, are already located on the coasts and are growing rapidly. New coastal infrastructure development, especially in delightfully sunny regions, is accelerating — but with little if any consideration of sea level rise. Between 1958 and 2007, for example, the population of the aptly-named Gold Coast (Queensland, Australia) exploded from less than 40,000 people in 1958 to over 480,000 people in 2007, and with about 3.8 million visitors per year in 2008–2009.[14] Implicit in this growth has been the belief that the stable sea levels of the geologically-recent past will continue indefinitely.

In one worst-case scenario (defined to mean that while the number of people living in coastal areas continues to increase rapidly, no effective steps are taken to adapt to with sea level rise), it has been estimated that — postulating a relatively modest sea level rise of only 3.5 feet (1.07 meters) by 2100 — some 200 million people will face flooding each year.[15] The official forecasts made by the IPCC in 2007 must give us pause because trouble is clearly brewing on the horizon.

It is now self-evident that coasts are highly vulnerable to the adverse consequences of climate change and sea level rise. As mentioned earlier, these impacts are certain to be overwhelmingly negative. They will be exacerbated by increasing human-induced pressures. Extreme events, e.g., storms, will also impose substantial costs on coastal societies. Although adaptation costs for vulnerable coasts will be much less than the costs of doing nothing, our best guess is that for a variety of political, economic, and social reasons very little will done by most societies. The Netherlands may well be the only major example to the contrary. It is already thinking hard about a major sea level rise: see Appendix 6, "Possible Dutch responses to a sea level rise of 16.4 feet (5 meters)."

In the long run, sea level rise around the globe is very likely to conflict seriously with human development patterns and aspirations as we know and practice them today. This is evident when we see that many of the world's deltas, barrier islands, and estuaries have already experienced heavy population growth. Barrier islands, salt marshes, and mangrove forests are being converted for use in agriculture, aquaculture, silviculture, industry, urban development, and mass recreation. The natural abilities of these areas to collect and transform nutrients, smooth out waves and storms, collect sediments, and support diverse ecological communities thus comes under heavy stress.[16] In many areas, tourism will be impacted, too. For example, Hilton Head Island, South Carolina, is a lovely centerpiece of South Carolina's beach-based tourism but it is also highly vulnerable to land loss from sea level rise and accelerated rates of shoreline erosion.[17]

In our view, by far the best way for the world to cope with sea level rise is by a continuous process of adaptation. This, however, is much easier said than done. The IPCC, for example, has listed eight major impediments to the success of adaptation in coastal zones. Lightly edited, they are:

- Our inability to predict how the edges of the sea will respond to sea level rise.
- Insufficient or inappropriate shoreline protection measures.
- Divergent information management systems hamper data exchange and information.
- Lack of definition of key indicators and thresholds relevant to coastal managers.
- Inadequate knowledge of coastal conditions and appropriate management measures.
- Lack of long-term data for key coastal zone descriptors.
- Fragmented and ineffective institutional arrangements, often coupled with weak and corrupt governments.
- Last but definitely not least: *social resistance to change*. As the IPCC puts it in accurate but leadenly-bureaucratic terms, "Socio-economic and cultural

conditions frequently present barriers to choosing and implementing the most appropriate adaptation to sea level rise."[18] Translated into straightforward English, this means that adaptation to sea level rise will not happen unless the local inhabitants really want it to happen and are prepared to pay for it.

VII

Cities and Countries of the Atlantic Ocean Basin

Many cities and countries are already facing or will soon be facing serious problems as the sea level rises. In the interests of brevity, we shall examine only 25 of them in this book, but there are of course many others in the world, too.[1] We will discuss our selections in three separate chapters. Each chapter will focus on some of the cities and countries situated around or in one of three great oceanic basins—namely, the Atlantic Ocean Basin, the Pacific Ocean Basin, and the Indian Ocean Basin. Each chapter will attempt to explain their respective sea level rise problems in simple but technically accurate language.

To begin this process, we will now look at nine Atlantic basin cities and countries (including the Mediterranean and the North Sea), namely, New Orleans, Miami, New York (all in the United States); Rotterdam (Netherlands); the Thames Estuary and London (United Kingdom); Venice (Italy); Lagos (Nigeria); Alexandria (Egypt); and, finally, Recife and the northeast coast of Brazil.

New Orleans

Let us begin with a succinct overview of this region as a whole. It is estimated that approximately 22,393 square miles (58,000 square kilometers) of land along the Atlantic and Gulf coasts lie below the 4.9 foot (1.5 meter) height contour. Louisiana, Florida, Texas, and North Carolina account for more than 80 percent of this total. Louisiana alone has more than 9,554 square miles (24,724 square kilometers) of land below this contour line.[2] The Insurance Information Institute valued Louisiana's coastal insured property at $224 billion.[3] Climate change scientists Orrin Pilkey and Rob Young describe southern Louisiana in these graphic terms. It is, they tell us, a region where

a unique assemblage of natural and human-induced changes has combined to produce a landscape that has been drowning for decades.... In areas where the land surface is sinking (or subsiding), the actual local rate of sea level rise can be much greater than the rate of rise on a stable coast. Such is the case for southern Louisiana.[4]

The IPCC adds a specific warning about the subsiding deltaic plain of south-eastern Louisiana. Sediment starvation and increases in the water levels and salinity of coastal marshes there, due to human development projects, have occurred so quickly that large stretches of the intertidal coastal marshes and adjacent lands have now been converted to open water. By 2050, an additional 501 square miles (1,300 square kilometers) of coastal land loss is projected if, as it seems likely, current global, regional, and local trends continue unabated.

The projected increases in sea levels and in the intensity of tropical storms can only exacerbate these losses.[5] For example, a 2011 analysis by Core-Logic (an American corporation providing financial, property, and consumer information) of possible storm surge inundation to residential property in 10 major U.S. cities concluded that a Category 5 hurricane (the most powerful category) striking the greater New Orleans region would flood over 278,000 homes at a cost of $39 billion.[6] If levees fail at this time, as they did during Hurricane Katrina in 2005, the impact to residential property would be much worse.

New Orleans itself is located on the banks of the Mississippi River about 105 miles (169 kilometers) upriver from the Gulf of Mexico. The city has a total area of 350.2 square miles (907 square kilometers), of which only 51.55 percent is land, i.e., 180.56 square miles (467.6 square kilometers). The United States Geological Survey tells us:

> New Orleans is now sinking [at the rate of] two inches [5.1 centimeters] per decade, and it is anticipated that it will sink roughly one meter [3.2 feet] in the next 100 years relative to mean sea level. The ocean is also rising.... Within the next century if nothing is done to modify the existing infrastructure [in fact, the rebuilt, post–Katrina levee system will be stronger than its predecessor] some areas of the city that did not flood as a result of Hurricane Katrina will likely flood in a future storm due to subsidence and sea-level rise.[7]

Over the past few centuries, one quarter of the wetlands forming part of the Mississippi Delta has been lost to the ocean.[8] The city was first settled along the natural levees or on the high ground along the Mississippi River. Since then, it has waged a never-ending war against the water, e.g., by levees constructed since 1879 by local sponsors and by the U.S. Army Corps of Engineers. As the city began to expand into low-lying areas and more levees were built, water had to be pumped out of these areas when it rained. In the process, the underlying sediments were sucked dry of water; they compacted significantly, causing the land to sink. As a result, much of New Orleans and its neighboring area is now well below sea level — in some places even 6.5 to 9.8 feet (2 to 3 meters) below sea level.

This fact was dramatically illustrated in 2005 by Hurricane Katrina, when there were over 50 catastrophic failures of levees, floodwalls, and pump stations. About 80 percent of the city was flooded. The areas that were not flooded were either protected by a levee segment that did not connect with those that broke, or they were located on higher ground adjacent to the Mississippi River, i.e., on the so-called "natural levee" of the river. Local residents refer to it as the "sliver on the river" and joke that, in New Orleans, "water flows away from money." In fact, the neighborhoods that did escape flooding included the expensive uptown area; the downtown commercial district; and the tourist Mecca for which New Orleans is world-famous— the French Quarter. On the other hand, a very expensive area known as Lakeview, which is located about 7 feet (2.1 meters) below sea level, was completely drowned.

New Orleans is encircled by levees, which are designed to withstand hurricane storm surges of up to 19.6 feet (6 meters) or more. They can be built even higher if necessary. Hence the likely sea level rise, as projected by experts today, will not flood the city itself (unless, of course, the levees break or are overtopped) but will wash over all of the low-lying dry land. Much of the marsh that now surrounds the city is less than 19.6 inches (50 centimeters) above water, so it is virtually certain that it will be flooded.

In terms of remedial efforts, there is great concern felt by many in the scientific community but little consensus on what to do. Engineering solutions to rebuilding the coast call for transporting sediment from the Mississippi River or the current coastal zone and continental shelf to places where the land is disappearing. In point of fact, however, there is simply not enough sediment to rebuild the coast: the sediment load of the Mississippi River has been reduced by 50 percent due to dam construction in the Mississippi Basin.[9]

Nevertheless, some people still hope that that the coast can be rebuilt in its entirety. Unfortunately, the solutions that would rebuild the most land, and are therefore better for the coast as a whole, are not the same solutions that would rebuild land to protect New Orleans itself from future storm surges. Experts therefore conclude that significant coastal drowning is inevitable in the future because, even if sediment loads could somehow be restored, the sea level is now rising at least three times faster than it was when the delta was originally formed.

Indeed, it is now estimated that the maximum sea level rise, including a possible 0.31 inches (8 millimeters) of subsidence per year, might be as much as 4.5 feet (1.4 meters) by the year 2100. In the absence of sediment input, some 3,861–5,212 square miles of land (10,000–13,500 square kilometers) will be submerged by 2100 owing to subsidence and sea level rise.[10] This is an area that is 11 to 15 times larger than the city of New Orleans.

On a more positive note, the Inner Harbor Navigation Canal surge barrier wall, dubbed "The Great Wall of Louisiana" by the local press, is now complete.[11] This impressive barrier, over 7,600 feet long and rising 26 feet above the adjacent wetlands, was built in only 15 months. Part of the greater Hurricane and Storm Damage Risk Reduction System, the "Great Wall" will help provide 100-year level risk reduction for southeast Louisiana. Specifically, by providing protection from storm surges coming from the Gulf of Mexico and Lake Borgne it will reduce the risk of storm damage to some of the region's most vulnerable areas, e.g., New Orleans East, metro New Orleans, the 9th Ward, and St. Bernard Parish. The designers tell us that this surge barrier design can be adapted for use elsewhere in the world to deal with surge conditions caused by sea level rise, hurricanes, floods, and other wind-driven water rises.

Miami

The Insurance Information Institute cited earlier valued Florida's coastal insured property at $2.5 trillion, with the greater Miami region being a significant part of that total. Miami and its suburbs are situated on a broad plain which extends from the Florida Everglades to the west, to Biscayne Bay to the east, and from Florida Bay north to Lake Okeechobee. This low-lying region is never more than 40 feet (12 meters) above mean sea level. It averages about 6 feet (1.8 meters) in elevation in most neighborhoods, especially those closest to the coast.

As noted earlier in this book, a sea level rise of 3.2. feet (1 meter) would flood 18 percent of Miami, while a 19.6 foot (6 meter) rise would put 98 percent of the city underwater. Any significant rise would have major effects on many people. In terms of land area (much of its territory is water), Miami packs more than 400,000 human beings into only 35 square miles (92 square kilometers) of land, making it one of the most densely populated cities in the United States.

The limestone bedrock underlying the Miami area was formed as a result of drastic sea level changes caused by ice ages. About 130,000 to 120,000 years ago, the sea was about 20 feet (about 6 meters) above its present level: all of southern Florida was then covered by a shallow sea. After 120,000 years ago, glaciation began lowering the sea level (frozen water was locked up on land instead of being in the oceans) and exposed the floor of the Miami lagoon which had formed behind a reef line. By about 18,000 years ago, the sea had dropped to 420 feet (120 meters) below today's level. Subsequently, it rose quickly, slowing within a meter of its present level about 2,500 years ago and leaving the mainland of South Florida barely above sea level. However, it is not going to stay that way forever.

A study published in 2007 by Tufts University estimated that in a business-as-usual case (defined here to mean steadily increasing greenhouse emissions and "bad luck with the uncertain impacts of extreme weather"), sea level will rise by 27 inches (68 centimeters) by about 2060. This would flood 9 percent of Florida's land, including significant portions of the Florida Keys. In addition, part of Florida's most populous region — Miami — would be underwater. Remedial measures may well prove to be costly and ineffective. The very porous limestone and sand substrate of Miami-Dade County, which now provides excellent drainage, also limits the effectiveness of any wide-spread use of levees and dikes to hold off the encroaching sea.[12]

In a 2008 report, the Science and Technology Committee of Florida's Miami-Dade County Climate Change Task force issued a "Statement on Sea Level Rise in the Coming Century," which concluded that the *minimal* figure for sea level rise over the course of the 21st century is likely to be 3.3 to 5 feet (1 to 1.5 meters.)[13] If so, this would inundate large areas of Miami-Dade County, southern Broward County, and Everglades National Park. But despite some thoughtful reports on this subject,[14] little if anything is now being done to deal with this eventuality. Indeed, to make an old joke of a potentially serious new situation, we can only say that the local politicians are now devoting their energies simply to "rearranging the deck chairs on the Titanic."

Their head-in-the-sand approach is indeed a shame, because, measured by the commercial value of property that would be threatened by a 3 foot (0.9 meter) rise, Miami is near the top of the list of the most endangered major cities in the world. Such a rise would flood all of Miami Beach and would reduce downtown Miami to an island, disconnected from the rest of Florida. The economic and human losses of this event would be enormous. The risk to property in Miami is high even at today's sea levels. The firm CoreLogic, cited earlier, concluded in 2011 that a Category 5 hurricane striking the greater Miami region would inundate over 247,000 homes at a cost of about $45 billion, not including the costs of a collapsed local economy which would greatly increase that estimate. Even a Category 1 hurricane would damage 52,000 homes at a cost of $16 billion.

A scientist in Florida who studied a series of articles in 2011 on the potential impacts of sea level rise on Florida's natural and human communities stated that

> The main lesson that emerges [from this review] is that sea level rise, combined with human population growth, urban development in coastal areas, and land-scape fragmentation, poses an enormous threat to human and natural well-being

in Florida. How Floridians respond to sea level rise will offer lessons, for better or worse, for other low-lying regions worldwide.[15]

New York

New York City has a watery past and will have a watery future. It is situated at the mouth of the Hudson River in southeastern New York State and has a fine, deep, naturally-sheltered harbor which was the keystone of its prosperity. As Herman Melville described the city in *Moby Dick* (1851),

> There now is your insular city of the Manhattoes [i.e., the Indians living in what is now Manhattan], belted round by wharves as Indian isles by coral reefs—commerce surrounds it with her surf. Right and left the streets take you waterward.... Look at the crowds of water-gazers there.... Posted like silent sentinels all around the town, stand thousands upon thousands of mortal men fixed in ocean reveries. Some leaning against the spiles [the wooden posts supporting the piers]; some seated upon the pier-heads; some looking over the bulwarks of ships from China; some high in the rigging, as if striving to get a better seaward peep.[16]

The city's history as a European settlement began in 1609 when the Englishman Henry Hudson, then working for the Dutch East India Company and searching for a non-existent westerly route to Asia, sailed his ship, *Halve Maen* (*Half Moon*), through the Narrows into Upper New York Bay. The abundant beaver population he found in the region would spark the founding of Dutch trading colonies in the New World: beaver pelts were in great demand for making best-quality felt hats for gentlemen. One of these trading colonies, named New Amsterdam, would evolve into New York City.

The city today is vulnerable to storm surges from winter Nor'Easters (i.e., the strong northeasterly winds associated with extra-tropical cyclones that occur along the East Coast of the U.S. and Canada) and from summer hurricanes, as well as from the prospect of sea level rise. Much of the metropolitan region is less than 16 feet (4.8 meters) above mean sea level. It is estimated that, by the 2050s, adding as little as 1.5 feet (0.46 meters) of sea level rise to the forecast storm surges from a Category 3 hurricane which follows a worst-case track would cause extensive flooding in many parts of New York City.

Hurricanes are categorized on the Saffir-Simpson scale which ranges from 1 to 5, with 5 being the most powerful and the most destructive. The 1893 "New York Hurricane"—a Category 2 storm—was the last great storm to hit the city directly. The storm surge it caused pummeled the coastline and completely obliterated the Long Island resort town of Hog Island, New York.

In the Category 3 hurricane discussed above, areas subject to flooding would include the Rockaways, Coney Island, much of southern Brooklyn and

Queens, portions of Long Island City, Astoria, Flushing Meadows-Corona Park, lower Manhattan, and eastern Staten Island from Great Kills Harbor north to the Verrazano Bridge. As part of this process, there might be storm surges of up to 25 feet (7.6 meters) at JFK Airport, 21 feet (6.4 meters) at the Lincoln Tunnel entrance, 24 feet (7.3 meters) at the Battery, and 16 feet (4.8 meters) at La Guardia Airport.[17] Parts of New Jersey, e.g., Newark International Airport, are also highly vulnerable.[18] In 2008, the Insurance Information Institute, which we have already mentioned, valued New York's coastal insured property at $2.4 trillion, with the New York City/Long Island metropolitan area making up most of that total. A major hurricane hitting this region has the potential to dwarf the damages caused by Hurricane Katrina, which was the costliest disaster in U.S. history.

New York continues to study sea level rise, though no specific remedial actions have been proposed or undertaken yet. In 2010, the New York City Panel on Climate Change issued a report which, among other things, called attention to the future problems which will very likely be caused by sea level rise and by storm surges. The report stated in part:

> Climate change poses challenges to planning for coastal waterfront development in New York City, given the uncertain but significant risks of progressive sea level rise and enhanced flooding of low-lying neighborhoods and infrastructure, increased transportation disruptions, impaired operations, increased beach and shorefront erosion, and loss of wetlands.... Temperature increases and sea level rise are already occurring and, along with other climate changes, will continue to occur and accelerate in the future.[19]

In a February 2012 study, researchers modeled potential future storm surges for New York City and concluded:

> Struck by many intense hurricanes in recorded history and prehistory, NYC is highly vulnerable to storm surges. We show that the change of storm climatology will probably increase the surge risk for NYC; results based on two GCMs show the distribution of surge levels shifting to higher values by a magnitude comparable to the projected sea-level rise (SLR). The combined effects of storm climatology change and a 1 m SLR may cause the present NYC 100-yr surge flooding to occur every 3–20 yr and the present 500-yr flooding to occur every 25–240 yr by the end of the century.[20]

In 2007, the New York State Legislature created a Sea Level Rise Task Force to assess the impacts of rising seas on the state's coastlines and to recommend protective and adaptive measures. This task force labored mightily but, at the end of 2010, it brought forth only a mouse. Here are some key points taken from the Executive Summary of its report to the New York State Legislature.[21]

- A thorough analysis of the costs and benefits associated with sea level rise and potential adaptation strategies was beyond the scope of this report.
- The findings and recommendations of this report needed to be further analyzed to evaluate their applicability to specific sites and their effect on economic development, greenhouse gas mitigation efforts, the environment, and other factors.
- Members of the Task Force held very divergent views and were thus unable to reach agreement on some of the report's recommendations. For example, the City of New York, as well as some private commentators, argued that the recommendations of the Task Force were not supported by thorough scientific, environmental, or cost-benefit analysis and did not recognize the important differences between undeveloped areas and densely-populated cities.

Rotterdam

Located at the mouth of the Rhine River, the Maas River, and their tributaries, Rotterdam is the Netherlands' second largest city (after Amsterdam). It is also the lowest city below sea level in the country and the point where sea-and-river-borne traffic mix and mingle. The port of Rotterdam is the largest port in Europe. (From 1962 to 2004 it was also the world's busiest port but it was then overtaken, first by Shanghai and then by Singapore.) Given the small size of the Netherlands, Rotterdam cannot ever be considered in isolation but only as one of the theaters of Netherlands' perpetual war against the water.

More than any other country in the world today, the Netherlands is already taking expensive, comprehensive, well-organized steps to prepare for a future with much higher sea levels. About 27 percent of the Netherlands lies below sea level, so the price of failure would be exceeding high. As an old saying has it, "God made the world but the Dutch made the Netherlands." There is much truth in this witticism.

Indeed, it is only thanks to their unrelenting efforts—which continue year-round, day and night—that the Dutch have been generally successful at keeping the water at bay. Eternal vigilance is, however, the price of their victory. No one has described the situation better than the Dutch poet Hendrik Marsman (1899–1945). He wrote:

> *en in alle gewesten*—And in every region
> *wordt de stem van het water*—The voice of the water
> *met zijn eeuwige rampen*—Telling of endless disaster
> *gevreesd en gehoord.*—Is feared and heard.

The Dutch will never forget what happened in 1953. In that year, a combination of a high spring tide and a severe northwesterly gale caused a storm surge which exceeded 18.3 feet (5.6 meters) in parts of the Netherlands. Dutch sea defenses were quite overwhelmed; 1,835 people were killed in the Netherlands and about 70,000 had to be evacuated. To prevent a similar disaster in the future, the Dutch have built a formidable flood defense system known as the Delta Works. It will be discussed later.

As for Rotterdam itself, a Dutch study published in 2011 offered the following comments:

> The possible consequences of the combined impacts of local sea level rise, storm surges, and peak river discharges [e.g., from the Rhine] become apparent when considering the situation near Rotterdam. Its harbour is protected by the Maeslant Storm Surge Barrier [we will discuss this barrier in more detail later on], which closes automatically when the local water level reaches a prescribed criterion — an event that [initially] was expected to occur on average every 10 years. If the high-end projection for sea level rise [described in the study] becomes reality, the storm surge barrier which is expected to close five to fifty times more often. This would severely hamper the accessibility of Rotterdam harbor, resulting in large economic losses.
>
> In addition, the projected increases in sea level and peak river discharge will significantly enhance the probability that the storm surge barrier will have to be closed while the river discharge is large. During closure, the river system behind the barrier rapidly fills, increasing the local flood risk.[22]

In our judgment, the Netherlands is now head-and-shoulders in front of any other country in the world when it comes to *actually doing something* about sea level rise on a highly organized national level. Because of its very long experience with water management, its careful planning for the future, its well-trained labor force, and its general prosperity and political stability, the Netherlands can be expected to do an excellent job coping with sea level rise in the decades to come.

The Thames Estuary and London

In his finest short story, *Heart of Darkness* (1902), Joseph Conrad evokes the Thames Estuary and London in these magisterial cadences:

> The *Nellie*, a cruising yawl, swung to her anchor without a flutter of the sails and was at rest.... The sea-reach of the Thames stretched before us like the beginning of an interminable waterway. In the offing the sea and the sky were welded together without a joint.... The air was dark above Gravesend, and farther back still seemed condensed into a mournful gloom, brooding motionless over the biggest, and the greatest, town on earth [London].[23]

The Thames Barrier now stretches 570 yards (520 meters) across the River Thames. It is located at Woolwich (downstream of central London) and is the world's second largest moveable flood barrier (after the Oosterscheldekering — in English, the Eastern Scheldt Storm Surge Barrier — in the Netherlands). Its purpose is to prevent London from being flooded by exceptionally high tides and storm surges moving up from the sea.

Both the Thames Estuary and London itself are potentially vulnerable to severe flooding. The River Thames is at sea level where it runs into the North Sea; the lowest point in the city of London itself is only about 20 feet (6 meters) above sea level. As the United Kingdom's Environment Agency explains,

> When an area of low pressure, perhaps hundreds of miles across, moves eastwards across the Atlantic Ocean towards the British Isles, it raises the level of the seawater beneath it by up to a third of a meter [1 foot]. If this "plateau" of sea water passes north of Scotland and then into the shallow basin of the North Sea, perhaps further heightened by strong winds from the north, it can cause excessively high surges tides in the Thames Estuary of up to 4 metres [19.5 feet] leading towards London. When a surge tide also coincides with a spring tide (which occur twice monthly), flooding would be a serious possibility. The problem is made much worse when floodwater from upstream meets a high surge tide coming up from the Thames Estuary.[24]

The threat of flooding has increased over time because the southeastern corner of the British Isles is slowly tilting downward (due to post-glacial rebound in northern Britain where there were glaciers in the past) and because sea levels are rising. As a result, the high tide in central London is creeping up at a possible rate of 29.5 inches (75 centimeters) per century.[25]

Today, maintained and operated by the Environment Agency, the Thames Barrier is protecting about 48 square miles (125 square kilometers) of central London and some 1.25 million people. It only needs to be raised during high tide; at ebb tide it can be lowered to release the water that backs up behind it. Based on future estimates of sea level rise, this barrier should, with some modifications to give it a higher effective crest level, be able to cope with projected sea level rises until about 2070.[26] In the very long run, if changing climate conditions and future sea level rise dictate the need to do so, it would technically be possible to build an "outer estuary barrage" all the way across the Thames Estuary near Canvey Island.[27]

Venice

Located on the northeastern coast of Italy, Venice is at the northern end of the long, narrow, rectangular-shaped Adriatic Sea.[28] It is very low-lying:

the low parts of the city are only about 2.9 feet (0.89 meters) above sea level. One of its most famous sights—Piazza San Marco (St. Mark's Square)—is so low that it is flooded regularly by the frequent and damaging *acqua alta*— "high water" in Italian. This phenomenon will be explained very briefly later on.

Venice was built on islands inside a lagoon which is separated from the Adriatic Sea by three barrier islands. The lagoon is the place where fresh and sea waters mix, mingle, and circulate. The first peoples who moved into the lagoon were those looking for a safe place to live — one which gave them protection from marauders. Since then, for hundreds of years the inhabitants of Venice have directed their efforts to maintaining a fragile equilibrium, playing with the forces of nature to influence and orient, according to their needs, the evolution of a fragile, delicate ecosystem.

Over the last century, the city has lost approximately 10 inches (25 centimeters) in height relative to sea level. This loss has been due a variety of causes: natural subsidence caused by shifting of tectonic plates or by compaction of deltaic deposits; intensive human activities, including groundwater extraction; man-made changes in the lagoon environment, such as dredging navigation channels and building sediment-diverting jetties; and eustatic sea level rise. If, as seems quite possible, deglaciation and the melting of Greenland and Antarctic land ice will accelerate in the decades ahead, the waters surrounding Venice will rise at an even faster rate than the Italian authorities now expect.

There are, alas, no easy solutions to Venice's watery problems. The first mention of a big flood in the Venetian lagoon dates from a report by "Paul the Deacon" in the year 589. The first documented description of *acqua alta* in Venice comes from 782. Nevertheless, the Venetians literally rose above such challenges, to the extent that by the late thirteenth century Venice had become the most prosperous city in the whole of Europe. At the apex of its fortunes, it could boast that its 36,000 sailors and 3,300 ships dominated commerce in the Mediterranean. Venice well deserved then its title as "Queen of the Seas."

No glory lasts forever, however, and now Venice is best known as the tourist capital of Italy. In modern times, it has been increasingly subject to winter flooding by the high surges of water (*acqua alta*) that sweep into the city during certain wind, tide, rain, and lunar conditions. Rising seas, for their part, now threaten the Venetian lagoon. Along a few canals, the ground-floor windows of some of the buildings nearest to sea level have had to be cemented shut to keep out the waves. There can be no doubt that something dramatic must be done if the city is to be saved from the sea. The Italians have therefore turned to sophisticated technology to rescue the lagoon.

Doorways on the Grand Canal in Venice during high water in October 2010 (courtesy Steve Easterbrook).

Their chosen tool is known as MOSE, the acronym in Italian for Modulo Sperimentale Elettromeccanico ("Experimental Electromechanic Module"). Finally approved by the Italian government in 2003, this is the biggest public works project in Italian history. Perhaps to lighten the heavy technical and financial burden of this ambitious project, the Italians joke that MOSE is also a play on the Italian name for Moses (Mosè)—bringing to mind his biblical parting of the Red Sea.

MOSE will consist of 79 hollow floodgates, located at the three inlets that link the Venice lagoon to the Adriatic Sea. When these giant gates are at rest, they will lie on the bottom of the inlet channel and will not be visible from the surface. Each gate will be up to 92 feet (301.8 meters) long, 65 feet (213.2 meters) wide, and will weigh 300 tons (272 tonnes). When a dangerously-high tide is forecast, compressed air will be released inside the gates and will drive out the water which fills them. They will then rise to the surface and block the flow of the tide. If funding continues without interruption and if no other problems intervene, MOSE is scheduled to be completed in 2012.

We must note, however, that this project has long been, and still is, highly controversial. Its many critics denounce it as irreversible and as likely to be outdated within a relatively short space of time. They claim that it was designed without taking into account the most recent predictions on rising sea levels over the next century and that it poses environmental problems of its own. Regarding this latter point, they worry that, given the ever-rising seas, MOSE officials may have to close the gates so often that the normal ebb and flow of the cleansing tides, which flush Venice's sewage out of the lagoon, will be much reduced. As result, they believe, aquatic life within the lagoon would be adversely affected and, in a worse-case scenario, Venice itself might even be made unlivable for periods of time.

The Italian government and the MOSE supporters, for their part, assure the world that all is well, that this project has been studied with the utmost care, and that it is the only feasible solution to Venice's watery problems. However, all that seems certain right now is that, eventually, the sea will reclaim its prize. Thanks to sea level rise, even the most drastic human intervention can only stave off — say, for, 100 to 200 years — the permanent flooding of Venice.

It is very probable, therefore, that this famous city will, in the long run, become a textbook case on the perils of building human settlements on the low-lying coastal fringes of the world at a time when seas are rising. Throughout our own lifetimes, however, Venice will probably still continue to be the lovely and courageous city it is today. Indeed, Thomas Mann might well have had it in mind when he wrote in his novella, *Death in Venice* (1912):

> Forbearance in the face of fate, beauty constant under torture, are not merely passive. They are a positive achievement, an explicit triumph.[29]

Lagos

The city and port of Lagos is located in southwestern Nigeria on the Atlantic coast in the Gulf of Guinea, west of the Niger River delta. This is very hot, very flat, and very humid part of the world. Rivers sluggishly meander toward the sea and form swampy lagoons behind long coastal sand spits or sand bars. Lagos is still the economic and financial center of Nigeria; inland Abuja is now the capital.

In the wake of the 1970s Nigerian oil boom, Lagos held out the dream of untamed, unlimited economic growth and rapid social advancement. The city thus attracted, from all parts of Nigeria and from other African countries, very large numbers of young people and families, most of them poor, who were seeking a better life. As a result, Lagos is now a huge, sprawling metropolis — the second most populous city in Africa (after Cairo) and is thought to be one of the fastest growing cities in the world. There is no accurate count of its population but it has been estimated at about 11.5 million people.

Coastal erosion has long been a serious problem in Lagos State (an administrative division of Nigeria, located in the southwestern part of the country). This erosion has both natural and man-made causes. The natural causes include waves, littoral drift (sediments are carried by the strong long-shore and rip currents), shelf width (the narrower the shelf width, the greater the wave effect), and storm surges. The man-made causes of this coastal erosion include climate change and sea level rise, subsidence, harbor-protecting structures, and shipwrecks.[30]

A Nigerian study published in 2011 found that empirical evidence of sea level rise and flooding recorded in Lagos included severe coastal erosion, disruption of traffic, flooding of roads and property thanks to the uncontrolled increase of impermeable surfaces (a result of the very rapid growth of the city), washing away of protective granite boulders, and a very dramatic if temporary sea level rise during storm surge periods, e.g., a rise of 4.9 feet (1.5 meters) above normal within two days in 2006. Thus Lagos is clearly one the megacities cities most vulnerable to sea rise.[31]

It has been estimated that a permanent sea level rise of only 7.8 inches (200 millimeters) might create as many as 740,000 homeless people in Nigeria.[32] If so, one result would almost certainly be an intensification of the social conflict already prevalent in the area.[33] In the meantime, Nigerian beaches have been lost; buildings have been flooded; and roads, drains, and water pipelines have been destroyed.[34] Nevertheless, hope springs eternal in Nigeria and, quite remarkably, plans for a new coastal community near Lagos have been put forward.

It would be called "Eko Atlantic City" and would be built on about 3.4 square miles of land to be reclaimed from the Atlantic Ocean. Some of this land is said to have already been reclaimed. To protect this proposed community from fierce ocean surges and rising sea levels, a 4-mile-long (6.5 kilometer) sea barrier — locally and jokingly called the Great Wall of Lagos— may be erected. Its advocates claim that it will be able to withstand "the worst storm imaginable in a thousand years."[35]

Promoters of Eko Atlantic City assert that 250,000 people will be able to live there and that 150,000 more can commute to work there each day. They also claim that this project will be environmentally-friendly because it is designed to return the coast to its position in the 1950s and 1960s, reversing the extensive coastal damage done by erosion. Finally, they assert that the danger posed by future sea level rise has been studied very carefully and that the inhabitants and workers of Eko Atlantic City will be able to carry on with their lives, safely and securely, behind the Great Wall.

However, because Nigeria is still very much a developing country, it can be difficult or impossible for outsiders to get reliable information from Nigerian sources on many aspects of life there. This has been our own experience with Eko Atlantic City. Fortunately, we have been able to get the gist of a study undertaken by the Dutch firm of Haskoning Nederland in Rotterdam, the primary consultant to this project with regard to sea level rise. Lightly edited, the study makes the following key points[36]:

- The impact of potential sea level rise has been carefully considered during the planning and design of the sea revetment protecting the reclamation. An increase in water levels due to sea level rise will result in a minor increase in wave heights at the toe of the revetment, which could affect the stability of the primary armor protection and the frequency at which waves overtop the defenses.
- Tests conducted in Copenhagen show that the design for the revetment is robust and able to withstand an increase in the design wave height of 27.5 inches (0.7 meters) without significant damage to the armor. As an increase in water levels to 3.2 feet (1 meter) is likely to increase wave heights by a similar margin, it is concluded that the stability of the revetment will not be adversely affected by sea level rise.
- In the future, an increase in water levels will result in an increase in over-topping. To counter this effect, the wave wall is being designed so that mod-ifications (e.g., an increase in crest level) can be undertaken in the future to maintain overtopping at present-day levels.

If Eco Atlantic City is not in fact built to rigorous design and engineering specifications, this will turn out to be a serious mistake: sea level rise is certain to be a problem for Nigeria. For example, as early as 1998, it was estimated that in Nigeria 3.2 million people could be displaced from their homes as a result of sea level rise. Over 2 million of these people live in Greater Lagos and other urban areas.[37] A 2010 study of the likely impact of a relatively modest 3.2 feet (1 meter) sea level rise on the Nigerian coast predicted that such a rise would affect nearly 900,000 people and 375 square miles (973 square kilometers) of coastal lands.[38]

As for Eco Atlantic City itself, we believe it is still too early for outsiders to hazard a guess now on what the long-term prospects for this ambitious undertaking may be. Perhaps the most prudent course for us is simply to wait and see how matters stand in 2016, when Eko Atlantic City is supposed to be finished.

Alexandria

Founded by Alexander the Great in 331 B.C., the city and port of Alexan-dria is located on the edge of the low-lying Nile Delta of Egypt, one of the most densely populated and intensively cultivated areas on earth. Historically, the entrance to Alexandria's harbor was overshadowed by a famous lighthouse (*Pharos*), reputed to have been as much as 450 feet (138 meters) high. It was one of the seven wonders of ancient world; remarkably, its ruins were discovered, under water, in 1994. Such ruins show that Alexandria was one of several now-submerged Mediterranean cities, all of which fell victim to various combinations of global ocean expansion, land subsidence, relative sea level rise caused by local tectonic forces (e.g., earthquakes), and storms.[39]

Today, Alexandria has a population of more than 4.1 million people and is the second-largest city in Egypt (after Cairo). It is the country's biggest seaport, handling about 80 percent of Egypt's imports and exports and is also a key industrial center, thanks to the natural

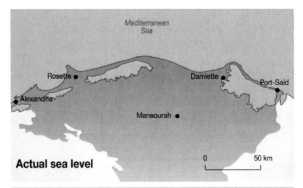

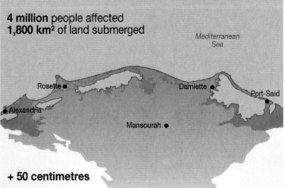

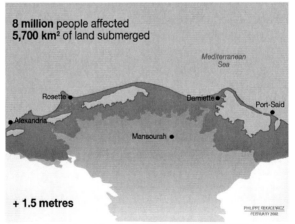

Sources: The Sea elevation model has been calculated by Otto Simonett (UNEP/GRID, Arendal and Nairobi) at the beginning of the 1990s.
See also http://blog.mondediplo.net/2008-01-22-Le-delta-du-Nil-menace-par-les-eaux

Impact of sea level rise on the Nile delta (Phillipe Rekacewicz, Otto Simonett, in UNEP/GRID-Arendal Maps and Graphics Library, 2009, http://maps.grida.no/go/graphic-/impact-of-sea-level-rise-on-the-nile-delta).

gas and oil pipelines running into it from the city of Suez. Alexandria sprawls for about 20 miles (32 kilometers) along the coast. Since much of it, and the Nile Delta as a whole, is less than 6.5 feet (2 meters) above sea level, the region is quite vulnerable to sea level rise.

The Nile Delta is already subsiding at a rate of 0.11 to 0.19 inches (3–5 millimeters) per year. Coming on top of this subsidence, a 3.2 foot (1 meter) rise in the Mediterranean Sea could inflict enormous damage. Some likely consequences[40]:

- The Alexandria coast is now protected from flooding only by a 0.62 to 6.2-mile-wide (1–10 kilometer-wide) sand belt. Rising seas will further erode part of this sand belt, which has been shaped by sediment discharges from the Rosetta and Damietta branches of the Nile. The sand belt has already been considerably weakened because of reduced sediment flows from the Rosetta and Damietta. This reduction is due to the construction, further upstream, of the Aswan High Dam in 1970.
- Without a viable sand belt, water quality in the Delta's freshwater lagoons will be adversely affected, jeopardizing one-third of Egypt's fisheries there; groundwater will be salinated; and beach and beach facilities, now very popular, will be severely damaged, thus harming the tourism industry.
- More than 6 million people could be displaced; 1,737 square miles (4,500 square kilometers) of cropland would be lost; industrial production would tumble (40 per cent of Egypt's industry is now located in Alexandria alone); and Egypt's Gross Domestic Product (a measure of a country's overall economic output) could decline by more than 6 percent.

A reasonable guess now is that if no effective remedial actions are taken, a sea level rise of between 1.64–3.2 feet (0.5–1.0 meters) will flood about 30 percent of Alexandria.[41] Some remedial work is already underway: Egypt is spending $300 million to build concrete sea walls to protect Alexandria's beaches from the rising seas. Whether this will be enough to safeguard the city in the years to come remains to be seen.

Recife and the Northeast Coast of Brazil

Brazil's coastal zone constitutes one of the major socioeconomic areas of the country.[42] Many areas there are already experiencing acute environmental problems, e.g., coastal erosion, pollution, degradation of sand dunes, and saline intrusion of coastal aquifers and rivers. In the future, accelerated sea level rise can only intensify these stresses and will almost certainly cause extensive flooding of coastal lowlands, erosion of sandy beaches, and destruction of coastal wetlands. Thus sea level rise will be one of the main negative impacts of climate change in northeast Brazil.

Recife itself is located on the northwest coast of Brazil where the Berberibe River meets the Capibaribe River and flows into the Atlantic Ocean. It is a major port. Its Metropolitan Center extends over a sedimentary plain with an average altitude of 13.1 feet (4 meters). Recife has been dubbed "the Brazilian Venice" because of its many rivers, small islands, and more than 50 bridges. The Metropolitan Center is characterized by low topography, intense urbanization, high demographic density, and ecological, tourist, and economic attractions.

Because it embodies several conflicts in coastal land and shoreline uses, it was one of the first regions in Brazil to be the subject of integrated studies of coastal erosion and is now being studied in terms of sea level rise impacts. It is estimated that in Recife a 3.2 foot (1 meter) sea level rise would flood about 12.7 square miles (33 square kilometers) of the city.[43] A Brazilian study published in 2010 concluded that

> The Metropolitan Center of Recife, due to its physical characteristics and its current erosion and flood problems, presents itself as a region highly vulnerable to an increase in sea level. Additionally, it has unfavorable social characteristics for responses to flooding, including high demographic density and intensified vertical growth on the coast, as well as occupation of riverside areas. The impact associated with the relative sea level rise may intensify if relief measures are not taken.[44]

Recife is not, of course, the only part of Brazil subject to damage from sea level rise: the coastline of the country is some 7,491 kilometers (4,654 miles) in length. To take but one tiny portion of it, we can note that, roughly 300 miles (482 kilometers) northwest of Recife, the Apodi River runs through Apodi, Mossoro, and other cities before emptying into the Atlantic Ocean.

The Apodi is one of the most important river systems that flow into this part of the Brazilian continental shelf. This region is also includes one of the primary Brazilian oil producing fields exploited onshore. Other economic activities there include shrimp and other fisheries, agriculture, tourism, and industrialization. If sea level there rises 3.2 feet (1 meter), about 15 percent of the total land area of this region will be flooded. Cities and towns, natural vegetation and agricultural land, industrial areas, beaches and salt marshes— all these will be impacted.[45] Similar statements could doubtless be made about many other parts of the long Brazilian coastline.

VIII

Cities and Countries
of the Pacific Ocean Basin

Ten key areas or cities are discussed in this chapter; all of them are vulnerable to rising seas. They include the San Francisco Bay Area (California); cities of the China coast; Vietnam's coastal regions; Bangkok (Thailand); Tuvalu and Kiribati (Pacific atoll nations); Osaka/Kobe (Japan); and Australia-New Zealand.

The San Francisco Bay Area

Fabled in song and story, San Francisco Bay, with its Golden Gate Bridge, is simultaneously both a *bay*, i.e., an inlet or cove providing a physical refuge from the sea, and a shallow, biologically-productive *estuary*, i.e., a place where freshwater meets an ocean or sea. It has a remarkable environmental history which is worth mentioning here.[1]

Often referred locally simply as "the Bay," San Francisco Bay varies in size somewhere between 400 and 1,600 square miles (1,040 to 4,160 square kilometers), depending on which sub-bays and wetlands are counted. It is the largest eastern Pacific estuary. The main part of the Bay is 3 to 12 miles (5 to 20 kilometers) wide, east to west, and approximately between 48 miles to 60 miles (77 kilometers to 97 kilometers) long, north to south. The average depth of the Bay is only about 12 feet to 15 feet (3.7 meters to 4.6 meters), though its deepest part (under and west of the Golden Gate Bridge) is 300 feet (91 meters).

After gold was discovered in California in the foothills of the Sierra Nevada mountains in 1848, miners found that the more gold-bearing gravels they could process, the more tiny specks of gold they were likely to find. They began to use very high-pressure hoses to wash entire hillsides through huge sluices to recover these bits of gold. By the mid–1880s, about 11 million ounces of gold, worth about $15 billion at 2011 prices, had been recovered by hydraulic mining during the California Gold Rush.

The bad news was that hydraulic mining had a devastating and lasting effect on the environment. Sediment from the rivers settled in parts of the Bay that had little or no current. Later, other wetlands and tidal inlets of the Bay were deliberately filled in for agricultural and industrial purposes. The upshot was that, from the mid–19th century through the late 20th century, more than 30 percent of the original Bay had become land. It is worth noting that the deep, damp soil of these areas is subject to liquefaction during earthquakes, that is, the ground can lose its stability and can no longer support the structures built on it.

Water levels in the Bay have risen about 7 inches (0.18 meters) over the last century and the rate of sea level rise is accelerating. Moreover, large portions of the South Bay are now below current sea level because of land subsidence.[2] In 2007, the San Francisco Bay Conservation and Development Commission (BCDC) produced maps showing the likely effects on the Bay of (1) a mid-century sea level rise of 16 inches (0.4 meters) and (2) an end-of-century rise of 55 inches (1.3 meters).[3] These maps show that large parts of the northern, eastern, and southern sections of the Bay would be inundated.

One difficult but fundamental question which residents and policymakers of the Bay Area must address is whether new developments along the very edge of the Bay make any sense now that sea levels are rising.[4] Cargill, an agribusiness company, believes that its 1,400-acre tract of salt ponds near Redwood City, California, is suitable for building a planned community to be known as Redwood City Saltworks. Officials at the Saltworks did not reply to our question asking what, if anything, they plan to do about sea level rise. Local environmentalists, for their part, want the salt ponds restored as wetlands so they can be buffers against the rising sea. What is known is that if the Bay rises 16 inches (0.4 meters) by 2050, as is now thought likely, an estimated 270,000 people and $62 billion in assets could be at risk from flooding, including both the San Francisco airport and the Oakland airport[5], plus major Silicon valley companies such as Google and Intel.

California now seems to take the threat of sea level rise more seriously than in the past. In 2010, the Adaptation Advisory Panel to the State of California officially recommended that information be collected and made available on a statewide basis on the following climate change topics (among others):

Sea level rise and wave measurement, monitoring of salt water intrusion in coastal aquifers, salinity changes in bays and estuaries, beach dynamics, coastal erosion rates, tectonic uplift rates, and changes in flooding patterns and wetland inundation, sedimentation, and species.[6]

While this recommendation is indeed commendable, the officials and residents of the Bay still have a long way to go in order to come to grips with sea level rise. The first comprehensive assessment of this problem was done by the Pacific Institute, with the support of the Stockholm Environment Institute, in 1990. Eighteen years later, in 2008, the Pacific Institute reported that

> the good news is that the conclusions [of the 1990 study] are still remarkably robust. The bad news is that 18 years has elapsed and we've hardly progressed in taking action. The sea is 1 to 2 inches higher already.[7]

It will indeed be interesting to see what the State of California ultimately decides to do about this problem. On the one hand, given the severe financial problems California is facing now, an ambitious, expensive program to "save the Bay" seems most unlikely. On the other, it is predicted that a 6-inch rise in the water level of San Francisco Bay will mean that a relatively routine once-in-10-year storm would wreak as much havoc there as a far more serious "100-year storm" would have caused before such a rise.[8]

On a positive note, in 2011 the San Francisco Bay Conservation and Development Commission unanimously passed a development plan for land located within 100 feet of the coastline, thereby giving the Commission a badly-needed tool to deny permits for development in coastal areas which are subject to flooding. The plan was, as is inevitable in these cases, a compromise between competing factions. On the one hand, the Building Industry Association of the Bay Area, which represents developers, pronounced itself pleased with the plan. On the other, the Sierra Club, a leading environmental-advocacy group, accepted the plan but added that while the vote was a "step in the right direction, these policies could and should be made more robust."[9]

In broader terms, a 2011 study of the potential impacts of increased coastal flooding in California as a whole painted an alarming picture of the consequences of 4.5 foot (1.4 meter) rise in sea level. Some of its key conclusions were[10]:

- Such a rise would put 480,000 people at risk, including large numbers of low-income people and communities of color.
- A wide range of critical infrastructure is vulnerable to sea level rise. This includes nearly 140 schools; 34 police and fire stations; more than 330 hazardous waste facilities or sites; an estimated 3,500 miles of roads and highways; 280 miles of railways; 30 coastal power plants, 28 wastewater treatment plants; and both the San Francisco and Oakland airports.
- Protecting vulnerable areas from flooding by building seaways and levees would cost more than $14 billion, with an additional $1.4 billion per year in maintenance costs. Continued development in vulnerable areas will put additional assets at risk and will raise protection costs.

Another study in 2011 looked at future coastal hazards of erosion and flooding along the California coast. It found that, given a 4.5 foot (1.4 meter) sea level rise, there would be 82.6 square miles (214 square kilometers) of land loss by 2100. Maximum potential erosion distances of up to 1,312 feet (400 meters) were predicted along cliff-backed shorelines and up to 1,968 feet (600 meters) along dune-backed shorelines.[11]

Cities of the Chinese Coast

Given the growing importance of China in almost all fields, we may usefully begin this section by quoting an authoritative American study on the impact of climate change on China. It was written in 2009 by the U.S. National Intelligence Council and made the following points, among others, in an Executive Summary:

> China is well known for its size; it has the world's largest population, the third largest land area, the fourth (nominal) or second (purchasing power parity) largest economy and is the second largest primary energy producer and the largest carbon dioxide emitter. As a major global player in human-caused climate change, China is vulnerable to the adverse impacts of climate change....
>
> Over the past 30 years, the sea level and sea surface temperature have increased 90 millimeters [3.5 inches] and 0.9 degrees Celsius.... By 2030, sea level rise along the coastal areas could be 0.1–0.16 meters [3.9–6.2 inches], increasing the possibility of flooding and intensified storm surges, leading to degradation of wetlands, mangroves, and coral reefs....
>
> Due to their flat and low landscapes, China's coastal regions, the engine of China's economic achievement, are highly vulnerable to storm, flood, and sea-level rise.... China has been actively developing early warning systems and related monitoring systems and improving the design standards of sea dikes and port docks. These efforts may help buffer some risk of natural weather extreme events.[12]

Over the course of history, many cities have been founded on sites of natural harbors and other avenues of access to long-distance and ocean-going shipping: China is no exception to this rule. For many centuries, the enormous benefits offered to the Chinese by coastal sites, e.g., lower transportation costs, have had to be balanced against the great risks to which these sites were exposed — for example, pirates, invasions, and weather and other ocean-related risks. Sea level rise must now be considered to be one of these risks because so much of the Yellow Sea coastal region has an elevation of appreciably less than 32.8 feet (10 meters).[13] This region is now home to some of China's largest cities, e.g., Tianjin and Shanghai, with many smaller cities in the surrounding areas.[14]

Another way of putting this is to note that, on the Eastern Pacific seaboard, about 60 percent of China's 1.3 billion people live in coastal provinces.[15] A number of Chinese cities have appeared on lists of cities likely to be impacted by sea level rise — for example, Guangzhou (formerly known as Canton), Shenzhen, Hong Kong, Ningbo, Shanghai, and Tianjin. Rather than discussing them one-by-one, it is easier and more productive to look at them collectively here, especially since current information on them (in terms of sea level rise) is not very readily available in English.

China's coastline is about 9,009 miles (14,500 kilometers) in length[16] and is washed by four seas — the South China Sea, the East China Sea, the Yellow Sea, and the Bahia Sea (the latter is the innermost gulf of the Yellow Sea). Increasingly, climate change has become a source of concern for Chinese all along the coast and also for the Chinese government.

They worry about the threats posed by powerful storm surges sweeping ashore on top of a rising sea level. In addition, some coastal lands are sinking due to the pumping-out of ground water for drinking water and irrigation. The mammoth Three Gorges hydroelectric dam on the Yangtze River will control flooding on the deltaic plain of the river but will, at the same time, decrease sediment accumulation there. This is process is likely to accelerate saline inundation of a vital breadbasket of China.[17]

At the governmental level, the Chinese are taking the threat of sea level rise seriously. In 2004, this is what China's National Coordination Committee on Climate Change had to say about changes in sea level along China's coast:

According to the Bulletin on the Sea Level in China in 2000, China's coastal sea level has risen at an annual rate of ~1.0~3.0 mm [~0.03~0.11 inches] on average. In 2000, China's coastal sea level rose by 51 mm [2 inches] compared with normal sea level [defined as the mean sea level between 1975 and 1986]. The general trend of the change in sea level rise is that the change along the southern coast is relatively great, while that along the northern coast is small.[18]

In 2010, Xu Sheng, director of China's National Marine Data and Information Service, stated in an interview with *China Daily*:

The Yangtze River Delta, the Pearl River Delta, the Yellow River Delta, and coastal areas of Tianjin are the country's most economically developed regions and are potential areas that could suffer from the impact of sea level rise. Local authorities should build higher dams [as used here, "dams" is probably a collective term covering seawalls, river embankments, and dikes] and take environmental protection measures to slow down the rise of the sea level.[19]

Total Chinese losses from a 3.2 feet (1 meter) sea level rise have been estimated, very roughly, at about $98 billion (i.e., 655.6 billion yuan).[20] Zhao Xitao, a Chinese climate-change scientist, has even referred to sea level rise as a "Damocles Sword" hanging over China's head.[21] He may well have had the Shanghai area in mind when he used this analogy.

According to an analysis of this region by Jie Yin et al. in 2010,

> At the possible maximum tide levels of 9.82 m [32.2 feet] by 2030 and 10.04 m [34.1 feet] by 2050, all river embankment crests would be exceeded or destroyed by flood intrusion. Almost all land cover ... and about 24 million people ... in Shanghai would be under direct risk of flooding. By then, Shanghai would be another New Orleans.[22]

Coastal Areas of Vietnam

It is easiest for us here, as in the case of China, to look at Vietnam's coastal regions collectively rather than individually. The urban areas and farms of the Vietnamese coast will suffer grievously, in terms of people displaced and homes and croplands lost, from a 3.2 foot (1 meter) sea level rise. Indeed, Vietnam is listed by the World Bank as one of the countries most threatened by rising waters brought about by higher global temperatures; moreover, climate change is also turning the rivers of the Mekong Delta salty, spelling trouble for millions of poor farmers there.[23]

Vietnam's two main deltas are those of the Red River and the Mekong River. They are low-lying; densely populated; and, agriculturally, very productive. A 3.2 foot rise would flood some 1,930.5 square miles (5,000 square kilometers) of the Red River Delta and 7,722 square miles (20,000 square kilometers) of the Mekong Delta. Indeed, it has been estimated that such a rise would displace more than 10 percent of Vietnam's people, inundate 12 percent of its land, and cut food production by 12 percent.[24]

Ho Chi Minh City (the former Saigon) is located in the delta of the Saigon and Dong Nai rivers, is now home to about 7 million people, and is at increasing risk from flooding and from sea level rise. Rapid growth has resulted in the expansion of its urban area into the surrounding marshlands. The result is that about 60 percent of the urban area is now less than 4.9 feet (1.5 meters) above sea level so this area is quite vulnerable to sea level rise.[25] During the last 50 years, sea level at Ho Chi Minh City has already risen by 7.8 inches (20 centimeters) and is expected to rise another 11 to 12.9 inches (28 to 33 centimeters) by 2050.[26]

To protect the city from the rising waters, an ambitious Master Plan for Tide Control was approved by the Vietnamese government in 2008. It advocates construction of a polder system around Ho Chi Minh City. (As noted earlier, polders are low-lying tracts of land, enclosed by dikes." Almost 123.4 miles (200 kilometers) of dikes and hundreds of tidal gates are being planned for Ho Chi Minh City.[27]

The Vietnamese government has made a considerable effort to learn from other countries which have more expertise in water management issues. In the spring of 2010, for example, it sent a high-ranking delegation to the Netherlands to profit from the Dutch experience in dike-building and polders. In the summer of that same year, it sent out another delegation, which visited the Netherlands, Belgium, Germany, and Italy.

A Vietnamese press release covering this latter trip used a question-and-answer format. The reporter put a question along these lines to the leader of the Vietnamese delegation:

> Dealing with climate change and sea level rise is an important issue for [the Vietnamese port of] Haiphong. On this trip, what did the delegation of senior Haiphong officials learn from the host countries?

The Vietnamese leader replied along these lines:

> In the Netherlands, the delegation learned about the sea dike system, along with water and environmental management. We also learned a number of lessons about building computer models to address these issues. I think that Haiphong should creatively apply these experiences to cope with climate change and sea level rise…. We can also learn from Belgium's experience in building and maintaining sea dikes. Belgium has a long, wide sea dike system, based on meticulous research and construction, and carried out with high technical skill and methodology to meet the requirements of environmental and ecological protection.[28]

Dr. Pham Si Liem of Hanoi's Institute for Urban Studies and Infrastructure Development has emphasized the importance of sea level rise, stating that:

> More than twenty Vietnam coastal cities with a population of ten million are directly subjected to the impacts of a rising sea level. As this is a very slow-onset event, the risk perception of the society is weak…. [Nevertheless,] sea level rise poses a great threat to Vietnamese coastal cities and will have a macroeconomic effect on the country. Our disaster adaptation policy should be considered as being a continuing "learning-by-doing" process. The best way for Vietnam to cope with sea level rise is to develop, with the support of international response organizations, into a developed country in the near future.[29]

Bangkok

Located in the northern extremity of the Gulf of Thailand, the greater Bangkok region contains more than 16 million inhabitants and is one of the biggest urban areas in the world. It was founded 225 years ago on a swampy floodplain and, indeed, the Chao Phraya River is still the city's dominant geographical feature. Bangkok has been called the "Venice of the East" because of the great number of canals and waterways threading through the city. After a heavy rain during the monsoon season, water in canals and the river can overflow the banks and cause massive floods. Moreover, subsidence has occurred in Bangkok at rates of up to 3.9 inches (10 centimeters) per year.[30] This is not surprising because, fundamentally, Bangkok sits on top of a swamp with a base of compactable clay.

The Bangkok Metropolitan Administration has built higher banks along some of the canals to keep the water from reaching street level, but it will be fighting a losing battle against sea level rise. Some of Bangkok is already below sea level; much of it is only about 3.2 feet (1 meter) above it; and its highest natural (i.e., not man-made) point does not exceed 5 feet (1.5 meters) in elevation. While the land is steadily subsiding, the level of the sea is inexorably rising. For this reason, an article in the *Straits Times* in 2010 predicted this result in a worst case scenario: "Within the next 40 years, vital installations and tens of thousands of homes and offices and factories will face major floods."[31]

In that same article, Dr. Anond Snidvongs, one Thailand's foremost experts on climate change, warned that Thai government policies and regulations "still do not take climate change into consideration at all": most designs and plans for infrastructure and buildings are still based on the premise that "everything is constant." He therefore called for an open debate and exchange of ideas in Thailand on how best to protect Bangkok against the imminent risks posed by the combined forces of sea level rise, land subsidence, and extreme storms.[32]

Although educated Thais are aware of the dangers posed by sea level rise, this realization does not seem to have led to much remedial action by the government. In 2011, a Western businessman with long experience in Bangkok (he must remain nameless here) told us privately that "very little is being done to anticipate flooding in Bangkok. Land use planning is a rarity in this part of the world." The outlook for Bangkok is therefore not encouraging. As early as 1990, a Thai study predicted that

> In the Bangkok Metropolis area, a combination of subsidence and sea-level rise will seriously affect residential areas, pollution of surface water and groundwater, flooding, wastewater drainage and treatment, agricultural land, and industrial and commercial activities in the foreseeable future.[33]

Moreover a 2011 case study found that, compared with the serious floods of 1995, the overall inundation area of Bangkok may increase up to 26 percent in 2050 due to a sea level rise of 12.5 inches (32 centimeters) and then to 81 percent in 2100 due to a sea level rise of 34.6 inches (88 centimeters). The number of affected buildings there is likely to increase by a factor of 1.5 in the 75 years from 2025 to 2100.[34] In the meantime, the floods of 2011, which required the Thai government to deploy some 50,000 soldiers and 30,000 policemen, left more than 500 people dead.

Two Sad Cases of Sea Level Rise: Tuvalu and Kiribati

In the vast reaches of the South Pacific there are some 260 atoll islands, i.e., rings of coral reefs enclosing a lagoon. Many of these atolls are exceptionally vulnerable to sea level rise because they have an average elevation of only 6.5 feet (2 meters) above sea level. Ultimately, as the sea rises, most of those that are inhabited will probably have to be abandoned and their tiny populations will have to be moved to higher, safer locations.[35]

From a sea level-rise perspective, the most well-known of all these atolls — or at least the one which has received the most press coverage — is the island nation of Tuvalu (formerly known as the Ellice Islands). This is a Polynesian island nation located midway between Hawaii and Australia. It consists of only 10 square miles (26 square kilometers) of land — i.e., four reef islands and five true atolls — and about 10,472 people.

One of the reasons why Tuvalu is so well-known in terms of sea level rise is that at one point it threatened to sue both Australia and the United States in the World Court for causing the global warming that is affecting its viability as a nation. This threatened suit was eventually abandoned, in about 2006, due to the lack of scientific evidence to support it, e.g., it could not be scientifically proven that the sea level rise troubling Tuvalu was in fact caused by Australia and the United States.

A sea level rise of only 8 to 16 inches (20 to 40 centimeters) over the next 100 years will make Tuvalu uninhabitable. The South Pacific Applied Geoscience Commission (SOPAC) confirms that Tuvalu is vulnerable, not only due to sea level rise but also due to its rapid population growth and poor coastal management. If, eventually, worse comes to worse and the population must be evacuated, Australia, New Zealand, or Fiji are possible destinations for resettlement.

Tuvalu is thus one of the places on earth most vulnerable to the negative effects of global warming. Sea level rise may well bring disaster to the Tuvaluans. As Saufatu Sopoanga, the Prime Minister of Tuvalu, explained in New York at the 58th Session of the United Nations General Assembly on 24 September 2003:

> We live in constant fear of the adverse impacts of climate change. For a coral atoll nation, sea level rise and more severe weather events loom as a growing threat to our entire population. The threat is real and serious, and is of no difference to a slow and insidious form of terrorism against us.[36]

Tuvaluan children watch with sadness as extra high tides flood their neighborhood (© Gary Braasch/ WorldViewOfGlobalWarming.org).

If Tuvalu is the first sad case of sea level rise, Kiribati is the second. An island nation located in the central tropical Pacific Ocean, Kiribati consists of 32 atolls and one raised coral island. Historically, it is remembered for being the scene of the Battle of Tarawa during World War II. On 20 November 1943, U.S. Marines landed on Tarawa and suffered heavy losses from Japanese soldiers firing from entrenched positions on the atoll. The Marines finally captured the island after 76 hours of the must brutal fighting, during which about a total of about 6,000 men (Japanese and Americans) died during 76 hours of intense combat.

In our own times, Kiribati has the distinction of being the first country in the world where its entire land territory will disappear due to sea level rise. In 2008, Kiribati's president said: "To plan for the day when you no longer have a country is indeed painful but I think we have to do that."[37]

Osaka-Kobe

Historically, Kobe was the commercial capital of Japan and the national center for rice trading. As an aside, we should note here that sea level rise can inundate rice-producing lands in Japan and in other countries as well, notably in Bangladesh, Taiwan, Egypt, Myanmar, and Vietnam. Moreover, climate

change can also impact global rice yields. If this happens, world rice production will almost certainly decline and the price of rice will almost certainly
increase.[38] Osaka itself continues to function as a center of the Japanese economy. In daytime, its population is 3.7 million people, second only to Tokyo.
Its nighttime population is 2.6 million.

Kobe was one of the Japanese cities initially opened for trade with the
West at the end of Japan's long, self-imposed policy of isolation. This city
suffered a severe earthquake in 1995, which caused more than $102 billion in
damage. Before the earthquake, Kobe was one of the world's busiest ports;
since then, despite repairs and new construction, it has failed to regain its
former status as Japan's principal shipping port. Nevertheless, it is still a
prominent port city.

In terms of sea level rise, a 2007 report by the Organisation for Economic
Co-operation and Development (OECD) listed Osaka-Kobe as one of the top
10 cities of the world in terms of its exposed population, and also as one of
the top 10 cities in terms of exposed assets.[39] A higher sea level will intensify
erosion of natural beaches and can have a particularly serious impact on sandy
beaches. A Japanese study has estimated that a sea level rise of 1.6 feet (50
centimeters) will result in the disappearance of about 70 percent of the sandy
beaches in Japan. A rise of 3.2 feet (1 meter) will inundate about 90 percent
of the sandy beaches in the country and all of the sandy beaches in Osaka
Province.[40]

Kobe is now reviewing the height of its existing seawalls. These were
designed to protect the city from the impacts of tsunamis, but they also had
the secondary purpose of keeping storm surges at bay. Critics, however, claim
that no matter how high Kobe's seawalls are raised, there will always be the
danger of a higher wave that will overtop them all.

Australia–New Zealand

The IPCC confirms that climate change is already affecting these two
countries.[41] For example, since 1950, there has been more warming, more
heat waves, fewer frosts, more rain in northwest Australia and southwest New
Zealand, less rain in southern and eastern Australia and northeastern New
Zealand, an increase in the intensity of Australian droughts, and a rise in sea
level of about 2.7 inches (70 millimeters).

Moreover, by 2050, coastal development and population growth in popular areas, such as Cairns and southeast Queensland (both in Australia) and
Northland to the Bay of Plenty (both in New Zealand), are expected to exacerbate the risks expected from sea level rise. Expected increases in the severity
and frequency of storms, and greater coastal flooding there, can only make

matters worse. The people of the Australian coast will be at some risk for the following reasons[42]:

- The Australian population is concentrated along the coastline. Six million people live within 1.2 miles (2 kilometers) from the beach, i.e., about 27 percent of the country's population. An estimated 425,000 Australians will be affected by sea level rise. Moreover, recent studies of a test area along some 124 miles (200 kilometers) of the coast of southwestern Australia show that while a modest sea level rise of about 1.6 feet (0.5 meters) will have only a minor impact, this impact will become much more serious when added to any extreme sea level event, e.g., a storm surge.[43]
- Over the past 10 years there has been an increase of over one million people moving to the coast. Coastal town dynamics are constantly changing as people move to the coast to experience a "sea change."
- The is no official national policy for coastal issues in Australia. The country's three-tier governmental system has contributed to a fragmentation of policies and laws governing coastal developments. The fluctuating population of coastal regions with semi and permanent residence means local councilors and planners face constant pressures to find a balance between the sense of place that local people demand, applications for new developments, and financial pressures for infrastructure.

New Zealand's Ministry for the Environment, for its part, lists the following impacts as likely to occur in New Zealand as a result of climate change[44]:

- Coastal defenses will be overtopped by waves or high tides more often.
- Severe storms will increase in intensity; storm surge levels will rise.
- Some sandy beaches may continue to accrete, but more slowly than before.
- Some gravel beaches are more likely to erode.
- Waves in Wellington may be 15 percent higher by 2050 and 30 percent higher by 2100.
- Areas with small tidal ranges, such as Wellington, the Cook Strait area, and the East Coast, will have more problems as the high tide mark is exceeded more frequently.

One of the biggest challenges now facing both Australia and New Zealand — and, of course, many other countries as well — is educating people about the potential hazards of buying coastal property. Because such property can be both highly desirable and highly lucrative, changing how it is bought and sold is not at all an easy or a non-controversial matter.

A final issue, and one impossible to forecast with any certainty, is that, in the years to come, climate change — especially sea level rise — may conceivably trigger significant population shifts in the Asia-Pacific region. If this does occur, increased migration pressures on both Australia and New Zealand cannot be ruled out.

Although coastal communities are vulnerable sectors in both countries, the good news is, as the IPCC tells us, that both Australia and New Zealand have well-developed economies, extensive scientific and technical capabilities, disaster implementation strategies, and biosecurity measures. That said, considerable costs and institutional constraints are still likely to be encountered when these two countries begin to implement adaptation measures.[45]

IX

Cities and Countries
of the Indian Ocean Basin

In this chapter we will look at six areas vulnerable to sea level rise: the coast of Bangladesh; Mumbai and Kolkata (both in India); the Maldives; Jakarta (Indonesia); and Karachi (Pakistan).

The Coast of Bangladesh

As noted earlier, the Bangladesh region is exceptionally vulnerable to rising sea levels. In the Bay of Bengal there have been 23 storm surge events, with over 10,000 people killed in each one since 1737. The most severe impacts were in 1737 (300,000 people killed), 1864 (100,000 people killed), 1876 (100,000 people killed), 1897 (175,000 people killed), 1970 (300,000 people killed), and 1991 (about 140,000 killed and 10 million made homeless).[1] Population pressures in Bangladesh are so great, however, that people find themselves forced to resettle on very vulnerable islands—even when a storm has recently drowned the previous inhabitants. In so doing, they are not only putting themselves in harm's way: their resettlement often destroys more mangroves, thus further increasing flood risks inland.[2]

Most of Bangladesh is less than 39.3 feet (12 meters) above today's sea level; if the sea rises by only 3.2 feet (1 meter), about 50 percent of Bangladesh will be under water. A rise of 4.9 feet (1.5 meters) will impact 17 million people (15 percent of the population) and 8,494 square miles (22,000 square kilometers) of land.[3] Because the country is so low-lying and so densely populated, three tropical cyclones during the twentieth century each killed more than 100,000 people. The Bangladesh "supercyclone" of 1970 generated what may be the greatest climate-related death toll on record—about 300,000 people. This was primarily due to storm surges flooding low-lying deltas. In the future, storm surges coming ashore in Bangladesh atop higher sea levels are also certain to be deadly.

One truly remarkable and endangered area in the region—the Sundar-

91

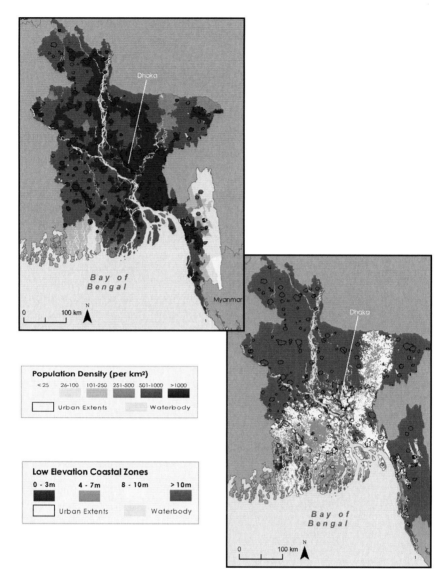

Bangladesh population density and low elevation coastal zones (Socioeconomic Data and Applications Center, 2009).

bans (its name means "beautiful forest" in the Bengali language) — embraces the largest single block of tidal mangrove forest left in the world. It lies in the huge delta formed by the confluence of the Ganges, the Brahmaputra, and the Megha Rivers in southern Bangladesh and in neighboring West Bengal, India. This vast forest covers a total of about 3,861 square miles (about 10,000 square kilometers) in Bangladesh and India; about 2,316 square miles (6,000 square kilometers) are in Bangladesh. Since 1997 the Sundarbans has been a UNESCO World Heritage Site and is a home of the Royal Bengal tiger. In 2010 it was estimated that there were only about 440 adult tigers left in the Sundarbans.[4]

Long-term prospects for the Sundarbans are, unfortunately, not very good. A 2007 UNESCO report predicted that a 17.7 inch (45 centimeter) rise in sea level — which is thought to be very likely by the end of the 21st century, if not well before — could, when combined with other forms of human-caused stress, lead to the destruction of 75 percent of the Sundarbans mangroves.[5] If so, the tigers will not be the only ones to suffer. The Sundarbans also plays a key role in protecting the millions of people living in and around the enormous urban areas of Kolkata (formerly known as Calcutta) from the extensive flooding which often accompanies cyclones. Scientists at the Coast, Port & Estuary Division of the Institute of Water Modeling in Dhaka, Bangladesh, have summed up prospects for the future in these words, which have been lightly edited:

> Increasing rates of sea level rise caused by global warming are expected to lead to permanent inundation, drainage congestion, salinity intrusion, and frequent storm surge inundation. Sea level rise is a growing threat for the coastal regions of Bangladesh.... [We estimate] that about 11 percent more land will be permanently inundated over the next century. [By 2100], the Sundarbans ... will be lost due to high salinity and permanent inundation from projected sea level rise. An increase of wind speed 10 percent greater than the severe cyclone of 1991 will increase the storm surge level by 1.7 meters (5.5 feet) along the eastern coast of Bangladesh.[6]

Mumbai

Formerly known as Bombay, Mumbai is located on the west coast of India and has a deep natural harbor. It is the most populous city in India, with approximately 14 million people, and is also the richest city in the country. Mumbai is the commercial and entertainment capital of India and the home of key financial institutions and many Indian and multinational companies. Despite its successes, however, this city will face a serious challenge from climate change, including sea level rise. By 2015, Mumbai's population could number as many as 22.6 million people. Not surprisingly, the OECD lists it as one of the top 10 cities of the world which have large populations that will be exposed to sea level rise.

In 2009, Dr. Sanjay Tomar, a Fellow at New Delhi's Climate Change Institute, had this to say about prospects for Mumbai:

Mumbai faces profound consequences of climate change ... the extent of vulnerability is dependent not only on the physical exposure to sea level and the population affected, but also on the extent of economic activity and coping capacities....

[The subsistence fisher folk of Mumbai, known as the *kolis*, will be directly
affected by climate change. Ironically, trying to protect the interests of such traditional fishing communities, a change in India's coastal law in 2011 opened up
the coastline to more people, thus placing populations with the least adaptive
capacity at more risk from climate change and sea level rise.[7]] They need to be
made aware about the profound impacts of rising sea level, particularly on
human lives, livelihood, and property. They should be made to understand how
important it is to be prepared to face such situations. These communities, especially the women, should resort to saving schemes and insurance schemes to
guard against any financial shocks in case of any unforeseen event.[8]

While we may hope for the best, a reasonable guess is that, given the
financial and logistical problems Mumbai is already facing, the recommendations of a climate change study published in 2010 will almost certainly be
ignored. It concluded that

the predicted consequences of climate change will exacerbate the city's ongoing
vulnerability to flooding if urgent measures are not taken to improve storm
water drainage systems and shore up other flood control defenses.[9]

In addition, frequent flooding and salt water intrusion may well affect
the structural stability of the high-rise buildings which have mushroomed in
Mumbai at an increasing rate in recent years. Since almost 25 percent of
Mumbai is at or below mean sea level, the long-term prospects for the low-
income residents living in these low-lying areas are not very good. As a 2008
report by an official of the National Environmental Engineering Institute in
Mumbai put it with considerable understatement,

Mega coastal cities like Mumbai could face profound consequences from climate
changes. Mumbai has a high exposure level due to population density, and its
major industrial and financial installations. Furthermore, the major proportion
of its reclaimed land is in low-lying areas and *the high population of its urban
poor has limited coping capacity to face the consequences of climate change.*[10]

Kolkata

Kolkata is still referred to as Calcutta in many publications. It spreads
out in a linear fashion along the banks of the Hooghly River in eastern India.
Since this area is low-lying and is adjacent to Bangladesh, it will share many
of the same sea level rise problems as its eastern neighbor. It lies in a very
vulnerable part of the world. In the northern Bay of Bengal, barotropic surge
simulations which are driven by climate change projections reveal that

changes in storminess will cause changes in extreme water levels. When added to scenarios on relative sea level rise, these changes can result in increases in extreme water levels across the Bay, especially near Kolkata itself.[11]

Kolkata was originally founded on marshy wetlands and some of it is still near sea level. The average elevation of the city is only about 17 feet (5.1 meters). It is very densely populated: there are now more than 15 million people living in the Greater Kolkata urban agglomeration. In 2009, this is what the WWF-World Wide Fund for Nature had to say, among other things, about climate-change prospects for this teeming city:

> Due to Calcutta's location and size it is particularly at risk of climate change impacts ... Sea-level rise and storm surges will inundate large proportions of the city and surrounding areas over the next few years. In fact, a 1 m [3.2 feet] rise in sea level could potentially inundate 5,763 square kilometers [2,225 square miles] in India. In addition to sea-level rise, a ground subsidence of 0.6 to 1.9 mm [0.02 to 0.07 inches] per year is adding to the risk in the Ganges Delta. Due to the combined effects of sea-level rise and subsidence, the Ganges Delta will likely see salt water intrude 100 km [62 miles] from the coast, greatly impacting ground water supplies.[12]

Commenting on this report, Shrish Sinha, head of the climate change and energy division of WWF-India, said:

> We do not want to create panic but Calcutta is definitely vulnerable to climatic events [due to] its position, population stress, poor drainage condition with continuous filling-up of wetlands and water bodies and, above all, the city's lack of preparedness to counter such disasters.[13]

The IPCC, for its part, confirms that Kolkata will face additional sea level difficulties in the future. The IPCC notes that although inundation due to higher sea levels over the 21st century will be a problem for unprotected low-lying areas like Kolkata, the most devastating impacts will be due to extreme sea levels resulting from the passage of storms, i.e., storm surges. The IPCC's barotropic surge models, driven by climate change predictions, predict sea levels of 2.3 feet (0.7 meters) or higher off Kolkata as early as 2040–2050.[14]

An interesting footnote on sea level rise in this area is the short life of a little island, known to the Indians as New Moore Island and to the Bangladeshis as South Talpatti Island.[15] This island was a small, uninhabited offshore sandbar located in the Bay of Bengal off the coast of the Ganges-Brahmaputra Delta. It emerged from the Bay of Bengal after the Bhola cyclone in 1970, attained a maximum size of about 110,000 square feet (10,000 square meters) at low tide, and was less than 6.5 feet (2 meters) above sea level.

The mini-island soon became an international issue and the subject of lengthy bilateral negotiations. Both India and Bangladesh vigorously claimed sovereignty over it because of speculation about the alleged presence of oil and natural gas in the region. India reportedly hoisted the Indian flag on the island in 1981, established a temporary base there for a contingent of its Border Security Forces, and regularly sent naval gunships to the area.

In 2010, however, Professor Sugata Hazra of the School of Oceanographic Studies at Jadavpur University in Kolkata announced that satellite images showed that, at some unknown point, the island had vanished entirely. He explained that sea level rise, changes in monsoonal rain patterns (which alter river flows), and land subsidence were all contributing to the loss of land in the northern Bay of Bengal. As Professor Hazra joked about the short life and death of this tiny island, "What these two countries [India and Bangladesh] could not achieve from years of talking, has been resolved by global warming."[16]

Maldives

The Maldives, an island nation set in the Indian Ocean, consists of about 1,200 islands and atolls, 26 of which are coralline and are spread out for about 960 miles (960 kilometers) across the top of an undersea volcanic ridge, some 400 miles (643 kilometers) southwest of the tip of India. The population of the country is roughly 373,000 people. The capital and biggest city is Malé, which has a population of about 103,000 people. The Maldives is the smallest Asian country (both in terms of population and area) and, with an average elevation of only 4.9 feet (1.5 meters) above sea level, it may also be the lowest-lying country in the world. This latter fact makes it quite vulnerable to sea level rise. In 1992, the President of the Maldives, Maumoon Abdul Gayoom, told the United Nations Earth Summit:

> I stand before you as a representative of an endangered people. We are told that as a result of global warming and sea-level rise my country, the Maldives, may sometime during the next century, disappear from the face of the Earth.[17]

In response to the threat posed by sea level rise, the Maldives decided in 1997 to raise the elevation of Hulhumalé Island, which is located in the Malé region. Sand was dredged from the ocean floor and dumped into a shallow lagoon in order to create a flood-resistant site for housing, industrial, and commercial development. The first phase of this ambitious project was finished in 2001. The target date for completion of the remainder of the project is 2020.

The Maldives' decision to face up to and prepare for sea level rise was a very wise one. In 2005, Church et al. studied sea level rise at tropical Pacific and Indian Ocean islands. They concluded that

Clearly sea level in this region is rising, and we expect the direct and indirect (e.g., increased frequency of extreme events) effects of this rise and the observed increase in the rate of rise ... will cause serious problems for the inhabitants of some of these islands during the 21st century.[18]

Malé's Environment Minister, Abdulla Shahid, told an interviewer in 2009 that his country's most important problems are storm surges and beach erosion. The Maldives has appealed to the UN Office for Outer Space Affairs for free photos from outer space, which commercially cost $4,000 each, so that the Maldives will have enough information to help it adjust to sea level rise. Shahid also mentioned that it would cost between $25 billion and $30 billion to build a seawall entirely around the Maldives to help protect this island nation from storm surges coming ashore on top of rising sea levels.[19] Given the prohibitive cost of this concept, we very much doubt that it will ever be undertaken.

The Maldives has become a vocal campaigner in the struggle to deal with rising sea levels. Making a dramatic gesture in 2009 to highlight the problems that the Maldives—and, by extension, what the IPCC calls the other Small Island Developing States (SIDS)[20]—will face in the future, President Mohamed Nasheed, dressed in full scuba gear, conducted a 30-minute *underwater cabinet meeting*, at a depth of 20 feet, off the Malé coast. The government arranged a horseshoe-shaped table to be installed on the seabed for the cabinet ministers, who communicated using white boards, indelible ink, and hand signals. Of the 14-member cabinet, only three ministers did not take part in the dive (two had medical conditions, the third was traveling).[21]

Jakarta

Jakarta, the capital and biggest city of Indonesia, is located on the northwest coast of Java. It is the country's economic, cultural, and political center. The population is about 9.6 million people. The city sits in a low, flat basin, which averages 23 feet (7 meters) above sea level. Some 40 percent of Jakarta, especially its northern region, is below sea level. Pervasive problems include sea level rise, worsening flooding, land subsidence, poverty, and overcrowding.

Since the 1930s, there have been discussions about the merits of relocating Indonesia's central government to a different part of Java itself, or perhaps to another of the country's many islands (there are about 17,508 of them), but at the moment there are no plans to move the seat of government. If it is not moved, the World Bank may be right in estimating that by 2025 the sea could be lapping at the gates of the presidential palace in the center of Jakarta.[22] Although Indonesian President Susilo Bambang Yudhoyono favors shifting the capital to a new location, an Indonesian architect told a reporter in 2010, "It's always a dream to start a new city. But if they [the Indonesian government] can't get Jakarta to work now, I'm doubtful they can make a new city work."[23]

The long-term outlook for Jakarta is not at all good. For example, a 2009 study by Indonesian and Japanese scientists made these predictions:

> Considering the sea level rise phenomenon, coastal subsidence in Jakarta will certainly affect coastal development in Jakarta. Considering the relatively flat nature (i.e., 0–2 meters [6.5 feet] above MSL [Mean Sea Level]) of most coastal areas of Jakarta, this combined effect of land subsidence and sea level rise will certainly have disastrous consequences for habitation, industry, and fresh groundwater supplies from coastal aquifers. During high tides, tidal flooding is already affecting some of these coastal areas. The extent and magnitude of subsidence related to flooding will worsen with the likely continuation of sea level rise along the coast of Jakarta, which is bordered by the Java sea. [A chart illustrating this study shows that, assuming continued subsidence and continued sea level rise off Jakarta, 12,716 acres (5,146 hectares) will be inundated by 2020 and 40,122 acres (16,237 hectares) by 2050.][24]

Karachi

The biggest city and the industrial and financial center of Pakistan, Greater Karachi has a population of about 18 million people. The Port of Karachi and Port Bin Qasim are two of the region's largest and busiest ports. Karachi is known to local Muslims as the "City of Lights" and as the "Bride of the Cities" because of its lively pace. These admirable qualities, however, will not by themselves be enough to protect Karachi from the sea.

In 2010, after carrying out a survey of the low-lying areas of Sindh province (where Karachi is located), Pakistan's Meteorological Department found that a sizeable part of this province, including Karachi itself, could be inundated by a major cyclone because sea level has been rising during the past decade. The Meteorological Department added that if the sea level continues to rise for the next 10 years, the population of the coastal belt of Sindh will be forced to move elsewhere. In the meantime, it said, the lowest areas of Sindh, including parts of Karachi, are quite vulnerable to tsunamis and sudden high tides.[25]

A related issue in Pakistan involves the Indus River, one of the major river systems of the world. About 10 miles southeast of Karachi is the very low-lying — indeed, very *swampy* — Indus River Delta. A study completed at some point in about 2002 by Pakistan's National Institute of Oceanography found that while no direct measurements were available on actual subsidence rates in this delta, these must have increased because the Indus is now depositing much less sediment there — due both to the increasing drawdown from the river of fresh water for irrigation, and to the construction of many barrages, dams, and link canals.

As a result of subsidence, the study suggested, the delta may experience a relatively rapid sea level rise of 0.31 to 0.39 inches (8 to 10 millimeters) per year in the future.[26] Another study, also completed in 2002, used the slope of the Indus delta, sea encroachment, and land area inundation to forecast an eventual sea level rise of 3.2 to 6.5 feet (1 to 2 meters).[27]

X

The West Antarctic Ice Sheet

Antarctica can be described in just two words: cold and big. It is the most frigid place on our planet: the coldest natural temperature ever recorded on earth was -128.6 degrees Fahrenheit (-89.2 degrees Celsius) at the Russian Vostok station in Antarctica. It is the fifth-largest continent in area (after Asia, Africa, and North America and South America). Ninety-eight percent of its surface — 5.4 million square miles, or 14 million square kilometers— is covered by ice. This ice sheet averages about 1 mile (1.6 kilometers) in thickness and stores roughly 70 percent of all the fresh water on earth. The West Antarctic Ice Sheet (WAIS) itself comprises about 10 percent by volume of the entire Antarctic ice sheet and in volume is equivalent to a 16.4 to 19.6 foot rise (5 to 6 meters) in sea level.

In geographical terms, the continent of Antarctica is divided into two parts by the Transantarctic Mountains close to the neck between the Ross Sea and the Weddell Sea. That portion lying west of the Weddell Sea and east of the Ross Sea is known as West Antarctica; the remainder is called East Antarctica. As mentioned earlier, if all the ice in Antarctica melted this would raise global sea level by about 190 feet (52.8 meters), although that would probably take thousands of years to occur.

Of the two major ice sheets draped over Antarctica, the East Antarctic ice sheet is the oldest and biggest. It is entirely grounded above sea level and is relatively stable.[1] Since it shows no promise of changing significantly in the foreseeable future, it does not occupy the policy limelight right now in terms of potential sea level rise. Although some minor scale instabilities have been observed there, the same cannot be said for its sister ice sheet, the WAIS.

The WAIS is a smaller, marine-based ice sheet. This means that its bed lies well below sea level and its edges flow out into floating ice shelves. The volume of the WAIS is about 479,873 cubic miles (2.2 million cubic kilometers). Through a process known as isostatic depression, its great weight has forced the rock beneath it to sink by between 0.31 and 0.62 miles (0.5 to 1

ANTARCTICA OVERVIEW MAP

This map shows the major geographical features on the Antarctic continent and the USA and UK
research stations, to accompany the Landsat Image Mosaic of Antarctica (LIMA). For information
about LIMA and to access the imagery, go to **http://lima.usgs.gov**

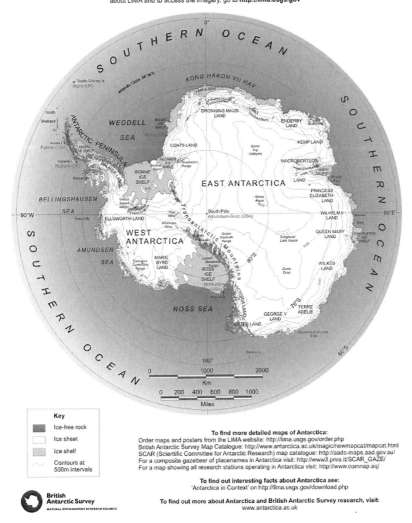

Key	
▓	Ice-free rock
☐	Ice sheet
▒	Ice shelf
∿	Contours at 500m intervals

British Antarctic Survey
NATURAL ENVIRONMENT RESEARCH COUNCIL

To find more detailed maps of Antarctica:
Order maps and posters from the LIMA website: http://lima.usgs.gov/order.php
British Antarctic Survey Map Catalogue: http://www.antarctica.ac.uk/magic/newmapcat/mapcat.html
SCAR (Scientific Committee for Antarctic Research) map catalogue: http://aadc-maps.aad.gov.au/
For a composite gazetteer of placenames in Antarctica visit: http://www3.pnra.it/SCAR_GAZE/
For a map showing all research stations operating in Antarctica visit: http://www.comnap.aq/

To find out interesting facts about Antarctica see:
'Antarctica in Context' on http://lima.usgs.gov/download.php

To find out more about Antarctica and British Antarctic Survey research, visit:
www.antarctica.ac.uk

The major geographical features on the Antarctic continent and the USA and UK research stations to accompany the Landsat Image Mosaic of Antarctica (LIMA) (NASA/LIMA, 2011).

kilometers). Under the force of its own weight and urged along by the inexorable tug of gravity, the WAIS slowly deforms and flows over the rough bedrock. Moreover, its ice can flow more rapidly in ice streams—a start-and-stop process which is still not fully understood. (As explained earlier, ice streams are relatively faster-moving "rivers" of ice bounded by walls of slower-moving ice.)

The WAIS does not need to melt completely to cause sea level rise — indeed, all is has to do is to decompose enough to slide into the ocean, where by displacement it will cause sea level rise. What now causes some scientists great concern is that large parts of the WAIS lie on an underwater bed which slopes downward and inland. In theory, this ice sheet is potentially unstable. Indeed, it is conceivable that some imperfectly-understood changes in the WAIS might destabilize it enough to lead to relatively quick (in geological terms) disintegration. A senior NASA scientist, Dr. James E. Hansen, warned in 2006 that "Once a sheet starts to disintegrate, it can reach a tipping point beyond which break-up is explosively rapid."[2]

That said, however, Dr. Natalya Gomez and others argued in a highly-technical paper in 2010 that their own studies showed this:

> Gravity and deformation-induced sea level changes local to the grounding line contribute to a *stabilizing influence* on ice sheets grounded on reversed bed slopes. We conclude that accurate treatments of sea level change should be incorporated into analyses of past and future marine-ice-sheet dynamics."[3]

To add a further note of uncertainty about the WAIS, Dr. Jonathan Bamber and others wrote in 2009 that, in their opinion, the potential contribution to eustatic and regional sea level would be about 10.8 feet (3.3 meters), with important regional variations. For example, the maximum increase in this rise might be concentrated along the Pacific and Atlantic seaboards of the United States.[4]

In any case, we should take note of reports that the WAIS is losing mass at an increasing rate in the Pine Island[5], Thwaites, and Smith Glaciers. The Pine Island Glacier is a large ice stream that flows west-northwest into Pine Island Bay in the Amundsen Sea. This glacier drains a large portion of the WAIS. Much of the ice in the basin sits below sea level, but there is enough ice above sea level so that if the entire basin were lost to the ocean, global oceans would rise about 3.2 feet (1 meter). This will not happen overnight, but scientists are now studying the dynamics of this rapidly changing system so that its future can accurately be predicted.[6]

What is evident now is that much of Antarctica's current net ice loss takes place along the Amundsen Coast, where the comparatively warmer 33.8 degree Fahrenheit (1 Celsius) Circumpolar Deep Water runs into the continental shelf. (Circumpolar Deep Water is a mixture of deep water from all oceans. It forms the core of the Antarctic Circumpolar Current.) At the continental shelf, this warmer water erodes its base, causing tens of meters of thinning and melting each year beneath the floating ice shelves which stretch seaward from the grounded WAIS. A 2010 study by experts at the Polar Science Center in Seattle and at the Courant Institute of Mathematics in New York explained that

> How the resulting thinning of grounded ice will evolve is one of the major uncertainties in 21st century sea-level projections.... Arguably, nowhere on the Antarctic Ice Sheet is change more apparent than at Pine Island Glacier, which has been described as the "weak underbelly" of Antarctica.... Too little is currently known about the process controlling the CDW [Circumpolar Deep Water] flowing onto the continental shelf to draw further conclusions at this point.[7]

Melting in this region appears to be increasing. In a June 2011 paper published in the journal *Nature Geoscience*, researchers found that, in 15 years, melting beneath the Pine Island Glacier ice shelf had risen by about 50 percent. The glacier is currently sliding into the sea at a rate of 2.5 miles (4 kilometers) per year, while its ice shelf is melting at about 19 cubic miles (80 cubic kilometers) per year.[8]

One of the most thorough studies of the state of WAIS science was provided in 2010 by the Antarctic Treaty Meeting of Experts.[9] It made the following key points, which have been edited and annotated here for ease of reading:

• There are currently no continental-scale ice sheet models that are considered to be reliable enough for predicting decadal or century-scale changes. In the glaciological community, there is thus no consensus now on the future of the WAIS. Its future evolution is best described as "a discursive approach which draws both on scientific literature and on policy-oriented ideas on how to deal with sea level rise."
• If the WAIS does indeed disintegrate in its entirety, this will raise global sea level from between 10.8 and 19.6 feet (3.3 to 6 meters), or perhaps even more.[10] Even a partial collapse of the WAIS could lead to a rise of 4.9 feet (1.5 meters).[11] The high degree of uncertainty in these estimates is due to differing scientific opinions on the extent of this marine-based ice sheet's instability. The period of time over which such a rise might occur, as well as the possible rate of rise, are also important but still-unknown variables.
• While there may well be a tipping point for the WAIS, it is also possible that there will be no specific tipping point: the WAIS may gradually lose ice simply as a result of a warmer world. If not, there is a wide range of scientific estimates on the temperature rise needed for a potential tipping point. It has been argued, for example, that perhaps the WAIS is already destined for a collapse — that is, for disintegration independent of anthropogenic global warming. (As used here, the term "collapse" connotes the loss of most or all of the WAIS over a relatively long period of time, e.g.,

over hundreds or even thousands of years, rather than in a matter of weeks or months.[12]) Alternatively, it has also been asserted that rising global temperatures will eventually push the WAIS over the brink of some undefined tipping point.

- Disintegration of the floating Wordie, Wilkins, and Larsen A and B Ice Shelves has already been observed. Glaciers in the Amundsen Sea/Pine Island Bay are now changing rapidly. Along the Ross Sea/Siple coast glaciers, some ice streams are accelerating, while others have stalled. Some areas of the WAIS show no major changes.

- Recent measurements indicate that the Antarctic ice sheet is losing mass, and that this loss, which is largely from the Antarctic Peninsula and West Antarctica, is accelerating. More research is therefore needed, and on several fronts. Important topics here include (1) the role of subglacial lakes and other water flowing at the base of the ice, and (2) the role of ice streams in regulating discharge (most of the discharge of the WAIS is via major ice streams entering the Ross Ice Shelf, plus the Rutford Ice Stream entering Ronne-Filchner shelf of the Weddell Sea, and the Thwaites Glacier and Pine Island Glacier entering the Amundsen Ice Shelf). Broader subjects needing more work include ocean-ice interactions, and continental and ocean warming.

- The environmental and socioeconomic effects of worst-case scenarios and extreme outcomes for the WAIS would clearly be monumental and devastating. As mentioned earlier, climate change induced by carbon dioxide emissions will last for many centuries, even if these emissions are totally halted tomorrow. As a result, the oceans will gradually become warmer. A warming of the intermediate-depth ocean around Antarctica could eventually lead to a collapse of the WAIS. Even if this is not likely to happen soon, such a high-risk event nevertheless now deserves our full attention: the potential dangers are simply too great for us to ignore it.

Fortunately, the WAIS is now being studied very carefully. The WAIS Divide Ice Core Project is a deep ice coring project funded by the United States' National Science Foundation.[13] (An ice divide is similar to a watershed divide, i.e., an ice sheet divide separates opposing flow directions of ice on an ice sheet.) The goal of this project is to study the last 100,000 years or so of the Earth's climate by drilling and recovering a long, deep ice core from the ice divide in central West Antarctica. The ice is 3,789 yards (3,465 meters) thick at the drill site, which is located 1,018 miles (1,639 kilometers) from McMurdo Station.

Ice core science has dramatically advanced our understanding of how the earth's climate has changed in the past. For example, ice cores collected from Greenland have already revolutionized scientists' grasp of climate changes there over the last 100,000 years. The WAIS Divide ice core will provide the first comparable Southern Hemisphere climate and greenhouse gas records. It will be used to test models of WAIS history and stability, and to investigate the biological signals hidden in deep Antarctic ice cores. This core may also give scientists some clues about the past stability and the future prospects of the WAIS.

One of the best recent studies of the WAIS, published by Drs. Richard Katz of Oxford and M. Grae Worster of Cambridge in 2010, deftly summarized the state of scientific knowledge as of that time.[14] These scientists noted that recent studies of the WAIS have revealed rapid changes in the mass balance of its component glaciers. To understand this, we need to understand a few technical terms.

Mass balance is the difference between the amount of snow accumulated during the winter and the amount of snow and ice removed by melting during the summer. The *grounding line* is the line separating grounded ice from floating ice. *Grounding-line recession* is the inland motion of the grounding line. The *theory of unstable recession* is, in its simplest terms, the idea that the bedform of a marine glacier makes it unstable to small changes in the grounding-line position.

Changes in the WAIS raise the question of whether changing climatic conditions have triggered a dynamical instability in the ice-sheet-ice-shelf system itself. Since the WAIS is, in large part, grounded on rock lying below sea level, the "ungrounding" of a relatively small part of the ice sheet, and its attendant change in mass balance, could result in a significant rise in sea level. The most challenging question is now this: will gradual modulation in the environmental conditions of Antarctica lead to massive, irreversible grounding-line recession and to the disintegration of the WAIS? At present, this question cannot be answered definitively but we should note that unstable grounding-line recession may already be occurring at the WAIS's Pine Island glacier and that observations at the WAIS are consistent with the theory of unstable recession.

XI

The Greenland Ice Sheet

Greenland is the world's largest island. We have already mentioned the Greenland ice sheet on several occasions thus far. Ice melt there is not potentially as dramatic as the West Antarctica Ice sheet but it still deserves, and will receive, our undivided attention in this chapter. First, a brief description.[1]

Despite its forbidding nature, the vast Greenland ice sheet can exhibit an austere beauty. In winter, it takes on a blue/green color. In summer, the top layer of ice melts, leaving pockets of air that change the appearance of the ice sheet into a milky white. Meltwater lakes, which form on the surface of the ice sheet in summer, form cobalt blue highlights, set against the endless white. Meltwater cascading down into crevasses known as *moulins* is a frothy and lighter blue.

Putting these visual charms aside, we can note that this ice sheet is the second biggest body of ice in the world (the Antarctic ice sheet is the biggest); is about ll0,000 years old; and covers about 80 percent of the surface of Greenland. It totals some 666,235 square miles (1,710,000 square kilometers) and is almost 1,500 miles (2,400 kilometers) long in a north-south direction and 680 miles (1,100 kilometers) wide near its northern margin. Its thickness is usually more than 1.24 miles (2 kilometers) but ranges up to a maximum thickness of 1.86 miles (3 kilometers). It is not the only ice mass on Greenland: there are also isolated glaciers and small ice caps elsewhere.

What is most important for our purposes here is that some scientists believe global warming may eventually push the Greenland ice sheet over an as-yet-undefined threshold, after which the entire sheet conceivably may melt comparatively rapidly (in geologic terms), e.g., in less than a few hundred years. Indeed, if the entire 683,751 cubic miles (2,850,000 cubic kilometers) of ice melts, this will result in a sea level rise of 23.6 feet (7.2 meters).[2] Such a rise would of course flood almost every coastal city in the entire world.

Large outlet glaciers, which are tongues of the ice sheet, now flow through valleys around the edges of Greenland and calve off into the ocean. This calving process is what generates the icebergs that can be a danger to the North

Atlantic shipping lanes: witness the loss of the *Titanic*. Outlet glaciers can move with surprising speed. For example, at its terminus, the Jakobshavn Isbrae glacier (Greenland's most prolific ice stream) flows at 65.6 to 72.2 feet (20 to 22 meters) per day. This glacier alone accounts for more than 6 percent of the ice loss from Greenland's interior ice cap — an amount that has doubled in the past decade.[3] Breakup of the small ice tongue terminating the Jakobshavn Isbrae glacier has caused a doubling of the flow velocity of this glacier.[4]

The Greenland ice sheet is vulnerable to global warming because the Arctic climate is now warming rapidly. This ice sheet has experienced record melting in recent years; and much more melting is forecast in the years to come. It is difficult to measure the mass balance very precisely but most studies indicate that, at lower elevations, mass loss from Greenland accelerated since the 1990s.

The GRACE (Gravity Recovery and Climate Experiment) satellite has shown that there is an ongoing ice mass loss in Greenland, which is tied to the acceleration of the glaciers draining Greenland's interior.[5] Using GRACE data, Dr. I. Velicogna determined that ice loss increased from 137 billion tons per year to 286 billion tons per year in 2009.[6] In short, this huge island is now shedding mass at an increasing rate.

All along the coastline, glaciers are calving ice into the ocean more rapidly than increased snowfall at higher elevations is forming new ice. Snowfall is increasing because global warming is adding more moisture to the air. This results in more precipitation. Since interior Greenland is at such a high altitude — 4,921 feet or 1,500 meters — and has such a high albedo — it stays well below freezing. Thus precipitation there is always in the form of snow.

Mass loss is important because, according a 2011 study of the Greenland and Antarctic ice sheets which was led by Dr. E. Rignot of Earth System Science at the University of California (Irvine),

Ice sheet mass balance estimates have improved substantially in recent years using a variety of techniques, over different time periods, and at various levels of spatial detail. Considerable disparity remains between these estimates due to the inherent uncertainties of each method, the lack of detailed comparisons between independent estimates, and the effect of temporal modulations in ice sheet surface mass balance. Here, we present a consistent record of mass balance for the Greenland and Antarctic ice sheets over the past two decades, validated by the comparison of two independent techniques over the last 8 years....

We find excellent agreement between two techniques for absolute mass loss and acceleration of mass loss.... The magnitude of the acceleration suggests that ice sheets will be the dominant contributors to sea level rise in forthcoming decades, and will likely exceed IPCC projections for the contributions of ice sheets to sea level rise in the 21st century.[7]

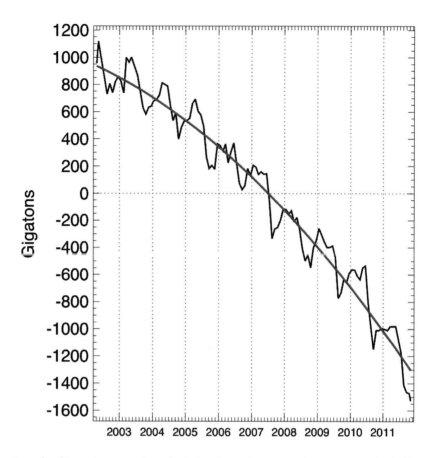

Greenland ice mass anomaly — deviation from the average ice mass over the 2002 to 2010 period. Smooth line shows long-term trend (courtesy Dr. John Wahr).

For example, if present melt rates are extrapolated forward to 2050, the cumulated loss could raise sea level by 5.9 inches (15 centimeters), for a total rise of 12.5 inches (32 centimeters). This latter figure includes 3.1 inches (8 centimeters) from glacial ice caps and 3.5 inches (9 centimeters) from thermal expansion.[8]

An excellent summary of the Greenland situation was provided in 2010 by Dr. Konrad Steffen of the University of Colorado. He told us:

We are seeing a transition from the slow, measured behavior long associated with polar ice sheets to the rapid rates of change more typical of big glaciers in Alaska and Patagonia. This transition is most apparent in Greenland, where a tendency of glacier acceleration is progressing northward, leaving Greenland's southern ice dome under threat from both increased summer melting near the coasts and increased ice discharge from glaciers that extend their influence far inland. If this continues, it is quite possible that the ice dome of southern Greenland will reach a tipping point, with accelerating positive feedback causing its ever more rapid decline and an associated sea rise level of about 85 cm [2.7 feet]. Continued northern migration of the tendency of glacier acceleration will also make the far larger northern dome vulnerable.[9]

In wake of the above study, Dr. Jay Zwally of the NASA Goddard Space Flight Center in the United States reported in 2011 that the Greenland ice sheet continued to grow inland and to thin at the margins between 2003 and 2007. Surface melting and accelerated flow significantly increased the marginal thinning compared with the 1990s. The bottom line of this study was that the net balance in Greenland changed from a small loss in the 1990s to an appreciably bigger loss between 2003 and 2007.[10]

A subsequent study by Dr. Stephen Price of the Los Alamos National Laboratory predicted a total sea level rise from Greenland, i.e., including both surface mass balance and ice dynamical effects, of 3.3 inches (85 millimeters) by 2100. The study warned, however, that its modeling implicitly assumed no change in the magnitude or spatial distribution of basal sliding in the future. If (as we think quite possible) such sliding does becomes more widespread on the Greenland ice sheet, this sea level rise estimate will have to be revised upward.[11]

XII

A Range of Options
to Cope with Sea Level Rise
Two Case Studies — The Netherlands
and the United States

Cnut the Great was a Viking king of Denmark, England, Norway, and some areas of Sweden in the early part of the 11th century. He met with repeated successes in politics, military affairs, and religion, but a pious legend tells us that, eventually, he met his match at the seashore. Henry of Huntingdon, a 12th century chronicler, assures us that Cnut purposively set up his throne at the very edge of the sea and, once seated, he ordered the rising tide to stop and not to wet his feet and robes. But when the tide failed to halt at his command, Cnut leaped backward, away from the water, and is said to have shouted:

> Let all men know how empty and worthless is the power of kings, for there is none worthy of the name, but He whom heaven, earth, and sea obey by eternal laws.[1]

Legend has it that Cnut then hung up his gold crown on a crucifix and never wore it again. The moral here an obvious one: even the greatest rulers are powerless when faced with a rising sea.

It is instructive at this point to look more closely at two highly-developed countries which will increasingly be faced with a rising sea and to learn what steps they may take to deal with this problem. The first country is the Netherlands, which has the most to lose from the rising sea and which, as a result, is taking an active role in efforts to deal with this issue.[2] The second country is the United States, which because of its enormous size and great range of topography, has much less to lose. Probably as a result, it has not moved very far beyond the "lots of talk, no action" option mentioned earlier. In this chapter, we shall discuss each the situation of each country in some detail.

The Netherlands

We have already referred to the Netherlands, especially the port of Rotterdam, several times in this book but a closer look is in order here.[3] The Netherlands is located on the western edge of the Eurasian land mass—on the North Sea and at the estuaries of the Rhine, the Maas, and the Scheldt rivers. It is flanked by Belgium on the south and by Germany on the east. The western and northern coasts of the Netherlands border the North Sea.

Some readers may remember the famous children's story of Hans Brinker, who is described as using his finger to plug a leak in a dike until help could come. This tale is much less well known in the Netherlands than it is in the United Kingdom or the United States because it is so far-fetched: if a dike threatens to give way, it takes much more than a boy's finger to hold back the water. As the Dutch author Han van der Horst has explained in *The Low Sky*, his excellent introduction to the Netherlands, if a break does occur,

> The water comes in like a wall ... boring a deep hole in the ground immediately behind the dike. It then spreads out, thundering and boiling, sweeping away everything in its part — trees, cattle, people....[4]

Although there is in fact a statue of little Hans in the village of Spaarndam, where his dike-plugging feat is supposed to have occurred, the only reason why the Netherlands is relatively dry today is that the Dutch have long excelled at non-stop feats of hydraulic engineering, i.e., water management. They need to be skilled at this undertaking because their country is, as they readily admit, *zo plat als een pannenkoek* ("as flat as a pancake"). They must always keep the sea at arm's length.

We mentioned earlier that about 27 percent of the Netherlands lies below sea level. Approximately two thirds of the country — one of the most densely populated on earth — is vulnerable to flooding. Its lowest point, near Rotterdam, is 22 feet (6.74 meters) below sea level. Its highest point, located at the southern tip of the country where the German and Belgian frontiers meet, has an elevation only 1,056 feet (322 meters).

Natural sand dunes and man-made dikes, dams, and floodgates protect the Netherlands from storm surges from the sea. River dikes prevent flooding from water flowing into the countryside from major rivers like the Rhine and the Meuse. An intricate system of drainage ditches, canals, and pumping stations makes the land suitable for homes and farms. This system is maintained by regional government bodies known as Water Boards, some of which date from the 13th century. They are charged with managing water barriers, waterways, water levels, and water quality in their respective areas of responsibility.[5]

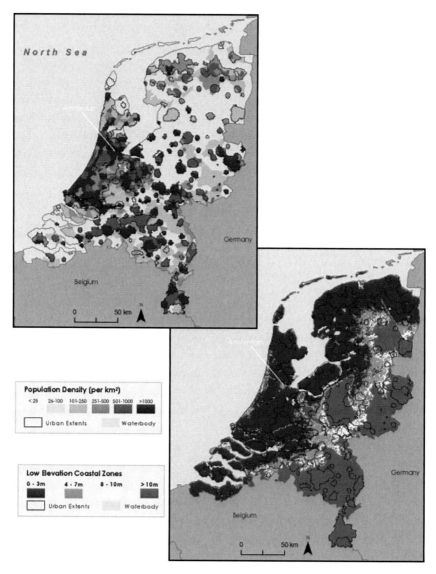

Netherlands population density and low elevation coastal zones (Socioeconomic Data and Applications Center, 2009).

The Dutch experience with hydraulic engineering began in about 500 B.C., when settlers now known as Frisians heaped up piles of earth called *terpen* and lived on them not far above the level of the water.[6] They had a hard life: the Roman naturalist Pliny tells us that they were a "wretched race." In the period before the invasion by the Romans, the inhabitants of what is now

Friesland (located in the northwestern part of the Netherlands) were building low dikes to protect themselves against flooding by the sea. After 800 CE [CE = Common Era], when water levels at high tides increased significantly, the growing population had to intensify its efforts to prevent flooding. The first dike construction works on a large scale in the Friesland area began in the first half of the 10th century.

The earliest dikes were low embankments about 3.2 feet (1 meter) high, designed to protect crops in the fields from occasional flooding and to safeguard the small villages which had sprung up. As the population grew, there was a greater need for arable land and also a greater number of strong backs available to build dikes under the supervision of the major landowners and, later, the monks.

In 1287, however, the Dutch nearly lost their war against the water, when big floods swept over the land and created the Zuiderzee ("Southern Sea" in Dutch), a large shallow inlet of the North Sea, located in the northwestern part of the Netherlands. (In 1932, a barrier dam would transform the Zuiderzee into the fresh-water Ijsselmeer, or "IJssel Lake" in Dutch.) The first drainage windmill was built in the Netherlands in 1414. After the St. Elizabeth's Day Flood of 1421, which killed some 10,000 people and inundated 20 villages, many more windmills were built. In the 17th century, the great hydraulic engineer Jan Adriaenzoon Leeghwater (fittingly, his surname means "empty water" in Dutch) used 43 windmills to help him construct polders north of Amsterdam. These windmills made it possible to regulate water levels by a series of drainage canals which crisscrossed the polders and thus dried out the land.

To prevent a recurrence of the disastrous flood of 1953, the Dutch created the Delta Works. Consisting of a complex series of dikes, dams, sluices, locks, and storm surge barriers, the overall goal of this ambitious and remarkable project was to shorten the Dutch coastline, thereby reducing the number of dikes that had to be raised in height. Most of the Delta Works were built between 1950 and 1997 in the southwest of the Netherlands to protect an extensive region of land around the Rhine-Meuse-Scheldt delta.[7] The final step in this project was only a small one — the official opening of a strengthened and raised water retaining wall near the city of Harlingen in 2010.

The last mega-undertaking of the Delta Works was the Maeslant Storm Surge Barrier on the Nieuwe Waterweg (New Waterway) near Rotterdam, which was finished in 1997.[8] This barrier, which closes automatically when needed, is one of the largest moving structures on earth and is designed to protect the 1.5 million inhabitants of Rotterdam and its surrounding area. The barrier is connected to a computer system which constantly monitors sea level data and controls the barrier appropriately.

Under normal sea level conditions, the two giant, hollow, semi-circular doors of the barrier remain open, giving seagoing ships plenty of room — a 1,181 foot-wide (360 meter-wide) gap — to pass between them. When a storm surge of 9.8 feet (3 meters) above normal sea level is anticipated in Rotterdam, however, the doors close automatically. The Dutch now believe that, due to the rising sea level, the barrier will have to be closed about once every five years to keep the sea out, rather than once every 10 years as initially expected. The barrier first closed its gates for a storm flood during 2007. It is tested every year before the 1 October–15 April storm season begins.

In 2008, the Netherlands' high-level Deltacommissie (Delta Commission), reflecting on the lessons learned in New Orleans from Hurricane Katrina and on the certainty of additional sea level rise in the future due to continued global warming, reported that the Netherlands needed a massive new building program to strengthen the country's defenses against sea and river water. The likely cost of this work, e.g., broadening coastal dunes and strengthening sea and river dikes, was estimated at more than $144 billion (100 billion Euros).

In its studies, the Delta Commission evoked, among other scenarios, a worst-case, low-probability sea level rise (due in part to land subsidence) of 2.1 to 4.2 feet (0.65 to 1.3 meters) by 2100, and of 6.5 to 13.1 feet (2 to 4 meters) by 2200. Although no one can be sure be sure how high the sea will rise in the years ahead, the Dutch are certainly facing this problem head-on. The Delta Commission also made 12 recommendations, of which the first was arguably the most important. It stated:

> The present flood protection levels of all diked areas must be raised by a factor of 10. To that end, the new standards must be set as soon as possible (around 2013). In some areas where more protection is needed, the Delta Dike concept is promising (these dikes are either so high or so wide and massive that the probability that these dikes will suddenly and uncontrollably fail is virtually zero). With regard to special or local conditions, this will require a tailor-made approach. All measures to increase the flood protection levels must be implemented before. After 2050, the flood protection levels must be updated regularly.[9]

Plans for mass evacuations in the event of worst-case scenarios are also being refined. The current sea defenses of the Netherlands are continuously being strengthened and raised to meet the safety norm of a flood chance of once every 10,000 years for the western part of the country (this is the most densely populated and economically most important region), and once every 4,000 years for other areas. Primary flood defenses are being tested against this norm every five years.

In response to the Delta Commission's work, a "Delta Commissioner" was appointed and given an appropriate staff. This official is tasked with making sure that a Delta Programme is drawn up and implemented every year and that progress reports are submitted. Thus, to use a metaphor from the sport of rowing, the Dutch are not resting on their oars. In its 2008 report, the Delta Commission concluded:

> Implementation of the recommendations [in the report] is a matter of urgency. The Netherlands must accelerate its efforts because, at present, even the current standards of flood protection are not being met everywhere. Moreover, the current standards are out of date and must be raised, the climate is changing rapidly, the sea level is probably rising faster than has been assumed, and more extreme variations in river discharge are expected. *The economic, societal and physical stakes in the Netherlands are great and growing still; a breach in a dike has seriously disruptive consequences for the entire country.*[10]

The United States

Although many shoreside East Coast and Gulf Coast cities are virtually certain to face serious problems from sea level rise over the coming decades, there is now no single, comprehensive national American program designed to deal with this issue. Some comparatively modest efforts are now underway at the Federal level (e.g., via the U.S. Geological Survey, the Federal Emergency Management Agency, and the U.S. Army Corps of Engineers), as well as at various state and city levels. But taking it all in all, the overall response by the United States to sea level rise has thus far been spotty and, on a national basis, not well coordinated.

Probably the most important reason is that, in the absence of any sea level rise disasters in the United States, the American public — and thus the American Congress — is unwilling to finance any major preventative measures (New Orleans excepted). Such measures are likely to be expensive and politically controversial. Many American decision-makers still function under the traditional assumptions that the level of the sea, and thus of the shorelines it washes, is inherently stable and that storms are a regular, normal part of nature.

At minimum, all of them know that no matter how important it may be in the long run, sea level rise is not now a problem that, in political terms, *simply must be dealt with this week.* Moreover, it is very difficult for legislators to convince Americans living in landlocked states in the middle of the country that their tax dollars must be spent to mitigate sea level rise along the distant coasts of the United States.

Nevertheless, despite these realities, at the technical level a good deal of in-depth research has already been conducted in the United States on sea level rise. One the best examples was a hefty (300-page) report coordinated by the U.S. Environmental Protection Agency in 2009.[11] This magisterial project, chaired by James G. Titus, focused on the mid–Atlantic region of the United States, e.g., on the coasts of New York, New Jersey, Delaware, Maryland, Virginia, and North Carolina. It remains the most thorough U.S. Government publication on the implications of sea level rise and is not likely to lose this heavyweight title soon. By drawing from it selectively and by allowing ourselves a little bit of editorial freedom in the process to improve readability, we can learn a number of interesting things[12]:

Perhaps the first and most important lesson is that although other coastal regions of the country (most notably the Gulf of Mexico and the Florida coast) are fundamentally more vulnerable to sea level rise, the mid–Atlantic coastal region, for its part, is a very prosperous, high-tech, densely-populated part of the United States coast that will be at greater risk as the sea rises in the years ahead. Farmlands, forests, wetlands, and developed lands in low-lying localities there will suffer the most from any future sea level rise of 3.2 feet (1 meter) or higher. When storm surges wash ashore on top of this kind of rise, there is going to be a great deal of trouble along the Mid-Atlantic coast.

Remarkably, however, the kind of comprehensive, high-resolution, precise analyses of the spatial distributions of population and infrastructure vulnerable to sea level rise in the Mid-Atlantic region which are essential for effective planning and response do not appear to exist at this time. Because of a wide variety of heavy financial, political, and bureaucratic restraints, most the public entities involved in this issue have not prepared for a rising sea. The Mid-Atlantic studies which do exist usually lack the required underlying land elevation data which is necessary for decision-makers to have full confidence in the results of possible efforts to deal with sea level rise.

Today, existing generalized data can give us only a very rough approximation of how many people may be affected by sea level rise in the Mid-Atlantic area. For example, between approximately 900,000 and 3,400,000 people (between 3 to 10 percent of the total population there) are believed to live on parcels of land or city blocks with at least some land less than 3.2 feet (1 meter) above monthly highest tides. As noted earlier, a sea level rise of about 3.2 feet (1 meter)—and perhaps even more—seems quite possible by 2100.

There are several ways—none of them perfect—to cope with sea level rise. These options include:

- In-shore protection (i.e., protecting buildings, etc., which are situated immediately inland of the shore).
- Shoreline armoring, for example, the use of seawalls, bulkheads, retaining structures, revetments (walls whose seaward side follows a slope), dikes, dunes, tide gates, and storm surge barriers.

- Beachfill (also called beach nourishment or sand replacement), which adds material to a beach to make it higher, wider, and less vulnerable to the sea.
- Physically raising existing structures: for example, after a severe hurricane in 1900, most of Galveston, Texas was elevated by more than 3.2 feet (1 meter).
- Erecting groins (hard structures placed offshore) and/or converting eroding mud or sand beaches to a cobble or pebble beach, which is more stable.
- Retreat (also known as relocation). The most ambitious relocation program in the Mid-Atlantic region was moving the Cape Hatteras Lighthouse about 1,475 feet (450 meters) inland in 1999.

A basic problem here is that almost all coastal communities and public structures in this region (and elsewhere, of course) were conceived, designed, and built without any realization that sea level would rise substantially. Although these communities probably expect that the Federal or state government will somehow stabilize their shores and maintain the coastal status quo, the economic costs of shore protection over a very long period of time are now unknown. Similarly, the long-term economic and social costs of retreat still remain to be quantified.

The need to prepare for a rising sea level is a function of numerous complicated and interrelated factors. Some of them are:

- the length of time over which a decision will have continuing consequences
- how rapidly the sea is expected to rise
- the degree of uncertainty about the pace of this rise
- levels of risk tolerance among the tax-paying and shore-using publics
- levels of risk tolerance among the decision-makers responsible for community action or inaction
- the implications of doing nothing at all at a given time.

Within the Mid-Atlantic region, most governmental organizations are not yet taking specific measures to prepare for sea level rise. Congress has given neither the U.S. Army Corps of Engineers nor the U.S. Environmental Protection Agency a mandate to change the present administration of wetlands by focusing on a rising sea. Understandably, these agencies are not able to move ahead on this issue without a green light from Congress. On the other hand, some private organizations that manage land for environmental purposes, e.g., The Nature Conservancy (the largest private holder of conservation lands in the Mid-Atlantic region), are now moving ahead unilaterally on this front.

Looking ahead, what can we say about the implications of sea level rise for the United States as a whole? Here are some of the ideas mentioned in the Environmental Protection Agency's report:

- More than one-third of the U.S. population now lives in the coastal zone, which continues to attract new residents and commercial development. Fourteen of the 20 largest U.S. urban centers are situated along the coast. Sea level rise, especially if accompanied by more frequent storm surges, will have significant and uniformly negative economic and social impacts.
- Some portions of the U.S. coast will be subject to inundation from sea level rise over the years leading to the next century. In a relatively early (1989) study, the U.S. Environmental Protection Agency forecast that a rise of only 3.2 feet (1 meter) could drown approximately 25 percent to 80 percent of the U.S. coastal wetlands. Such a rise would also inundate 5,000 to 10,000 square miles (12,949 to 25,899 square kilometers) of dry land if shores were not protected, and 4,000 to 9,000 square miles (10,359 to 23,309 square kilometers) of dry land if only developed areas were protected.[13]
- A great deal still remains to be done to quantify the likely effects of this rise and to spell out the dominant coastal change processes for each region of the U.S. coast. Understanding, predicting, and responding to the environmental and social effects of sea level rise will therefore benefit from a national program of integrated research that includes both the natural and social sciences. The findings of such a program (which does not yet exist) would be of great value to other coastal nations, too.
- In the process of such research, the historic and geologic record of coastal change should be used to improve our understanding of natural and human-influenced coastal systems. We need to increase our knowledge of sea level rise and coastal change over the past few millennia; to identify possible thresholds or tipping points in coastal systems; and to relate past changes in overall climate to specific changes along the coasts.

XIII

Impacts of Sea Level Rise

As stated earlier, the long range outlook for our planet is that sea level rise will increasingly conflict with humanity's established patterns of development and its ambitious plans for the future. What is critically important is that policymakers and citizens alike begin to understand, now, that sea level rise will not in fact come to a grinding halt after 2100, the year most often used to make climate change projections, but will continue for a very long time to come. We hope that this introductory survey, which is likely to appear in libraries and may therefore have a relatively long lifespan, will make a small contribution toward increasing public knowledge in this regard.

Because sea level rise will be such a long term, intractable problem, we must consider it in this light, and not simply as a temporary aberration of the familiar status quo. In fact, we should take our cue from the Dutch, who since 2008 have been studying very low probability but very high impact sea level rise scenarios, e.g., a sea level rise of up to 13.1 feet (4 meters) by 2200, and are beginning to make their national emergency plans accordingly.[1] Here we will look very briefly at four interrelated facts:

1. Some parts of the world, especially the megadeltas, are at much greater risk from sea level rise than other areas and will suffer more damage.
2. In the United States alone, as many as 180 municipalities may be adversely affected by sea level rise.
3. Climate change, and thus sea level rise, may well be more abrupt in the future than it is now.
4. Sea level rise will have important and probably now-unforeseen political and social impacts, as well as its more easily understood economic impacts. It may even have some military impacts, too.

First, a small caveat is needed here. There are only a handful of reasons why the seas will inexorably continue to rise. Global warming caused by greenhouse gas emissions will continue to expand ocean water. The mountain glaciers will melt further. If warming continues, the ice sheets will eventually melt away completely or slide into the seas. In some places, shoreside land will continue to subside.

At the same time, however, a large number of examples can be advanced to explain and elaborate on these few physical processes. Some of these examples, e.g., sea level rise prospects for Tuvalu, are so very clear and so dramatic that they have been cited repeatedly in the international climate change literature. For this reason, we will free to discuss them in this chapter, too, even if we may have already mentioned them earlier in this book or may do so again later on.

In terms of the major risks and major consequences of sea level rise, we — and, indeed, most of all, our descendants— must be especially concerned about the future of the world's megadeltas: namely, the Ganges-Brahmaputra Delta in Bangladesh, the Mekong Delta in Vietnam, and the Nile Delta in Egypt. These are the parts of the world most likely to suffer the gravest damage. We mentioned earlier that more than 1 million people may be displaced by sea level rise in each of these three megadeltas alone, and that in smaller deltas an additional 510,000 people may be displaced —for an overall total of about 3.51 million people, not including the expected increases in population in these regions that will certainly increase these numbers. In this chapter, drawing on IPCC reports and other sources, we will try to imagine some of the possible impacts of large-scale displacements in these megadeltas and in other regions.

Ganges-Brahmaputra Delta

With an area of 41,000 square miles (105,000 square kilometers), this is the world's biggest delta, being approximately 220 miles (350 kilometers) across at the Bay of Bengal. Kolkata and Haida (both in India), and Mongla and Chittagong (both in Bangladesh), are the principal seaports on the delta. The delta itself consists of a serpentine maze of waterways, swamps, lakes, and muddy flood plain sediments. Between 125 and 143 million people already live in this watery region, despite the pervasive and often lethal risks they face from floods caused by monsoons; from heavy runoff from the melting snows of the Himalaya Mountains; from tropical cyclones; and now, and increasingly in the future, from sea level rise.

Indeed, the threat of rising sea levels is arguably — after the endemic poverty of the region — the most insoluble challenge its people will have to face in the years ahead. This rise will be caused both by local subsidence and by global climate change. It is thought that a rise of only 1.6 feet (0.5 meters) might result in 6 million people losing their homes. Computer–generated United Nations Environment Programme (UNEP) graphs have forecast that, in the case of a sea level rise of 3.2 feet (1 meter), 15 million people will be affected and 6,563 square miles (17,000 square kilometers) of land will be submerged; in the case of a 4.9 feet (1.5 meter) rise, 17 million people will be affected and 8,494 square miles (22,000 square kilometers) of land will be flooded.[2]

With this kind of bleak future stretching out in front of it, how stable can Bangladesh hope to be over the long run? Since its independence in 1971, the country has already suffered from overpopulation, famines, natural disasters (the 1970 Bhola cyclone was the deadliest tropical cyclone ever recorded and may have killed as many as 500,000 people), widespread poverty, corruption, and political violence and instability. A reasonable guess is that, in the future, widespread flooding due to sea level rise will force large numbers of Bangladeshis to seek safer ground in neighboring India.

Today, Bangladesh is a secular republic and a parliamentary democracy with an elected parliament known as the Jatiyo Sangshad. Religion is a very important part of Bangladeshi life: nearly 90 percent of the population is Muslim and almost all of the remaining 10 percent is Hindu. The army has already played a key role in the recent history of Bangladesh. It does not require an overactive imagination for us to wonder whether, at a time of national disaster and enormous suffering caused by extreme sea level rise, a charismatic military-religious leader might not come to power and, in the process, sweep away all the trappings of parliamentary democracy and religious toleration.

What is certain is that coping effectively with extreme sea level rise in Bangladesh would require foreign assistance on a large scale. The problem here is that in any scenario where Bangladesh is very hard-hit by sea level rise, many other countries would be hard-hit too. If so, we doubt that they would have the will or the ability to do very much to help Bangladesh. Moreover, at the same time, Bangladesh could also being undergoing a political and economic fragmentation of its own. In this scenario, the writ, the competence, and the legitimacy of the central government might not extend to all of the country, making any international relief efforts much more difficult. To compound these problems, if large numbers of desperate Bangladeshi "sea level rise migrants" made their way into India, relations between India and Bangladesh would become severely strained.

Mekong Delta

Embracing a large part of southwestern Vietnam, the Mekong Delta, known in Vietnamese as the "Nine Dragon river delta," encompasses about 15,000 square miles (39,000 square kilometers) of land and water. During the

Vietnam War, this delta witnessed fierce fighting between Viet Cong guerrillas and units of the "brown-water navy" and hovercraft forces of the United States. ("Brown-water navy" refers to the small gunboats and patrol boats used by American forces along the rivers of Vietnam.)

Because it is such a low-lying coastal region, the Mekong Delta is particularly vulnerable to sea level rise. Studying the possible consequences of climate change in Vietnam, the Climate Change Research Institute at Vietnam's Can Tho University has predicted that, in addition to suffering from climate change drought brought on by seasonal decreases in rainfall, many provinces in the Mekong Delta will be flooded by 2030 due to sea level rise. The provinces of Ben Tre and Long An, for example, are very likely to be flooded if sea levels rise by only 3.2 feet (1 meter).[3]

"GIS," i.e., Graphic Information System, refers to a geographical information system which integrates hardware, software, and data to manage many kinds of geographically-referenced information. GIS is important to us at this point because a GIS–linked numerical model shows that the flood levels in the Mekong Delta depend on sea level rise; on the combined impacts of high river flows in the Mekong River; on storm surges; and, finally, on the future siltation of the Mekong Estuary, which will be the result of construction of dams in China and from the many other dams proposed throughout the remaining river catchment.

This GIS model suggests that engineering structures in the Mekong Delta, while helping to protect the local inhabitants, also increase flow velocities in the rivers and canals. This in turn leads to greater erosion of their banks. It also results in appreciably more water flowing through the rivers and canals, thus risking catastrophic flooding if the dikes should give way. The model warns the Vietnamese that the sea level rise caused by global warming will enhance flooding in the Mekong Delta and that this flooding will worsen in the long term due to estuarine siltation resulting from the construction of dams.

The bottom line, according to the study, is that in a worst-case scenario— which is defined here to mean only a very modest sea level rise of 1.6 feet (0.5 meter)—the combined impact of storm surges and sea level rise could flood 1,600 square miles (4,300 square kilometers) of the Mekong Delta to a depth of 8.2 feet (2.5 meters).[4] Any subsequent and higher sea level rise would of course have much more severe impacts.

Coastal engineering structures in Vietnam, including ports and sea dikes, will be more vulnerable to waves as water depth in front of the structures increases, as the seashore is eaten away by erosion, and as the protective forest belt disappears. In fact, the safety of many of Vietnam's sea dikes can no longer be taken for granted today. They are not high enough, and the hydraulic forces working on them, combined with seepage flows, may exceed their initial design capacities.

Sea level rise in Vietnam will also reduce the capacity for flood drainage into the sea. This will result in more serious flooding, which in the future will have negative impacts on agricultural production (especially on rice production) in the Mekong delta. Ho Chi Minh City and other urban areas will be at greater risk of being flooded — due to sea level rise, floods, high tides, or a combination of all of these. Saline intrusion will be a growing problem as well.[5] Sea level rise itself is not now a cause of migration in the Mekong Delta. Migration there is driven by other seasonal, economic, and social factors, with the majority of migrants moving internally, usually from rural areas to the cities. However, even for the Vietnamese who will eventually be directly affected by sea level rise, e.g., those citizens living in the Mekong Delta, there is very little awareness today of the importance of climate change and sea level rise. The Vietnamese government, for its part, is only now beginning to think about the enormous challenges it will have to face in the future when dealing these problems.[6]

What seems certain at this writing is that the impacts of sea level rise, no matter how severe, will not unseat the Communist Party of Vietnam, which remains the ruling and the only legal political party in the country. Based on the Communist Youth League founded in China by Ho Chi Minh in 1926, the Communist Party of Vietnam played the leadership role in Vietnam's remarkable defeats of two major and militarily vastly-superior Western powers—first the French between 1946 and 1954, and then the Americans between 1965 and 1973/1974.

Today it seems quite unlikely that any other foreseeable political grouping will be able to compete with or seize control from the Communist Party of Vietnam. It is equally unlikely that the Party will ever surrender its dominant position voluntarily. Coping with sea level rise in the years to come will, however, seriously challenge the Party's ability to motivate its own members, to mobilize the rest of Vietnam's citizens, and to attract foreign assistance.

Nile Delta

To add to what we have said earlier, let us revisit the fan-shaped Nile Delta, which is located where the Nile River spreads out and runs into the Mediterranean Sea. The delta begins slightly downstream from Cairo and is one of the world's biggest deltas, stretching some 149 miles (240 kilometers) from Alexandria in the west to Port Said in the east. Measured from north to south, it is about 99 miles (160 kilometers) in length.

This delta is one of the oldest intensively-cultivated areas on this planet and is one of the most fertile and densely populated. About half of Egypt's 80 million people life here. The delta's low-lying floodplains are surrounded by inhospitable deserts: only about 2.5 percent of Egypt's land area, i.e., the Nile Delta and the Nile Valley, is suitable for intensive farming. Much of a 31 mile (50 kilometer)-wide strip of land along the coast of the delta is less than 6.5 feet (2 meters) above sea level. This narrow strip is safeguarded from flooding only by a 0.6–6.2 mile (1–10 kilometer) wide sand belt. The sand belt was created and maintained by discharges from the Rosetta and Damietta branches of the Nile. Today the erosion of this protective sand belt is a serious problem, and one exacerbated by the construction of the Aswan dam.[7]

Computer-generated UNEP outline maps show that a very modest sea level rise of only 1.6 feet (0.5 meters) will impact 3.8 million people and 694 square miles (1,800 square kilometers) of cropland in the Nile Delta. A higher rise — 3.2 feet (1 meter) — will affect 6.1 million people and 1,737 square miles (4,500 square kilometers) of agricultural land. Rising sea levels may also destroy weak parts of the sand belt, which is essential for the protection of the lagoons and the low-lying reclaimed lands of the Nile Delta. Such destruction would have serious impacts. One third of Egypt's fish catches are made in the lagoons. Sea level rise will change the water quality and affect most fresh water fish there. Valuable agricultural land will be inundated.[8]

Recent, entirely unexpected, and far-reaching political changes in the Middle East make it unusually hazardous now to try to peer into Egypt's future, but three factors are likely to be dominant there in the years to come. The first is Egypt's very long-running tradition of authoritarian government: political repression has always been seen as the only reliable guarantee of national security and stability. The second factor is Islam: about 90 percent of Egypt's population is Muslim. The third factor is income inequality: there have always been a few very rich and some comfortably-well-off Egyptians, but today most of the people are still extremely poor and are very likely to remain that way.

The armed forces of Egypt, especially the Egyptian Army, have considerable economic power and political influence in the country today. The army would undoubtedly try hard to deal with the widespread displacement and suffering certain to be caused by sea level rise, but the army cannot command the Mediterranean Sea to retreat. Moreover, given the size of the delta and its large population, the army itself is relatively small (its active-duty strength is only about 380,000 men) and it is not equipped to mount large-scale humanitarian operations. For this, international help would be essential.

Our guess is that if a civilian government is in power in Egypt at a time of acute sea level rise, it would not be able to achieve very much and would face mounting public hostility for its failures. In this situation, we can easily imagine that the Egyptian Army would intervene, would take charge of the relief efforts, and would gradually become the *de facto* ruler of the country. If so, the army would probably not look with much favor any criticism of its activities. In this eventuality, a new round of political repression might not be far off.

Turning away at this point from any further speculation about the prospects for these three megadeltas, let us see what predictions the IPCC has offered regarding the impacts of sea level rise on other parts of the world.

According to the brief (and here lightly edited) summaries in the IPCC's 2007 Synthesis Report, regional impacts may be as follows[9]:

- In Africa, projected sea level rise toward the end of the 21st century will affect low-lying areas with large populations. African efforts to adapt to this rise could amount to at least 5 percent to 10 percent of Gross Domestic Product. (We will offer our own comment here: these efforts are not likely to be successful because of the magnitude of the problem and the very limited numbers of trained personnel and the few resources at the disposal of most African governments.)
- In Australia and New Zealand, coastal developments and population growth in some areas of these countries are projected by 2050 to exacerbate risks from sea level rise. There may also be increases in the severity and frequency of storms and in coastal flooding.
- In Europe, climate change will increase the risks associated with sea level rise and may lead to more severe storms and more coastal flooding. (As we have suggested earlier, the Dutch are now the world leaders in preparing for sea level rise. Other countries lag very far behind them.)
- In Latin America, coastal communities and habitats will be increasingly under pressure from climate change impacts, including sea level rise, which will interact with the unchecked development and increasing environmental problems of this region.
- In the Small Island Developing States, i.e., the Pacific Ocean islands and the Indian Ocean islands, sea level rise is expected to increase inundation, storm surges, erosion, and other coastal hazards. These will seriously threaten the vital infrastructure, settlements, and facilities needed to support island communities.

Looking beyond the IPCC report, we must also consider the possibility that, in the future, sea level rise in the Pacific Ocean itself may be appreciably faster and higher than it has been in the past. If so, this will certainly have negative impacts on the cities and countries of the Pacific Ocean basin. Why might this happen? The answer runs along the following lines[10]:

Mean sea level rise will have important and worldwide consequences for shoreline and beach erosion, coastal wetlands inundation, storm surge flooding, and the feasibility of additional economic development of the coasts. Remarkably, tide gauge and satellite altimetry sea height measurements show that sea levels along the Pacific Coast of North America have remained relatively stationary since about 1980 — in contrast to the increases observed globally and in the western Pacific. The reason is that in about 1980 a dramatic change in wind stress patterns occurred along the eastern boundary of the North Pacific, after a mid–1970s shift from "cool" to "warm" phases of the Pacific Decadal Oscillation.

We must pause here for some needed definitions:

- Wind stress is the shear stress exerted by the wind of the surface of large bodies of water, such as oceans, seas, estuaries, and lakes.
- The Pacific Decadal Oscillation is a pattern of Pacific climate variability that shifts on an interdecadal time scale, each phase usually lasting about 20 to 30 years. During a "warm" phase, the eastern ocean warms while the western Pacific cools; during a "cool" phase, the opposite occurs. Moreover, when the cycle shifts to its "cool" phase, coastal ocean waters are then characterized by downwelling, during which the amount of colder and denser water that is typically brought to the surface by upwelling is reduced. This process ultimately raises sea level through thermal expansion of the warmer surface water.
- Wind stress curl is atmospheric wind circulation that can force seawater downward or upward. In the context below, it means that wind stress curl was forcing water downward so that Pacific sea level rise was suppressed. Wind stress curl is one reason why sea level does not rise uniformly across the globe.

Beginning in about 1980, the predominant wind stress along the US West Coast suppressed regional relative sea level rise to less than the global rate. Mean annual wind stress curl over the entire North Pacific (which is associated with decadal basin-wide ocean circulation oscillations that probably have a Pacific Decadal Oscillation connection) and over the eastern North Pacific dropped to levels during 2008 not observed for the previous 30 years.

If this change in wind patterns persists, a new shift in the Pacific Decadal Oscillation phase may result in a resumption of sea level rise along the West Coast, approaching or perhaps even exceeding the global mean sea level rise rate. A persistent change in wind stress curl, causing changes in upwelling/downwelling regimes and in sea level rise along the West Coast, would have important negative impacts. It would affect coastal erosion and flooding, economic resources, and marine ecosystems.

What can we say now about the likely impacts of sea level rise in the coterminous United States? Here we are helped by a 2011 study which pointed out that a total of 180 municipalities (i.e. 20 municipalities with populations greater than 300,000, and 160 communities with populations between 50,000 and 300,000) all have land areas with elevations at or below 19.6 feet (6 m) and also have connectivity to the sea.[11] On average, approximately 9 percent of the land area of these coastal municipalities lies at or below 3.2 feet (1 meter), while 36 percent lies at or below 19.6 feet (6 meters).

Most of these 180 municipalities are located along the Gulf and southern Atlantic coasts, particularly in southern Louisiana and in southern Florida. The northern Atlantic and Pacific coasts, for their parts, have far fewer low-lying areas, though there are exceptions. For example, the Chesapeake Bay near Washington, D.C., and the San Francisco Bay and San Joaquin-Sacramento river delta in northern California all have areas at or below 3.2 feet and 19.6 feet (1–6 meters).

Examples of municipalities on the Gulf and southern Atlantic coasts that will be at most risk from sea level rise include Virginia Beach, Jacksonville, Miami, Tampa, New Orleans, and Houston. Indeed, color-coded outline maps of the east coast of the United States show that virtually all of the coast between Virginia Beach and the tip of Texas is low-lying and that there are many densely-populated, low-lying metropolitan areas located north of Virginia Beach, too. These include Washington, D.C.[12]; Baltimore; Philadelphia; New York; and Boston. Parts of Maine's rock-bound coast will be at risk from sea level rise as well.[13]

The long-term outlook for the shorelines of this region is not, alas, a positive one in terms of sea level rise. If, as seems certain, high levels of greenhouse gas emissions continue unabated around the world, then the ensuing rise in sea level cannot fail to affect some of the Americans living in the 180 municipalities mentioned above. It is now crystal-clear that settlements in American coastal lowlands— and, of course, settlements in lowlands in many other parts of the world as well — are especially vulnerable to risks resulting from climate change.

The bad news is that most of these lowlands are already densely populated and are still growing rapidly. Reducing the risk of impacts related to sea level rise in coastal areas will require a time-consuming, expensive, and politically-combustible mix of mitigation, adaptation, migration, and resettlement. There are now no signs that such a mix will prove to be at all acceptable to local residents or to their elected representatives. As a result, no progress can be expected on this front in the foreseeable future.

We said earlier that climate change, and thus sea level rise, will probably be more abrupt in the future than it is now. It is indeed regrettable that, in addition to the usual impediments to any significant political, economic, or social modifications of the status quo, it is not widely understood today that the climate has changed abruptly in the past and that there is no reason to suppose it will not do so again in the future.[14] Paleoclimatic records from the last 10,000 years reflect abrupt shifts in hurricane frequency, floods, and droughts. Examples in more recent times include the Dust Bowl drought of the 1930s in the United States and the massive social displacement it set in motion.

In the years ahead, abrupt climate change seems more likely than not. It could have profound impacts. A rapid sea level rise could threaten or inundate coastal populations. Significant changes in patterns of droughts or frosts could destroy forests or agricultural systems. Sudden temperature changes could make improperly insulated, heated, or cooled buildings inhabitable. Despite the need for more information on these fronts, the National Academies (which, collectively, serve as the scientific national academy of the United States in the fields of science, engineering, and medicine) stated in 2004:

> To date, however, relatively little research has addressed the ecological and eco-nomic impacts of abrupt climate change: most studies focus on gradual climate change. *Given the accumulating evidence of past abrupt changes and their capacity to affect human societies, some attention should be focused on potential abrupt change scenarios.*[15]

In addition to studying future abrupt changes, it might also be worth-while for governments or scientific institutions to fund a few studies of *totally unexpected* sea level rise developments. For example, it does not seem at all probable now that the sea could rise by as much as 9.8 feet (3 meters) any time soon, even though a high-end scenario of an 11.4 foot (3.5 meters) rise for the Netherlands, by 2200, has already been discussed in the literature.[16] Nevertheless, in our view well-sourced sea level rise estimates do deserve careful attention.

This path is of course fraught with difficulties. In order for a 9.8 feet (3 meter) or higher increase to occur, most of the water would have to come from the continental ice sheets of Greenland and Antarctica. There is no easy way, short of physical modeling, to tell how much would come from Green-land and how much from Antarctica. Moreover, that ratio might change over time. About all that can be said now with some certainty is that in such a case the equatorial regions would get more water than other regions.

This is because the disappearance of ice, i.e., mass, from the polar regions would lower the geoid there, while it would rise at the lower latitudes to com-pensate. (The geoid is a representation of the surface of the earth that it would assume if the sea covered the planet entirely, bearing in mind that mean sea level is not uniform in all parts of the globe.) More water — that is, higher sea levels — in the equatorial regions would certainly have negative impacts there. We believe that these possible impacts are worth studying, at least on a contingency basis.

We suggested at the beginning of this chapter that sea level rise will have important political and social impacts as well as economic impacts and that it may have some military impacts, too. These impacts will come about because, eventually, as the seas rise, some people will have to move. Such individuals have often been referred to in climate change literature and especially in the popular press as "environmental refugees." In our view, however, "environmental *migrants*" is not only a more accurate term but also one which sidesteps the thorny question of who is considered to be a refugee.

At present, environmental migrants are not held to be refugees in legal terms. The International Organization for Migration, for example, defines environmental migrants only as

> Persons or groups of persons who, for reasons of sudden or progressive changes in the environment that adversely affect their lives or living conditions, are obliged to have to leave their habitual homes, or choose to do so, either temporarily or permanently, and who move either within their territory or abroad.[17]

An underlying problem here is that no one now has any clear idea how many environmental migrants there may be in the future. One report has even implied that a maximum of 634 million people might be involved because this is the number said to live in coastal areas within 30 feet (9.1 meters) of sea level.[18] There is a fundamental reason for such a high degree of uncertainty: human migration of any kind is a complex phenomenon which depends on a wide range of socioeconomic, environmental, and political contexts. Climate change alone is rarely the sole motivation.

In any case, people will at first try hard to cope with climate change, e.g., sea level rise, in other ways, not simply by moving. Migration is truly the last resort. To the extent that people are successful in finding other ways, this will reduce their motivation to relocate and will hold down the potential number of environmental migrants. To the best of our knowledge, there is now no significant number of sea level rise migrants anywhere in the world, although in 2007 the government of Papua New Guinea announced that it planned to evacuate the small population of the Carteret Islands, which are succumbing to sea level rise and/or subsidence.[19]

It is easy for us to identify many of the likely hotspots of future environmental migration. The most obvious places, of course, are the small islands of the Pacific and Indian Oceans, the megadeltas, and the large urban conurbations all along the coasts of the world.[20] A 2011 study, for example, estimated that in the United States alone some 23 million people live in low-elevation coastal areas, defined in this case as the areas susceptible to a 3.2 to 13.1 foot (1–4 meter) increase in sea level.[21] The study added that the impact of sea level rise will far extend beyond these directly-impacted coastal counties, due to the intricate migration and economic networks that link inland and coastal zones and their populations.

Finally, the study listed 20 major metropolitan areas across the continental United States which will be at risk from higher sea levels. They include Portland, Maine; Boston, Massachusetts; Providence, Rhode Island; New York and the greater New York metro area, including Long Island; Wilmington, Delaware; Baltimore, Maryland; Norfolk-Hampton, Virginia; Charleston, South Carolina; Savannah, Georgia; Miami, Jacksonville, Fort Meyers, St. Petersburg, and Pensacola, Florida; Mobile, Alabama; New Orleans, Louisiana; Oakland, San Francisco, and Sacramento, California; and Seattle, Washington. It seems reasonable to suppose that, over time, climate change, including sea level rise, is likely to have military impacts of some kind, though it is not easy at this point to say precisely what they will be. As a result, discussions of this subject tend to be long on generalities and short on specifics. For example, this is what one think tank (policy institute) article said in 2007:

> Climate change can act as a threat multiplier in some of the most volatile regions of the world, and it presents significant national security challenges for the United States.... About two-thirds of the world's population lives near coastlines, where critically important facilities and infrastructure, such as transportation routes, industrial facilities, port facilities, and energy production and distribution centers are located. A rise in sea level means potential loss of land and displacement of large numbers of people.... During the Cold War, the United States established and maintained a large number of [military] bases throughout the world. Climate change could compromise some of these bases.[22]

In the same vein, another think tank offered these comments in 2011 in the executive summary of a study on "defining a risk management framework for climate security":

> There is a growing consensus in the security community that climate change presents significant risks to the delivery of national, regional, and global security goals. Through sea level rise, shortages of food and water and severe weather events, climate change will have significant impacts on all countries, which in turn could affect their social stability. In the coming decades such impacts will increase the likelihood of conflict in fragile countries and regions. Peaceful management of even moderate climate change will require investment in increased reliance in national and international security and governance systems.[23]

As the full extent of sea level rise becomes clearer in the years to come, we believe that governments and their analysts will need to give more thought to its likely political, economic, military, and social impacts. Earlier rather than later, they will also have to focus on maritime boundaries during the process of rising sea levels. This point deserves a word of explanation here.[24]

We have already mentioned the wide range of negative impacts which sea level rise is likely to generate, but we have said nothing so far about the identification of maritime areas where individual countries can exercise sovereignty, sovereign rights, or legal jurisdiction under the rules of the international law of the sea. The retreat of coastlines—a result of the submergence of low-lying areas, small islands, and atolls—could, when coupled with coastal erosion, significantly change the reference line for judging a coastal country's legal zones in the ocean. This reference line is known as the baseline.

Under the United Nations Convention on the Law of the Sea (UNCLOS) which entered into force in 1994, and under customary international law, this baseline is the starting point from which the breadth of a coastal country's four maritime zones is measured. These zones are: (1) the territorial sea (regarded as the sovereign territory of a coastal country), (2) the contiguous zone (where a state can exert limited control to prevent the breaking of certain laws), (3) the exclusive economic zone (where a country has exclusive commercial rights over all resources), and (4) the continental shelf (where a country has exclusive economic rights over resources or below the sea floor, but not in the water column).

The baseline is also of great importance in determining the equidistance and meridian lines that can be drawn between adjacent or opposite coasts to resolve conflicting maritime claims. The usual baseline is defined by the UNCLOS as the low-water line along the coast, as marked on large-scale charts officially recognized by the coastal state in question. (Where the coastline is deeply indented or sprinkled with islands, the baseline can be drawn by connecting more prominent points along the coast.)

International courts have ruled that, as in the case of a territorial dispute between Nicaragua and Honduras in the Caribbean Sea, that changes in the coastline of a country will affect the location of the baseline. As a result, sea level rise may therefore have a significant impact on the extent of a coastal state's maritime claims, as well as maritime demarcations between states with opposite or adjacent coasts. As David D. Caron, a scholar specializing in these issues, remarked in 1990 with a nice turn of phrase,

> The outer boundary of the exclusive economic zone, the contiguous zone, and the territorial sea are ambulatory in that they will move with the baselines from which they are measured.[25]

In the future, UNCLOS judgments on baselines will increasingly be subject to two potentially conflicting interpretations: static vs. dynamic. Under the former, the traditional 20th-century baselines would be maintained, regardless of sea level rise; under the latter, "ambulatory baselines" would be drawn up to reflect changing sea level conditions. Despite the apparent merits of such new baselines, the bad news is that they would cause appreciable legal uncertainties for the countries whose shores would be affected.

XIV

Getting to Know the Experts

The information found within this book is the result of research provided by numerous scientists from a variety of disciplines. The names of those scientists that personally helped us appear in the Acknowledgements. In this chapter, the reader will get to know six of the notable scientists who helped us to complete this book. By peering into their lives, one will see that they are motivated by an intense curiosity to solve nature's riddles. For most, their "lab" is the great outdoors where they trek across the globe in search of clues that will advance our understanding of climate change and rising sea level. Sometimes they face danger in order to get their job done, with one narrowly escaping death aboard a fire-ravaged submarine.

Scientists are first and foremost human, just like the rest of us. They have highs and lows in life, enjoy their families, and have a variety of interests and talents outside of their careers. While not out in the field or in the lab crunching the data, our scientists enjoy many activates such as, among others, surfing large ocean waves, competing in long distance ocean swimming events, and spending time either coaching or cheering for their children's sporting events.

Dr. Marci M. Robinson is a micropaleontologist with the United States Geological Survey (USGS). She studies very small (at most about a quarter of a millimeter in diameter) ancient fossils in order to better understand past climate. She has worked with the Pliocene Research, Interpretation and Synoptic Mapping (PRISM) project since 1994, first as an undergraduate student and now as a research geologist, and she earned her PhD in 2007 at George Mason University studying the coastal geomorphology of the Outer Banks of North Carolina. She has also researched ancient shorelines of the southern and western coasts of Australia to determine past sea levels.

Currently, Dr. Robinson is researching past ocean temperatures during the latter part of the Pliocene Epoch which occurred about three million years ago. During the Pliocene CO_2 levels were comparable to today's levels (near 400 ppm), but the climate was about 5.4 degrees Fahrenheit to 9.0 degrees Fahrenheit (3 degrees Celsius to 5 degrees Celsius) warmer than before the

Industrial Revolution, and sea levels were about 82 feet (25 meters) higher than today. Geographically, the Earth was also very similar to today so the Pliocene offers a glimpse of what the world may look like in the not too distant future. Her research includes understanding why the sea level rise was so dramatic back then in response to a relatively small temperature rise, and if sea levels might respond the same way in the near future.

Robinson's research has had profound implications for climate modeling. If climate models can accurately simulate a past climate (known as "hindcasting") then there is more confidence that they can accurately project future climate. Her work is included in reconstructions of past climate that have been transformed into digital data sets that are used by these climate models. During the Pliocene, data suggests that the ocean was much warmer around Greenland and Iceland and into the Arctic Ocean than it is today. So much so that if these ocean temperatures were to occur in the present, most of the Greenland ice cap would melt and there would be a large and rapid rise in global sea level. It turned out that none of the climate models could simulate this pattern of warming in the North Atlantic and this mismatch was a great concern for modelers. Because the models seem to be working correctly, and since the data seem trustworthy, Robinson started looking for other reasons for the mismatch. She read that the big underwater ridge that runs through Iceland (from Greenland to Scotland) was much lower three million years ago than it is now. In the modern ocean, the Greenland-Scotland Ridge acts as a barrier to deep water in the high latitudes that is trying to flow southward along the ocean floor. She worked with some modelers to erase the ridge from their experiments, and as a result, the surface temperatures in the model simulations were much closer to the data.

This means two important things: (1) Scientists now have a better idea why the northern North Atlantic/Arctic Ocean might have been so warm three million years ago (better circulation without that barrier could have led to more warmer water being pumped into the high latitudes), and (2) if this is the case, the temperatures in this area will not get that warm again in the near future (they'll get warmer than they are now, but not that warm) because the Greenland-Scotland Ridge changes very, very slowly; it will be near its current height for many thousands of years. Robinson is still fascinated by her research and fossils are not data to her as this quote illustrates:

> These organisms are amazing in the amount of information they contain, and most people don't even know that they exist. They are tiny and beautiful and complex, and working with them feels to me like I'm privy to a very special secret.

In fact, she has a tattoo of one of her fossils on her right wrist. It is a new species that she found in the Nordic Seas where the temperatures were so warm.

Even at a very young age, Robinson had always been interested in figuring out how things work and why they work the way they do, but she never considered calling her interest *science*. Surprisingly, she disliked science in grade school.

Robinson did not travel the traditional path of most scientists. She was a high school dropout because she got pregnant at 15 and left school after the 10th grade. She and her son lived below the poverty level for many years and she took advantage of every social program available. She did eventually graduate from high school and started college at 20. Because she was a working single mother, it took her six years to get her undergraduate degree.

Robinson never lost her scientific curiosity after becoming a mother. She enrolled in Geology 101 her freshman year at the College of Charleston. She asked her professor questions about how the earth worked that he could not answer, and this caused her to "fall in love with the mystery of it all." She kept getting A grades in her geology classes so she kept signing up for more. One might say that she became an accidental geologist.

While not doing research, Dr. Robinson volunteers weekly with a local Assisting Young Mothers program, helping previously homeless teen moms and their babies transition into a healthy, meaningful and independent lifestyle. She spends an awful lot of time sitting on high school bleachers, watching her younger two sons play football and basketball. She is a big Washington Redskins football fan and has a secret desire to join a roller derby league. She is an accomplished Southern cook, having been raised in the South Carolina low country. Given a few free moments, she crochets afghans and reads novels.

Dr. Richard B. Alley is the Evan Pugh Professor of Geosciences and an associate of the Earth and Environmental Systems Institute at Pennsylvania State University. His research, spanning the previous 30 years, is focused on how large ice sheets work and how to represent them in models so that humans can make scenario-based projections ("if humans do XXX then the ice sheets will do YYY to sea levels").

Dr. Alley's research has taken him to Antarctica and Greenland several times to look for clues to past climate. His discovery in Greenland that the last major cold event of the previous ice age, called the Younger Dryas (after a yellow flower named *Dryas*) may have suddenly ended in just three years, helped put the study of abrupt climate change on the map. His research shows that Earth's climate is dependent on "switches" and "dials" that are interconnected with each other, the most well-known being that carbon dioxide is the most important control on Earth's thermostat.

Dr. Richard Alley on the Franz Josef Glacier, New Zealand (courtesy Geoffrey Haines-Stiles, Earth: The Operators' Manual).

Alley has won numerous awards for teaching and research including most recently being honored with the prestigious Heinz Award and receiving the Stephen H. Schneider Award for Outstanding Climate Science Communication in 2011. The Alley Glacier in the Transantarctic Mountains was named in his honor.

In the following, Alley summarizes his views on climate:

The climate can be a little like a kayak. If you lean a little, the boat leans with you. Lean a little more, and so does the boat. Lean too far, and the boat tips over. Push on the climate, and it changes. Push a little more, and it changes a little more. Push too much, and it might "tip" into a new state. We humans have built things for the climate we have, so a huge change would have huge impacts on humans.

When we test our understanding of climate against the past, we find that our science is quite good, but occasionally when nature has pushed the climate, the climate has changed more, and more rapidly, than our models reproduce. In turn, this suggests that our projections of future challenges from climate change are either accurate or "conservative"—we might see changes that are larger and faster than we expect. The "argument" going on in public is often between our best estimate of what the future holds if we continue burning fossil fuels and releasing the CO_2, and a very optimistic view of that future in which our CO_2

has only a small effect. But, if anything, the history of climate says that we should be looking more closely at a more pessimistic view of the influence of our CO_2.[1]

Alley's interest in science dates back from his childhood fascination with gardens and rocks to his days in middle and high school where he attended local rock and mineral society meetings. During that time he spent his time cave-crawling and national park viewing. Although he also enjoyed reading and writing and considered journalism as a career, his love of science won out. As he explains, "Science is fun. My job involves discovering what no one knows, and sharing it with others to help them."

When not researching, Dr. Alley enjoys his family, plus playing and coaching soccer, bicycling, easy kayaking, bird-watching, hiking, gardening, and folk music, among others.

Dr. Henry Pollack is emeritus professor of geophysics in the Department of Earth and Environmental Sciences at University of Michigan in Ann Arbor, Michigan. He has been at the university for more than forty years and has conducted research on every continent. He was one of the many recipients of the 2007 Nobel Peace Prize for his work with the IPCC and is also currently the lead scientific advisor to former vice president Al Gore's Climate Reality Project. For more than five years, the Climate Reality Project has been training non-scientists around the world to deliver slideshow presentations on climate change. There are currently about 3,000 presenters world-wide.

Dr. Pollack's most important contribution to climate science is his work with borehole temperature data. Temperatures measured in deep holes drilled into the ground have been used to reconstruct past climate. Heat from the interior of the Earth makes it way up toward the cool surface and escapes to the atmosphere and space beyond. Temperatures of the rock in Earth's crust are influenced by this outward-bound heat, and a vertical temperature profile will reveal increasing temperatures with depth, displaying a straight-line slope. But near-surface temperatures are also influenced by heat from the atmosphere above and from the Sun. A warming or cooling climate will cause the rock near the surface to warm or cool, which in turn will cause the temperature profile to deviate from a straight line. These deviations can penetrate many meters into the underlying ground.

Pollack's research was not initially intended to be climate-related. Instead, he was looking for patterns in the heat flux from the Earth's interior to better understand the science of plate tectonics. His work on this topic is extremely important because his research has resulted in a very accurate measure of the heat loss from Earth's interior. Essentially he determined "the number" that is used on all global models as the boundary condition for Earth's heat loss.

The borehole temperature profiles he was analyzing showed some near-surface deviations from the anticipated straight line. At the time, Pollack assumed that the data contained irrelevant fluctuations that scientists call "noise." When he later decided to take a closer look at this noise, he realized that it was related to climate change, and in fact, he had found another method to measure global warming. It was this discovery that caused him to change his field of research to climate science.

Borehole temperature data has yielded climate reconstructions at more than 800 sites on six continents. Taken as a global ensemble, the borehole data indicate a temperature increase over the past five centuries of about 1 degree Celsius, half of which occurred in the 20th century alone. This estimate of 20th century warming is similar to the record of surface warming determined by meteorological stations.

Pollack's career in the geosciences was shaped very early on. As a six year old, he became enamored of maps because he frequently saw maps of the European and Pacific theatres of World War II in the newspapers as news organizations tried to relate the progress of that war to the general public. He began to draw his own maps during that time and believes that this childhood joy influenced his decision to change his research from a more local and regional scale to a global scale much later on in life.

While working on a ranch in Nevada in the summer before college, Pollack was exposed to mountains for the first time. He spent countless hours exploring the ghost towns of that arid region while also collecting minerals and rocks. This hobby caused him to sign up for a freshman-level geology course while attending college at Cornell University in upstate New York the following fall. During field trips in this course, he became hooked on the geosciences because it meant that his work would be "outside work" and not the typical office desk job. He always knew he would have a career in the sciences but the geosciences were especially appealing due to the extensive field-work that comes with it.

Pollack is clearly a family man. He has traveled the world with his wife and children to do his field work. When told he should consider retirement because then he could travel and spend time with family he replies that he has been doing that all of his life. Now in semi-retirement, for the past five years he has been involved in Research Experience programs that train undergraduate students in research methods. He does this without compensation.

Dr. Pollack says that sea level rise is an equal opportunity disaster and that humans must quickly mitigate the emissions of heat-trapping gases so that adapting to the changing climate will be easier and less costly.

Dr. Matthew England is a faculty member and co-director of the Climate Change Research Centre (CCRC) at the University of New South Wales.

The CCRC is one of the largest university research facilities in Australia focused on the key areas of Earth's climate: atmosphere, ocean and land-surface. He has authored over 90 peer-reviewed journal papers, and his research has been featured in the second and third IPCC Assessment Reports. He was also the Convening Lead Author of the 2009 Copenhagen Diagnosis.

Dr. England's research focuses on global ocean circulation and the influence it has on regional climate and climate processes, with a particular focus on the Southern Hemisphere. Using ocean and coupled climate models in combination with theory and observations, he studies how ocean currents affect climate and climate variability on time-scales of seasons to centuries.

His research career began in the late 1980s; at a time when the ocean circulation models used for climate projections did not accurately represent the large-scale overturning circulation. The models had particular difficulty capturing interior ocean flow patterns, including North Atlantic Deep Water (NADW), Antarctic Bottom Water (AABW) and Antarctic Intermediate Water (AAIW). These large-scale water-masses regulate the exchange of heat and carbon between the ocean and the atmosphere, so it is vital that they are accurately represented in climate models. His research as a PhD student uncovered several ways in which ocean models could be improved to capture these key water-masses. His work was featured in the IPCC Second Assessment Report. Today's models now include these important circulations with much greater resolution, therefore providing a better means of projection of future climate.

As a young boy, England was captivated with the oceans and marine life. He dreamed of one day becoming a marine biologist and travelling the world exploring marine ecosystems. In Australia his childhood revolved around the beach from an early age; by the time he was 10 he was swimming in weekly beach competitions through summer, and by 16 he was obsessed with board-riding and body surfing.

As a college student England majored in advanced mathematics and physics for the first two years not so much because he had a deep passion for these subjects, but more because the timetabling suited his passion for surfing and he found the courses relatively easy to study for. It was not until his third year at college that the watershed moment arrived that would point him to oceanography. While scanning for final year courses he spotted a photo of a large wave in the student handbook that grabbed his attention. He read further and decided to take a course in physical oceanography. It was during this course that he realized that his skills in math and physics could be applied to the oceans—his long-held but almost abandoned dream of being a marine scientist was resurrected. As a PhD student, England voyaged south toward Antarctica on an Australian research vessel one year and across the tropical

Pacific aboard a Japanese ship the next — his interest in geography, global affairs and the ocean environment further satisfied in a field he'd only just discovered three years previously. The rest is history, as they say.

Dr. England is still an avid surfer while also being a competitive open water ocean swimmer. He swims almost every day across a distance of one to two miles and regularly competes. Most recently he finished in the top 20 percent in the world famous Waikiki Rough Water Swim event which feature a 2.4 mile swim. In research and in leisure, the ocean is his constant companion.

Dr. John Marra is currently the National Oceanic and Atmospheric Administration (NOAA) regional climate services director, Pacific region. He has worked for over 20 years in both the private and public sector to bridge science, policy, and information technology (IT) to address issues related to natural hazards risk reduction and climate adaptation planning. His particular area of expertise is the development and dissemination of data and products associated with coastal inundation and erosion. He developed the Geographic Information System (GIS) and other IT–based tools to enable communities in the Pacific Ocean basin to make better, faster, and less costly decisions with regard to coastal inundation due to sea level rise caused by intense storms and climate change. These tools also increase awareness and education about the hazards that could potentially affect a community and actions that can be taken to help lessen the multiple impacts of these events.

Dr. Marra grew up in Montana miles away from the ocean so it might seem odd that he would end up in a career that was intimately tied to the ocean. However, it was the vastness, beauty, and splendor of the open spaces of Montana that allowed him to appreciate these parallel features of the Pacific Ocean. He loved being outdoors and even at a young age was interested in science. As a college freshman, he enrolled in a geology field course which merged his love of the outdoors with his affinity for science. After that course he decided he wanted a career as a geologist.

Marra does not like to think of himself as a "scientist" but instead as a coastal geologist who is trying to figure out nature's puzzles. He describes himself as having, over the years, "a slow, steady, and ever growing appreciation ... that evokes awe, and gratitude, and inspiration ... of the enmeshed nature of reality." Werner Heisenberg, the famous theoretical physicist, once said "The world thus appears as a complicated tissue of events in which connections of different kinds alternate, or overlap, or combine to determine the texture of the whole." He sees his work in much the same way with sea level rise and inundation being the expression of the superposition of multiple scales of unsteadiness.

Dr. Marra has been a competitive gymnast. He loves and lives to surf and his girls mean the world to him.

Dr. Peter Wadhams is a professor of ocean physics, and head of the Polar Ocean Physics Group in the Department of Applied Mathematics and Theoretical Physics, University of Cambridge. Since 1970 his research has been concerned with the physics of sea ice and its role in the polar oceans, especially fields such as ice thickness distribution measurement, wave-ice interaction, the role of ice production in convection and the thermohaline circulation, and iceberg and sea ice dynamics. He has conducted more than 40 field programs and is the recipient of several honors for his extensive work in the Arctic and Antarctic, including the Polar Medal in 1987 presented by Britain's Queen Elizabeth, and the Italgas Prize for Environmental Sciences in 1990.

Dr. Wadhams' most direct contribution to sea level rise research was a paper written with Walter Munk in 2004 where they found that sea ice melt back was adding about 144 cubic miles (600 cubic km) of fresh water to the ocean per year. That value matched the rate of freshening of the ocean as inferred from the widely cited Levitus[2,3] census hydrography data. However, that value left no room for a contribution from glacier retreat (which would cause sea level rise, whereas sea ice melt does not), yet clearly there is such a contribution as the observed rate of sea level rise is too great to be due to warming alone. He drew attention to this anomaly in his paper, but subsequently no convincing answer has been offered. His view is that there may be problems with the Levitus hydrography in not seeing all of the fresh water that is added at high latitudes.

Wadhams was one of the first scientists to use submarine data to observe thinning of sea ice and he wrote the first paper on sea ice thinning for *Nature* in 1990. He also discovered long-lived deep convective chimneys (plumes of vertical water movement) in the Greenland Sea that were observed to last for up to three years. These chimneys are not very well-understood but have climate implications because Greenland Sea convection is essential to preserving the Atlantic thermohaline circulation which moderates the climate of Western Europe.

Wadhams has had several "aha!" moments during his career and they are all connected. The first occurred when he was a graduate student analyzing a big set of wave measurements in ice. What appeared to be a random set of wiggly lines actually fit into a very simple mathematical law known as a *negative exponential*. He also saw this same negative exponential when observing sea ice thickness measurements from submarines. He sums up the experiences this way:

> It has always amazed me how geophysics, the science which looks at the apparently random collection of processes that occurs on the earth, so often comes up with processes that follow extremely simple mathematical laws to a high degree of accuracy. Of course, this is true throughout physics, and many mathemati-

cians and physicists, from Einstein downwards, have commented on how nature is beautiful because it is mathematically simple. Also that a theory that is not mathematically simple is probably not valid. This has serious philosophical implications of course. Is it just the way in which we have constructed our mathematics? Or is there something deeper and more purposeful going on?[4]

During the British East Coast floods of January 31, 1953 (caused by a storm surge in the North Sea, which killed about 2,000 people in the Netherlands and the UK), Wadham's family house in Tilbury, Essex, was flooded out. So at the age of four he had an early experience of sea level rise!

Wadham's love of science began when he was just 11 and went to grammar school in the United Kingdom where he experienced formal science teaching for the first time. The first lesson was an experiment in the school chemistry lab. The teacher had a test tube with a blue solution of copper sulphate and another test tube with a colorless solution of sodium carbonate. After mixing the two, to his amazement, a brown precipitate of copper carbonate formed where no such substance had been present before. He had seen his first chemical reaction and it was tremendously exciting. From then on he was hooked on science. As a child growing up on the banks of the River Thames in the 1950s, he had always imagined he would be a Merchant Marine officer like his two grandfathers. By becoming an oceanographer he could follow both his passions: going to sea and doing science research.

Wadham's first scientific paper, while a student, was on parapsychology, and he has kept an interest in the subject. He is also interested in painting, maritime history and archaeology.

The scientific method employed by all scientists is underpinned by data. That data either supports or discounts the hypothesis being considered. Much of the data used by scientists comes from field work which can occasionally place scientists in very dangerous situations.

Most sea ice field work is dangerous. Wadhams has had ice floes break up on him while his helicopter was on one side of the floe and he and the helicopter pilot were on the other. Luckily the two floe edges came together again, otherwise he might still be drifting down the Greenland coast.

The nearest he came to death was in March 2007 and in the supposedly safe environment of a nuclear submarine, HMS *Tireless*. The submarine was under the ice in the Beaufort Sea, surveying ice thickness, when there was an enormous bang and the vessel filled with smoke. The crew went to emergency stations and thought at first of reactor failure or collision. But gradually it turned out that there had been an explosion of a SCOG (self-contained oxygen generator), a slab of potassium chlorate which can be activated to generate oxygen at times when the boat's electrolysers are not working (they were frozen up). Two sailors were ordered to activate a SCOG slab, but it blew up and killed them both. This also blocked entry to the compartment that they were in and started a fire, so that some flooding was necessary. It was actually quite close to a fatal accident for the boat. Dr. Wadhams and the crew had to wear oxygen masks for about three hours until the boat could be brought safely to the surface through the ice and opened up to clear the atmosphere. He had a bad cough for about a year afterwards.

Dr. Pollack also has had occasional brushes with danger during his career and fortunately none of them have been injurious. For example, his field work in the Zambezi Valley on the border between Zambia and Rhodesia (now known as Zimbabwe) put him in very close contact with armed guerrillas. Pollack's group was headed towards a mining exploration area where boreholes had been drilled, and when they came to a fork in the road they asked a boy by the roadside where the mining camp was located. The young man did not understand English very well, but when he heard the word "camp" he pointed to the right fork in the road. Unfortunately, the camp was the local guerrilla camp and Pollack's group rode into a heavily armed village where men were being treated for wounds after a day of heavy fighting. His group was lucky when a man shouldering an AK-47 told them to go back and take the other fork in the road to reach the mining camp. What might have been that day had the guerrilla not been in an accommodating mood!

Dr. England says that oceanographic field work on the open seas has its dangers. Open ocean swells can reach well above 50 feet and if there is a strong crosswind there is a chance that the torque created by these opposing natural forces could capsize a vessel or snap a research vessel's hull. It is not uncommon for scientists to be lined up on deck, securely fastened with life vests, ready to board life boats if disaster strikes. Fortunately, none of the vessels he has ever been on have had emergency evacuations. He knows of ocean scientists whose vessel has gone down in the Antarctic ice zone and others doing research in the Indian Ocean whose vessels are equipped with weapons in case they are attacked by pirates. Ocean observing work is costly, challenging, and dangerous.

Dr. Alley has faced dangerous situations such as flying into remote places in military aircraft and landing on rough coasts in small boats. He has also traversed glaciers that contain giant crevasses, cracks that can be over 60 feet wide and nearly 150 feet deep, and extend for hundreds of feet in length.

For most individuals everyday life has its ups and downs. Scientists are no exception as expressed by the frustrations described by the researchers who have helped us with this book.

On her greatest fear, Dr. Robinson explains:

I have a terrible fear of public speaking. It's strangely out of character for me because I'm not shy and rarely get embarrassed. In fact, I'm quite competitive and never run from a challenge. But the idea of getting on a stage and speaking in front of people sends my heart racing and sweat pouring out all over me. My throat closes up, and I can't move. It's crazy. But scientists present their research in front of their peers, for discussion and critique, often on big stages at international conferences in front of the smartest people in the world.... So, I was going to have to figure out how to do this.

I started with elementary school students, bringing in lots of rock and mineral and fossil samples and helping their teachers complete their science curricula. Then I moved on to teaching Introductory Geology labs to college freshman, then moved to upper level Geology labs. I found that teaching is a wonderful way to remember what you already knew but also to ease into public speaking without so much dread. I'm still terrified when I give talks to a scientific audience, but people say they can't tell anymore. That's an improvement.[5]

In late 1984, Dr. Alley's team drilled an Antarctic ice core, which he had intended to ship home to use for his PhD research. Unfortunately, the contractor shipping the ice allowed it to melt before arrival, taking his first attempt at a dissertation with it.

Dr. Marra laments that in many cases logic does not prevail over emotion with regard to climate science. Dr. England agrees and is frustrated by the concerted campaign by lobby groups in his home country of Australia and in the United States to muddy the climate science findings of the past century.

Dr. Pollack appears to be the lucky one of the group. He claims he has no frustrations. He loves his job and cannot recall a single day when he did not want to go to work.

Scientists do not exhibit a tribal mentality where they all agree, but instead battle each other professionally to prove that the other scientists' data or conclusions are incorrect. This is the classic scientific method of peer-review where only the strongest data and conclusions survive the constant jousting.

Climate science is also being challenged from outside the scientific community. Climate change has become a particularly divisive discussion in the public arena, particularly in the United States, Canada, and Australia. These internal and external battles are illuminated by several of our scientists as they describe their experiences with people who held opposing views to their own.

One of the projects Dr. Alley started after his PhD melted was helping some brilliant geophysicists (Don Blankenship, and Sean Rooney, working with Charlie Bentley) interpret data from ice stream B, West Antarctica (now known as Whillams Ice Stream). This team came up with a model that the ice stream was lubricated by deformation within subglacial "mud" (till). They were following work by a few other pioneers, but this was a fairly radical view, and was greeted as a possible paradigm shift in glaciology. Some established scientists were unhappy with these ideas, and held to the older ideas that subglacial deformation was not important. Looking back from 25 years later, both were right. The older researchers had indeed noted that till could deform, but had data from places where this was not especially important. There are such places, so the older researchers were right about that. The model used by Alley and others was modified somewhat over time using newer data and ideas and now works quite well. And, some of the puzzles that had bothered the older researchers have been solved by these new ideas. The basics of ice flow are unchanged — a big pile of ice spreads under its own weight, flows in the direction of the downhill surface slope, and goes faster where the bottom is better-lubricated. Alley's work showed that sometimes that lubrication is a bit farther down into the mud than most people previously thought, and as a consequence the mathematical relation used between the gravitational stress driving flow and the ice velocity is somewhat different than that previously used.

Alley believes this offers an important lesson:

> Philosophers of science are often excited about "revolution." Some people thought that Newton's physics would solve all problems, and then Einstein gave us a very different view than Newton; a revolution overthrew Newton and replaced him with Einstein. But, you could honestly describe me as a Newtonian physicist — when I calculate how the ice flows in response to gravity, whether over a soft bed or a hard one, I use Newton and not Einstein because, for the velocities and masses and stresses we deal with, Newton is so incredibly accurate that adding Einstein would not change the results enough to be measured, and calculating with Newton is easy. Philosophically, something big happened, and for really huge, really small and really fast things there were important changes in our understanding (with quantum mechanics as well as Einstein's relativity), but for the things that Newton described well, we still tend to use Newton — in much of the practical world, Newton was not overthrown, but simply taken into a bigger picture. (Our GPS and computers use Einstein and quantum, but we use them to study ice flow that we describe with Newton's tools.) On a MUCH less-important scale, our deforming beds did not overthrow glaciology; we just added a bit.
>
> I am NOT a philosopher of science, but as a practical person, I observe that it has been a very long time since a major, well-accepted result of science was overthrown completely, as opposed to being subsumed into something bigger. For example, when my father had an ulcer, the doctor thought that it must have been diet, or stress, or some other cause from physics, chemistry, or his personal biology that caused the illness. Probably, his ulcer was caused by "external" biol-

ogy — an infectious agent (the bacterium Heliobacter pylori). The discovery of ulcer-causing bacteria forced a lot of doctors to reevaluate a lot of diagnoses, and a chunk of research, and was rewarded very quickly with the Nobel Prize. But, our fundamental understanding of how diseases are caused did not change — we knew that physics, chemistry, and biology inside and out can cause disease, and they still can. If you damage the lining of your stomach with non-living things, you may trigger an ulcer, so it remains just possible that my father's doctors were right, and it is also possible that a combination of the infectious agent and other issues was responsible. The bacterial cause of many ulcers was a huge discovery, greatly valuable and quickly rewarded, but aside from shifting one disease from "not infectious agent" to "usually infectious agent," and triggering searches for other such cases, the fundamentals of medical science were not shaken.[6]

Dr. England recalls when his first PhD student stood up and questioned him about a lecture topic being discussed. At first he was irritated that this much less experienced researcher would question established fact, but on further reflection he realized that this was what ultimately makes a great scientist — namely an enquiring mind. He realized that the very best scientists are highly skeptical of established ideas and are always questioning existing data and hypotheses.

When Dr. Robinson's research showing warm Arctic temperatures three million years ago was released, the USGS put out a routine press release. She was amazed at the angry accusations she received from people who admitted to not having actually read her article. Below is an example of the type of communication she received:

> Frankly, I see the climate warming community as little more than ill-informed and childish activists looking for a cause to campaign against, a community frequently led by opportunists looking for ways to line their pockets by selling snake oil to useful idiots willing to further their quest for effortless wealth at the expense of others.[7]

That experience showed Robinson that some people are just angry and looking for a venue to spout insults. She is not ill-informed; nor is she an activist or an opportunist. She is, in fact, a scientist with no agenda and with no hope of financial gain regardless of her research results. At USGS, scientists are forbidden to hold any interests in any mineral or energy resources. She chose to work for the USGS because she believes science belongs to the people and by working for a government agency, she is giving back to the people who assisted her when she needed help.

The final question posed to our team of scientists was: "If you had a magic wand and could change any one aspect of your field of study or how your results are used by society, what would it be?"

Dr. England wishes that climate science held the same esteem and respect as other scientific disciplines such as medicine and engineering. With greenhouse science based on fundamental physics and laws of thermodynamics he finds it difficult to understand how scientists can be pilloried for explaining simple facts. He wishes that the media, policymakers and the general public anticipated the latest IPCC reports with the same interest and apprehension as the latest budget reports. He hopes that national governments, businesses and the broader public better appreciated the scale of the climate change challenge; with a coordinated global emissions reduction strategy already well in place.

Dr. Marra would give people the ability to see into the future, much like Ebenezer Scrooge in Charles Dickens's *A Christmas Carol.* He thinks that if people could see where we are headed with respect to climate change and its impacts, they would change course.

Dr. Pollack wishes that more scientists would communicate with the general public about climate change and that they do so with more vigor and much earlier in their careers. A true success story for any professor is to enable their students to think clearly, write better, read with more comprehension, and to possess stronger mathematical skills. The course content is merely a vehicle to achieve those outcomes.

Dr. Robinson has a similar wish. She wishes to close the comprehension gap between science and society by improving general science education and by making scientists better communicators.

Dr. Wadhams wishes to improve British climate science:

If I could change the present I would like to see NERC (the Natural Environment Research Council, a UK Government body which is supposed to be a main supporter of environmental science) abolished and all research in the UK combined in a single research council (like NSF in the US) which would be large enough to be free of the current bias and cronyism. This would offer a real way forward for British climate science.[8]

Dr. Alley expresses this desire:

I'd like people to understand the basic physics of CO2 as a greenhouse gas have been known for more than a century, and were really worked out by researchers working for the US Air Force after WWII, who were not studying global warming but things such as sensors on heat-seeking missiles. Using that physical understanding to address climate shows that our climate would be much colder without CO2, and will be much warmer with much more CO2, unless some large "forcing" happens to occur to offset it, and we can't find any such forcing despite great effort. The history of climate, the modern state of climate, recent changes, fundamental physics and more attest to the warming effect of CO2. Simple bookkeeping and measuring show that we are raising CO2 rapidly, and estimates of fossil-fuel reserves show that we could raise CO_2 much more, enough to cause very large changes to climate. Science is always open to revision, but this basic understanding has been with us for decades now, and we cannot find any way out of it. In considering how to respond to this, there are many issues (jobs, taxes, national security, votes, etc.), so the science does not dictate policy. But, wishful thinking will not make the science go away, the odds that this understanding is fundamentally flawed are very low, and in my opinion the science is understood better than any of the other issues in the discussion.[9]

The life stories of these six scientists are typical. Climate researchers fall in love with nature at a very early age and their curiosity about how things work makes it almost inevitable that they will choose science as a career. Many choose this particular field of science because it allows them to work in the great outdoors. We are all fortunate that they work with such passion, sometimes even in the face of danger. It is their pursuit of the answers to Nature's riddles regarding the changing climate system that will be used to inform the world's policymakers about the crisis that is inherent in rising sea levels.

XV

Very Long Term Prospects for the World's Shorelines

This is a very speculative chapter — one designed not to offer climate change information but to encourage the reader to engage in thinking as creatively and as far ahead as possible. This chapter is a smorgasbord of five issues: flood myths; sea level rise over the past 2,000 years; effects of future sea level rises on natural systems; ethical aspects of coping with sea level rise; and why efforts to deal with these rises are very likely to fail.

To begin with, it is a remarkable fact that flood myths (or deluge myths) have been present in so many different cultures over such long periods of time. Many theories have been advanced to explain this fact. Our own guess is that these tales must reflect, if only very fragmentarily and imperfectly, some kind of reality, i.e., terrifying "watery events" of the primordial past, which have been embellished over the years by verbal and written evocations and endless retellings of these calamities. Here are some good examples of this genre[1]:

- The Puranas (ancient Hindu, Jain, and Buddhist religious texts) give us the story of Manu, who saved a small fish from death. When the fish grew up to an enormous size, it warned Manu that a great flood was coming and that he must build a ship to save himself. Manu did as he was told and then discovered, once the floodwaters had receded, he was the only living thing left on earth.
- In the Neo-Assyrian Gilgamesh flood myth, we learn that a local god warned the flood hero Utnapishtim that a great flood was coming and the he must build a ship to save himself, his relatives and craftsmen, his gold and silver, and domesticated and wild animals. He did so, and the storm raged for seven days. When it was finally over, Utnapishtim and his wife were the only human survivors. The gods granted them immortality.
- In Greek mythology, Zeus was appalled when the king of Arcadia sacrificed a boy to him. In his anger, Zeus unleashed a deluge: the sea flooded the coastal plain and the rivers ran in torrents. However, the flood hero Deu-

calion (son of the god Prometheus, who brought fire to mankind) built a chest with the help of his father and managed to save himself and his wife.

- An Algonquin (American Indian) legend relates that when the god Michabo was hunting one day with his pack of trained wolves, he had an amazing experience: when the wolves came to a lake, they simply disappeared into it. Michabo followed them into the water to retrieve them and, as he did so, the entire world flooded. He first dispatched a raven and then an otter to find some soil with which to make a new Earth, but they both failed to do so. Then he sent out a muskrat, who brought back enough earth to begin the rebuilding of the world. Michabo married the muskrat and they became the parents of the human race.

- In the Biblical and Quaranic account of Noah's Ark, Noah built this ship at God's command to save himself, his family, and pairs of the world's animals from the flood sent to cleanse the earth. When the flood ends, God places a rainbow in the sky. It symbolizes the divine promise never again to send a flood to engulf the Earth.

These folkloric accounts all share similar heroic and poetic qualities but they are relevant here for two more practical reasons. The first is that they reflect a deep-seated, cross-cultural understanding that, to quote the 20th century Dutch poet Hendrik Marsman again, "the voice of the water, telling of endless disaster, is feared and heard." The second reason is that human societies have managed to survive and, indeed, to flourish despite whatever grim experiences they may have had with the water in the distant past. At this point, however, let us consider what we can learn about sea level rise over the past 2,000 years.

A groundbreaking study by Kemp et al., published in 2011, shows that the rate of sea level rise along the Atlantic coast of the United States is greater now than at any time over the past two millennia.[2] The study also shows a consistent link between changes in global mean surface temperature and sea level.[3]

To measure sea level changes, scientists used a sample of 193 microfossils called foraminifera, which are preserved in sediment cores extracted from 10 coastal salt marches in North Carolina. These marshes are regularly flooded by the tides. As sea level rises, the salt marsh grows upwards because it traps sediments. The sediment layers accumulating in this way can be examined and dated, i.e., the age of the cores can be estimated by radiocarbon dating and other techniques.

In the study, these records were corrected for contributions to sea level rise caused by vertical land movements. The North Carolina coast has sunk steadily by about 6.5 feet (2 meters) in the past two millennia due to glacial isostatic adjustment, making it possible today to extract sediment cores roughly 8.2 feet (2.5 meters) long. The study found that sea level was relatively stable from 200 B.C. to A.D. 950. Then, in the 11th century, sea level rose by about 0.02 inches (0.6 millimeters) per year for about 400 years, an increase which is linked to a warm climate period known as the Medieval Climate Anomaly. This era was followed by a second period of stable sea level during a cooler period (the Little Ice Age), which lasted from 1400 until the late 19th century. Since then, sea level has risen at an average rate of 0.08 inches (2.1 millimeters) per year. This is the steepest century-scale increase of the past two millennia.

Because it is certain that sea level rise will continue far into the future, it is worth reviewing now what effects it is likely to have on natural systems. For our purposes here, we can identify five key effects: inundation/flooding, wetland loss, erosion, saltwater intrusion, and impeded drainage. An instructive matrix lists these five effects along one axis and then seven coastal socioeconomic sectors on another axis.[4]

It is easiest here to describe these interrelationships in print rather than trying to show them graphically. What the matrix demonstrates is that, as we might expect, the most important effect of sea level rise is inundation/flooding, which has strong impacts on all seven coastal socioeconomic sectors, namely, freshwater resources, agriculture and forestry, fisheries and agriculture, health, recreation and tourism, biodiversity, and settlements/infrastructure.

In terms of predictions, commentators on sea level rise can usefully be divided into the "pessimists" and the "optimists."[5] Both camps accept the reality and the high-impact potential of sea level rise, but the pessimists expect much bigger rises than do the optimists. The two sides differ most significantly on the world's prospects for adaptation to and/or protection against sea level rise. Pessimists believe that full scale protection is impossible, especially on an international scale. They think it is very likely that third world countries will be further weakened by sea level rise, which will ultimately result in greater political, economic, military, and social instability. The long-term prospects for the impoverished parts of the coastal world are therefore rather poor.

Pessimists focus on extreme events such as Hurricane Katrina; forecast high degrees of sea level rise; and conclude that the developed world's abilities to adapt to sea level changes are now very limited, not due to a lack of technological skills but rather to a widespread lack of political and financial will. Pessimists believe that several sea level rise disasters will be needed before this will begins to appear. They also note that earlier efforts by developed countries to deal with sea level rise typically have had a lead-time of 30 years or more. So, even if new defenses were designed, approved, and funded immediately, it would still be a very long time before they were actually in place.

In contrast, the optimists focus on much lower levels of sea level rise and argue that high-tech protection will indeed be possible and will be effective, especially in very highly developed countries such as the Netherlands. The optimists admit that adaptation costs are likely to be quite high and will require that investment in other fields be redirected to coastal adaptation. That said, they point to the fact that even though many of the world's megacities are now facing sea level rise and at the same time are also subsiding, they are nevertheless thriving in terms of their population growth and their economic activity. Optimists hope that these trends will continue.

What happens if adaptation is not implemented at all or if it fails? A 2011 study by Nicholls et al. estimated that, in this case, land loss around the world will total about 338,611 square miles (877,000 square kilometers) for a 1.6 foot (0.5 meter) rise and 690,736 square miles (1,789,000 square kilometers) for a 6.5 foot (2 meter) rise. This amounts to approximately 0.6–1.2 percent of the global land area. The net population displaced from this rise is much more significant, being estimated at 72 million to 187 million people over the century. This reflects the present very high population density of coastal area but it does not include continuing migration to the coasts. If, as seems certain, such migration increases in the years to come, the effects of sea level rise will of course be much greater.[6]

The vulnerability of certain parts of the world to sea level rise provides a persuasive argument for international action to avoid a much warmer world due to global warming. So far, however, as suggested earlier there have been only two serious national projects to deal with sea level rise. One is the Thames Estuary Project, which has focused on flood management in London and its environs. The other is the Dutch Delta Commission, which has investigated prospects for sea level rise in the Netherlands and on preventive measures that can be taken now. The British study looked at scenarios with a sea level rise of up to 16.4 feet (5 meters); the Dutch project studied those of 11.4 feet (3.5 meters) higher than today. Both undertakings concluded that improved and upgraded flood protection is the best long-term solution.[7] In our opinion, it would be a very good idea for other developed countries, e.g., the United States, to undertake similar studies.

Let us turn away now from purely scientific considerations and pay some attention to the ethical aspects of coping with sea level rise. This is an interesting issue and one which does not led itself to quick or easy solution. For example, in a 2010 paper on "The Ethical Implications of Sea-Level Rise Due to Climate Change," Sujatha Byravan and Sudhir Chella Rajan pose two intriguing questions:

> Does humanity have a moral obligation towards the estimated millions of individuals who will be displaced from their homes over the course of this century, primarily due to sea-level rise as the earth's climate warms? If there are sound reasons for the world to at on their behalf, what form should these actions take?[8]

This paper argues that although in some large countries, e.g., the United States and China, coastal communities threatened by sea level rise can simply move farther inland, this is not true for small islands in the South Pacific or, indeed, for densely-populated deltaic countries such as Bangladesh, Egypt, and Vietnam. People living in such vulnerable regions will ultimately be forced to retreat in the face of rising waters, with little possibility of ever being able to return to their ancestral homes.

The paper notes that under existing international law, environmental/climate migrants do not have any legal status as refugees. As a result, some victims of sea level rise may well face a crushing burden, namely, a breakdown or total forfeiture of prevailing physical, economic, and social support, with no "provider of last resort willing to help them. The paper therefore urges that the fairest solution is for the international community to grant to all those who will be displaced by sea level rise the legal right to migrate to safe countries as refugees.

The paper posits that the fundamental philosophical basis for such a solution should be what it calls "the principle of intergenerational trust," i.e., the belief each generation is collectively responsible for protecting and using natural resources in a sustainable manner so that future generations are not unduly harmed by their present misuse, e.g., by sea level rise largely caused by man-made global warming. While we think it exceedingly unlikely that the nations of the world will ever negotiate binding agreements based on this principle, ethical issues are something that governments in developed countries should factor into their planning for future sea level rises.

Another study—Stephen Gardiner's *A Perfect Moral Storm: The Ethical Tragedy of Climate Change* (2011)—also addresses these issues. Gardiner argues along these lines:

> Climate change is arguably the greatest problem confronting humanity, but we have done little to head off this looming catastrophe. Fundamentally, this represents an *ethical* failure, for three reasons:
>
> First, the world's most affluent nations are tempted to pass the cost of climate change to the poorer and weaker citizens of the world. [As we have seen, sea level rise is likely to have a heavy impact on the less developed deltaic countries.] Second, our own generation is tempted to pass the problem on to future generations. Third, our poor grasp of science, international justice, and the human

relationship to nature helps to facilitate inaction. As a result, we are engaging in willful self-deception when the lives of future generations, the world's poor, and even the basic fabric of life on the planet is at stake.[9]

To end this future-oriented chapter, let us examine why efforts to deal with rising sea levels may not be successful. We must begin by noting that there is a very low and uncertain probability that "black swan events" will occur from time to time.[10] The theory of such events was developed by Nassim Nicholas Taleb (born 1960), a Lebanese-American essayist and practitioner of mathematical finance, to discuss large magnitude, extremely rare events which lie beyond the range of our normal expectations and are therefore difficult or impossible to predict. By definition, they surprise everyone. Black swan events, according to Taleb, can play unexpected but decisive roles in our own lives and, indeed, in world history.

In Europe, black swans were presumed not to exist, since none had ever been seen. However, after a Dutch expedition discovered black swans in Western Australia in 1697, the term "black swan" has come to mean an apparent impossibility that turns out to be possible after all.

One must not push this concept too far, but it is easily conceivable that a rise in sea level may turn out to be something of a black swan event. If so, it might exhibit to a limited extent what Taleb identifies as the three defining criteria for such an event. He describes such an event in the following words:

> First, it is an *outlier*, as it lies outside the realm of regular expectations, because nothing in the [recent] past can convincingly point to its possibility. Second, it carries an extreme impact. Third, in spite of its outlier status, human nature makes us concoct explanations for its occurrence *after* the fact, making it explainable and predictable.[11]

Perhaps we can distinguish two types of mega-catastrophe scenarios that could be parts of a black swan event.[12] In the first scenario, climate change might suddenly and unexpectedly cross some kind of now-unknown threshold and thus trigger major and unforeseen events. In terms of sea level rise, perhaps the most important of these would be the collapse of the West Antarctic Ice Sheet, which, as noted earlier, is not likely in the short term but which would generate an appreciable sea level rise if somehow it happened.

In the second scenario, a series of initially minor but then accelerating and escalating "cascading catastrophes" might occur in quick succession. If so, these could have serious impacts. A purely hypothetical multi-stage example here is that a relatively sudden, unexpectedly high level of sea level rise first generates local food shortages in the Republic of Zoc, a fictitious third-

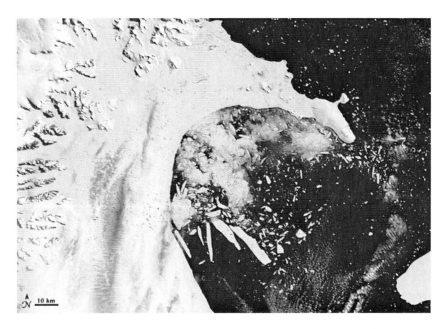

Collapse of the Larsen-B Ice Shelf as seen from satellite on February 23, 2002. (NASA, 2002).

world country. Before long, these shortages lead to food/ethnic riots and to the complete collapse of Zoc's already-shaky law and order apparatus. These riots force many of Zoc's desperate inhabitants to flee toward higher and safer ground, where they expect to receive food and other emergency aid from international donors. For logistical and political reasons, however, not enough aid arrives to satisfy Zoc's urgent needs for it. Finally, regional conflict breaks out as neighboring countries try to repel, militarily, the waves of migrants from Zoc who are desperately looking for food and safety anywhere they can find it.

To these scenarios, we may profitably add some of the personal opinions of Dr. Ted Scambos at the National Snow and Ice Data Center in Boulder, Colorado.[13] He thinks that one black swan event has already occurred, i.e., the break-up of the Larsen B Ice Shelf in Antarctica. In 2002, as mentioned in an earlier chapter, this huge section of ice disintegrated completely within six weeks. The speed of the disintegration and the immediate and significant response of the glaciers surprised most scientists.

Dr. Scambos suspects that other potential black swans are on the horizon now. For example, there is an indication that today's warmer conditions in the Arctic and the big losses of sea ice there correlate with more melt in Greenland. Moreover, significant mass loss of an East Antarctic ice outlet system is possible if there are changes in ocean circulation. Finally, we must not ignore the possible problems posed of ocean acidification and the toppling of major food chains in the oceans; soot and dust on snow, from coal, diesel, and livestock; and any new heat-trapping greenhouse gas, e.g., sulfur hexafluoride, which is used in the electrical industry, as an inert gas for the casting of magnesium, and as an inert filling for insulated glazing windows.

A British study published in 2010 addressed the implications for the United Kingdom of the impacts of sea level rise on critical coastal infrastructure overseas. It focused on potential impacts and threats to the United Kingdom and on potential benefits and opportunities. Edited to make its findings applicable to other developed countries as well, the study listed these impacts and threats[14]:

- Disruption of oil supply chains by more frequent coastal disasters.
- Security threats due to forced population movements, i.e., significant numbers of sea level rise refugees.
- A decline in the political prestige of the countries of the developed world, who may be blamed by some of the poorest countries for coastal disasters resulting from human-induced global warming.
- Direct and indirect impacts on some of the major finance, business, and insurance companies of the developed world.
- Potential impacts on former colonies in the developed world, who may turn to their former colonial rulers for help.

On a more positive note, the study also listed these benefits and opportunities:

- Markets for the coastal engineering and management expertise of the developed world.
- Possible benefits to the national prestige of developed world countries if they can in fact provide international aid in the short term and, in the longer term, if they can pioneer new ways to help the world to sea level rise.

In summary, Nicholas McKay, a climate change expert at the Department of Geosciences at the University of Arizona offers a prescient warning. He tells us:

The message is that the last time glaciers and ice sheets melted [this was during the Last Interglacial, a warm period that lasted from 130,000 to 120,000 years ago], the sea rose by more than eight meters [26.2 feet]. Much of the world's population [now] lives relatively close to sea level. [Sea level rise] is going to have huge impacts, especially on poor countries. If you live a meter [3.2 feet] above sea level, it's irrelevant what causes the rise. Whether sea levels are rising for natural reasons or for anthropogenic reasons, you are still going to be under water sooner or later.[15]

XVI

Conclusions: Looking Ahead

What does the future hold for the world in terms of sea level rise? Today, of course, no one can say for sure, but we think that it is permissible for us here to make some educated guesses. We thus will take the liberty of offering here, very briefly, our own opinions on four important points.

1. The Good News About a Sea Level Rise Disaster

The developed world's ability to mitigate and to adapt to sea level changes is very limited right now, chiefly due to a permeating and perhaps permanent lack of political and financial will. At the same time, the abilities of the less-developed world in this regard will continue to lag further and further behind those of the richer countries; indeed, as a practical matter, these abilities may never develop at all.

Pessimists believe that at least one sea level rise disaster will probably be needed if this political and financial willpower ever begins to gel in the developed world. In the United States, for example, in the absence of any such disaster, the American people — and thus the American Congress — will almost certainly be unwilling to finance any major new mitigation and adaptation measures, except perhaps for New Orleans. Such measures are certain to be complicated, expensive, time-consuming, and politically controversial. As a result, they are not likely to be undertaken in the foreseeable future — unless, of course, there is suddenly a highly visible, dramatic, and unmistakable need for them which cannot be ignored.

2. State and Local Governments in the United States Now Have Some Tools to Use to Cope with Sea Level Rise in Their Own Domains

Even without the very sharp spur that would be provided by a sea level rise disaster, state and local government in the United States already have a number of tools at their disposal. Here, for instance, are no fewer than 13 of them, as listed by Jessica Grannis of the Georgetown Climate Center. They include[1]:

- Comprehensive plans
- Zoning and overlay zones
- Floodplain regulations
- Building codes
- Setbacks/buffers
- Conditional development and exactions
- Rebuilding restrictions
- Subdivision and cluster development
- Hard-armoring permits (for hard-engineered structures that provide flood and erosion control)
- Soft-armoring permits (for "soft" coastal protection projects, e.g., beach buffers, living shorelines, or wetlands restoration)
- Rolling coastal management/rolling easement statutes
- Capital improvement programs
- Acquisitions and buyout programs (e.g., acquire property at risk from flooding or other hazards. Structures are typically demolished and the property restored; undeveloped lands are conserved as public parks or for natural resources)

Undertaking out some or all of these steps will have positive effects at the state and local levels. These steps, however, are inherently parochial and limited. There remains, moreover, that nagging problem of a lack of political and financial will. It is clear to us that what the world really needs in order to deal with sea level rise are *coordinated international efforts*, especially in terms of scientific studies and, eventually, binding international agreements.

3. A Long-Term International Program Is Needed to Improve Our Understanding of Sea Level Rise

Considerable progress has been made the last decade in measuring sea level changes globally and in understanding the climate-related causes of observed changes, but much more remains to be done. A thoughtful paper by Anny Cazenave and others, published online in 2011 as a result of the 2009 "OceansObs'09" conference in Venice on the marine environment, is entitled "The Challenge for Measuring Sea Level Rise and Regional and Global Trends."[2] It begins by making these fundamental points:

Global mean sea level will likely accelerate in the coming decades resulting from accelerated ocean warming and the melting of the massive ice sheets of Greenland and Antarctica. Unfortunately, long-term projections of sea level rise from coupled climate models [e.g., models that feature the physics for both the atmosphere and the oceans] are still very uncertain, both in terms of global mean and regional variability. This is due, in particular, to poor modeling of ice-sheet dynamics and inadequate accounting for decadal variability.

Improving our ability to project future sea level rise, globally and regionally, implies developments in both observing systems and modeling in various disciplines at different spatial and temporal scales. Although significant progress has been made in the last decade, *it appears timely to establish a long-term international program for sustaining and improving all observing systems needed to measure and interpret sea level change as well as improving future projections of global sea level rise and its regional impacts.*[3]

The paper then makes seven specific recommendations for action. We can shorten and summarize them thus:

1. An accurate multi-decade-long sea level record by altimeter satellites is essential, as is continued funding for the altimeter science team to provide leadership. A network of tide gauges with precise positioning should also be maintained, with emphasis on long record lengths and global spacial coverage.
2. Continuity of Gravity Recovery and Climate Experiment (GRACE)–type gravimetry observations is critically needed. New concepts for improving precision and resolution need to be developed.
3. Improved accuracy for the Glacial Isostatic Adjustment (GIA) forward modeling that are needed to provide corrections for GRACE, tide gauges, and satellite altimetry observations over oceans, land, and ice sheets should be made available.
4. Long-term maintenance of the Array for Realtime Geostrophic Oceanography (ARGO) network in its optimal configuration is imperative for measuring ocean temperature and salinity. New methods and systems should be developed to estimate deep changes in ocean heat content and thermal expansion.
5. High priority should be given to developing integrated multidisciplinary studies of present-day and last- century sea level changes, both regional and global.
6. Development and inclusion of realistic ice sheet dynamics is a key issue for projecting sea level change, since the potential contribution from ice sheets like Greenland and Antarctica is much larger than from any other sources.
7. Since local (relative) sea level rise is one of the major threats of global warming, it is of primary importance, among other things, to provide reliable local sea level forecasts on time scales of decades.

The paper concludes by stating that the above efforts are among the priorities of sea level rise studies. They will provide the necessary scientific background in support of political decisions for coastal management, mitigation, and adaptation to rising sea levels.

4. Towards "Meters of Sea Level Rise"

A 2011 study on the economic growth impact of sea level rise, commissioned by the United Kingdom's Foresight Project on Migration and Global Environmental Change, ended on this sobering note:

> To conclude, it is important to remember that sea-level rise is a very uncertain and very long-term process, which has just started and which will continue over millennia, to reach up to several metres. Most of the analyses that have been carried out so far have looked to 2050 or 2100, and considered sea-level rise of up to 1 meter [3.2 feet]. Assuming a continuing sea-level rise beyond 2100 and the idea that when a densely populated area is protected it has to be protected forever, then the cost of protecting world coastlines will keep increasing over time, maybe up to unsustainable levels that may significantly affect world economies.[4]

A 2012 study for the World Bank (written by the same author of the study quoted above) investigated the impact of sea level rise on economic growth and added this important warning:

> Importantly, the consequences of sea level rise do not need to be very strong to lead to reduced growth and out-migration. If sea level rise creates a comparative disadvantage of some coastal areas compared to other locations (inland zones and coastal areas that are easier to protect), it can be enough to lead to significant regional or local economic losses (compensated by gains in other locations). These losses can then easily turn into reduced investment (loss of physical capital) and out-migration (loss of human capital), making the overall macroeconomic and welfare impact much larger than expected from an analysis of direct losses from sea level rise.[5]

When asked what he thought are the most important points to be included in this last chapter, Dr. John Church told us:

> First, we will have to adapt to sea level rise. There is no way to prevent further sea level rise. Effective adaptation requires planning and acceptance of the reality of sea level rise. Sea level rise will continue long after we stabilize greenhouse gas concentrations.
>
> Secondly, the amount of sea level rise is up to us. To avoid large amounts of rise, we will need to reduce our greenhouse gas emissions urgently and very significantly. Without that action we will commit the world to sea level rise of meters.[6]

As suggested earlier, we ourselves do not believe that the political and financial will needed to reduce these emissions exists now or will arise in the foreseeable future. Indeed, it is far more likely that greenhouse gas emissions will continue to increase in the decades ahead. If so, it follows that "meters of sea level rise" now lie ahead for the world. We shall therefore end this final chapter by recalling the words of Dr. Church, which we quoted verbatim at the beginning of this book in the Preface.

Dr. Church tells us that while much of society's past development has occurred during a time of relatively stable sea level, we are now moving out of this period. Future coastal planning and development must therefore take into account the inevitable increases of regional sea levels. To these prescient words we will add a few of our own, namely: *it would be folly to do otherwise.*

Appendices

1: Climate Change Conferences: The 2009 Copenhagen, the 2010 Cancun and the 2011 Durban

It is clear that the international community has no appetite now for any binding remedial measures to deal with most aspects of climate change, including sea level rise. This fact was evident at the 7–18 December 2009 Copenhagen Conference, which was attended by representatives of more than 190 nations. The resulting "Copenhagen Accord" was hammered together at the last minute by only five countries: the United States, China, India, Brazil, and South Africa. Its many critics said that this skeletal three-page agreement failed to spell out any binding global emissions targets for 2020 and later years that would compel developed countries to reduce their greenhouse gas emissions. Moreover, they complained, it also failed to set up a payment plan for the $100 billion in financial assistance promised to countries that will be hardest hit by climate change.

The Copenhagen Conference satisfied very few participants. The more charitable ones hailed it as "a good start." The most that this meeting achieved was to confirm that there are no prospects for a binding, broadly-based global warming treaty any time soon. This point was, in effect, ratified by a United Nations climate change conference held in Cancun, Mexico, late in 2010.

At the close of the Cancun conference, the *New York Times* judged that these talks had resulted only in a "modest deal on emissions," an outcome which the American climate envoy at the conference damned with the faint praise as "a balanced package that lays the groundwork for future progress."[1] What was most evident was that the attending nations declined to take any action on any of the most important issues: they failed to enshrine any ambitious climate-change goals in any legally-binding agreements.[2]

The best summary we have seen of the 2011 conference in Durban was provided by *New York Times* correspondent John Broder, who made the following important points in his report:

> For 17 years, officials from nearly 200 countries have gathered under the auspices of the United Nations to try to deal with one of the most vexing questions of our era — how the slow the heating of the planet.
>
> Every year they leave a trail of disillusion and discontent, particularly among the poorest nations and those most vulnerable to rising seas and spreading deserts. Every year they fail to advance their own stated goal of keeping the average global temperature from rising more than 2 degrees Celsius, or about 3.6 degrees Fahrenheit, above preindustrial levels.
>
> This was the case again this year. The event, the 17th conference of the United Nations Framework Convention on Climate Change [ended] with modest accomplishments: the promise to work toward a new global treaty in coming years and the establishment of a new climate fund...
>
> There is no denying the dedication and stamina of the environment ministers and diplomats who conduct these talks. But maybe the task is too tall. The issues on the table are far broader than atmospheric carbon levels or forestry practices or how to devise a fund to compensate those most affected by global warming.
>
> What is really at play here are politics on the broadest scale, the relations among Europe, the United States, Canada, Japan and three rapidly rising economic powers, China, India and Brazil. These relations, in turn, are driven by each country's domestic politics and the strains the global financial crisis has put on all of them.[3]

2: The Impact on Ports of a 3.2 Foot (1 Meter) Sea Level Rise

The impacts of a 3.2 foot (1 meter) sea level rise on the major ports of the world would vary for each port and would depend on two main factors: elevation and exposure.[1]

Elevation is important because if the existing elevations of the port infrastructure are already within 3.2 feet (1 meter) of present day sea level, then the potential for routine inundation would be very high. Portions of various ports (docks, piers, construction decks, etc.) may be above 3.2 feet (1 meter) in elevation and would thus be at minimal risk — until after 2100 if sea level rise accelerates. However, many of these ports would still be at risk because much of the support infrastructure may be below 3.2 feet (1 meter) in elevation and thus susceptible to increased flooding. This includes access roads and railways, parking lots, storm water drainage, and storage areas that are away from the center of the port facility, but upon which continuous operation of the port depends. If these areas become inundated, even if only periodically, then port operations may become less efficient.

Exposure is also important because as sea level rises, ports that are exposed to extreme events such as storm surges and periodic astronomic high tides would become even more severely impacted in the future. Some coastal areas today are only inundated during the highest spring tides. With a sea level rise of 3.2 feet (1 meter), many areas would be inundated for a period of time on a daily basis, even without a storm effect. Even if storminess were not to increase in frequency or intensity due to climate change, sea level rise would still provide a higher background water level from which normal storm surge can build and become even more destructive. A 3.2 foot (1 meter) increase in this background water would give a significant boost to storm tide elevations. Any infrastructure that is now designed for a 100-year event threshold may become more exposed to even more frequent inundation in the future. Increased exposure could also come in the form of increased frequency of destructive waves and coastal erosion which would require ports to upgrade coastal protection structures.

In summary, there would be a full range of impacts to port facilities worldwide for a 3.2 foot (1 meter) rise in sea level by 2100. This could range from a need for a complete rebuild of the facility and supporting infrastructure to a minor infrequent inconvenience to normal operations. Ports and port facilities are highly competitive, however, and even a small incremental impact on port operations could have a large impact on their economic sustainability.

3: Extreme Event Analysis

Computer modeling systems can increasingly forecast the effects of climate variability and changes over space and time.[1] They can be used to describe baseline climates; examine current climate variability and extremes; assess risks, both present and future; investigate adaptation options; generate climate and sea level change scenarios; project sectoral impacts of climate and sea level change; study risks and uncertainties; and facilitate integrated impact analyses.

Past climate data can be used in these modeling systems as an extreme event analysis tool which can help determine the probability of a given extreme event, such as heavy rainfall or extremely hot or cold temperatures. The probabilities and return periods for extreme events can also be projected for the future by using the various IPCC scenarios of climate change. Developing this kind of information will be increasingly important for engineers designing structures to withstand future climate changes, as well for many other users, e.g., the insurance industry. Political leaders, activists, and interest groups, as well as the media, will be very interested in advances in extreme event analysis, too.

4: Sea Level Rise and Breakwater Damage

Breakwaters are structures built on coasts as part of coastal defense, e.g., to reduce erosion, or to protect anchorages.[1] These useful — and potential vulnerable -valuable structures are designed to absorb the energy of the waves that strike them. Caisson breakwater shelter moored vessels in ports, harbors, and marine terminals; protect coastal communities from flooding; and lessen the effects of coastal erosion. They use the mass of the caisson and the heavy fill within it to resist the overturning force applied by waves hitting them. Rubble mound breakwaters, cheaper to build in shallow waters, use the voids within their rocky structure to dissipate the waves' energy. All breakwaters, however, are subject to damage when they are overtopped by big storms. In the years ahead, rising sea levels are likely to increasingly cause such damage.

One fundamental problem here is that in the past the effects of climate change, e.g. sea level rise, were ignored when designing breakwaters. As a result, we may find that, over time and as they approach the end of their operational lives (50 years or more), they may no longer be as reliable as anticipated.

In 2006, for example, Japanese scientists studied the effect of sea level rise on caisson breakwaters and found that the probability of "sliding failure" could increase by up to 50 percent in the period ranging from 2000 to 2050. Moreover, a paper prepared for a UNCTAD Ad Hoc Expert Meeting in 2011 reported that, due to sea level rise, the potential damage to breakwaters built in shallower waters will increase towards the end of their lives. This study forecast that a breakwater designed in 2050 would be appreciably more expensive to build, e.g., about 8 percent for the deeper sections and 66 percent more expensive for the shallower sections, than a breakwater designed for the 20th century and which did have to not take sea level rise into account. The study warned that "the lack of certainty in the future [due to rapid anthropomorphic climate change] will not allow for economic designs based on past experience."[2]

5: Possible Dutch Responses to a Sea Level Rise of 16.4 Feet (5 Meters)

This appendix has been drawn from and selectively edited from a 2005 paper by Xander Olsthoorn et al. at the Vrije Universiteit of Amsterdam.[1] Their study was a background paper for the ATLANTIS Project, which was sponsored by the European Commission. (Atlantis was a mythical naval power which, according to Plato, sank into the ocean "in a single day and night of misfortune" after a failed attempt to invade Athens.)

The paper begins by asking what might happen to the Netherlands if, in 2030, sea level begins to rise and continues to rise for 100 years, eventually reaching a sea level of 16.4 feet (5 meters) above the current level. The cause of this rise is posited to be the disintegration of the West Antarctic Ice Sheet (WAIS). Two opposing scenarios are presented. The first, labeled "Markets prevail," essentially forecasts a continuation of political, economic, and social life as practiced in the Netherlands today. Under this scenario, there is only a very limited role in public services for the Dutch government. In the second scenario, labeled "Public institutions," the government plays a stronger role.

The study conceives of sea level rise as occurring in three hypothetical consecutive stages in the Netherlands:

Stage 1: Sea level rise begins to accelerate, 2030–2050

Sea level rise disasters have already occurred in other parts of the world. In 2049, the economic heart of the Netherlands (i.e., Rotterdam, The Hague, and Amsterdam) narrowly escapes a devastating flood due to a combination of high discharges from the Rhine, a high spring tide, a strong gale coming out of the west, and a modest amount of sea level rise. While, initially, there is little public belief in scientists' repeated warnings about the long term dangers posed by sea level rise, after the 2049 event it is widely accepted that sea level rise is indeed accelerating, though there is no consensus on its rate and maximum level. After the near-disaster of 2049, however, flood safety rises much higher on the Dutch political agenda. The government assures the public that any problems are quite manageable, i.e., there will be no need to surrender any of the hard-won Dutch land to the sea.

Stage 2: Accelerated sea level rise becomes a major public concern, 2050–2070

In one lifetime, sea level has risen 3.2 to 6.5 feet (1–2 meters) above the former sea level. In 2068, there is a serious dike breach north of Amsterdam.

A large part of the province of North Holland is flooded; there are many victims. The dangers posed by the WAIS are now well understood. There are growing doubts about the feasibility of keeping all of the Netherlands above water; thoughtful people begin to focus on the eventual need to abandon some of the polders (low-lying areas) to the sea. In Venice, there is such serious flooding that the city is virtually abandoned as a tourist destination. In the Netherlands, major programs are started to improve the country's civil engineering capacity. Roads will be elevated to help in flood protection and in emergency evacuations. After the flood disaster of 2068, the government votes for a patchwork of projects to preserve as much of the country as possible, while the public jokes about the new "Dutch Archipelago."

Stage 3: Sea level rise at its height, 2070–2130

At the beginning of this period, the geography of the Netherlands is much as it was before; at the end of the period, most of the low-lying and less populated areas are now under water. Agricultural production falls sharply, investments in vulnerable areas slump, the housing market swoons, and people begin to emigrate due to fear of further flooding. Abandoning vulnerable and less valuable parts of the country is increasingly suggested. After very lengthy and very acrimonious debates, these areas are in fact abandoned.

The study concludes that from a purely technical point of view it would be possible to maintain the territorial integrity of the Netherlands under a 16.4 feet (5 meter) sea rise. However, the study also suggests that the traditionally slow pace of political and social decision-making in the Netherlands makes it unlikely that such extremely difficult decisions can be made in time. Even if by then the Netherlands has adopted the "Public institutions" scenario mentioned earlier (in which the government plays a much stronger role in public affairs), the bottom line is that the territorial integrity of the country will nevertheless be lost due to sea level rise.

6: Using a Bayesian Network to Predict Coastal Vulnerability to Sea Level Rise

Thomas Bayes (c. 1702–17 April 1761) was an English mathematician and Presbyterian minister who took a deep interest in probability.[1] "Bayesian probability" refers to several related interpretations of probability, all of which have in common the concept of probability as something like a partial belief, rather than as a frequency. This allows the application of probability to a wide range of propositions.[2]

In practice, a Bayesian network provides an elegant mathematical structure for modeling complicated relationships among random variables, while at the same time presenting the reader with a relatively simple graph showing these relationships. Bayesian networks can be applied to uncertain knowledge in such diverse fields as sea level variations, medical diagnosis, and language.

Sea level rise in the 21st century — and long thereafter — will continue to have a wide range of effects on coastal environments; on living conditions for men, women, and children there; and on ports and other high-tech infrastructure. The very broad range of complicated factors at play here inevitably leads to a high degree of uncertainty in trying to predict the long-term impacts of sea level rise. A Bayesian network can be useful here: the Bayesian statistical framework is ideal for datasets derived from historical to modern observations of phenomena such as long-term shoreline change.[3]

For example, it can be employed to define the relationship between driving forces, geologic constraints, and coastal factors for the U.S. Atlantic coast that include observations of local rates of relative sea level rise, wave height, tide range, geomorphic classification, coastal slope, and rates of shoreline change. Such a network can be used to make probabilistic predictions about shoreline retreat rates in response to different future sea level rises. The bottom line is that Bayesian networks can help scientists make quantitative, probabilistic predictions about coastal changes in response to sea level rise that can be applied to coastal management decisions.

Notes

See the entries in the bibliography for full bibliographic data, e.g., URLs

Preface

1. Church, "Understanding Sea-Level Rise and Variability," p. 15. Italics added.

2. After Allison, et al, "Ice Sheet Mass Balance and Sea Level," p. 413.

Introduction

1. Quoted in French by Riché and Verger, *Des Nains sur des épaules de géants*, p. 13. The translation is by Hunt Janin.

2. The IPCC is organized into three working groups and one Task Force. The first working group evaluates the literature in the natural sciences which deals with climate and climate change. The second is concerned with the consequences of climate change and ways to adapt to them. The third working group evaluates methods to reduce emissions of greenhouse gases—an important step in limiting climate change. The Task Force is responsible for the National Greenhouse Gas Inventories Program.

3. The IPCC's Fourth Assessment consisted of three separate assessments, dealing with (1) the physical science of climate itself; (2) impacts, adaptation, and vulnerability; and (3) mitigation of climate change. The final report is a Synthesis Report that summarizes these three reports. The IPCC does not, in and of itself, conduct research. In essence, it assesses the available peer-reviewed literature and uses it to draw its own conclusions.

4. After IPCC, "Summary for Policymakers," pp. 2, 5, 10, 16.

5. National Research Council of the National Academies. "Advancing the Science of Climate Change," pp. 2, 21–22.

6. Wikipedia, IPCC Fifth Assessment Report, pp. 1–6.

7. The IPCC's Synthesis Report of 2007 addressed six topics: observed changes in climate and its effects; causes of change; climate change and its impacts in the near and long term under different scenarios; adaptation and mitigation options and responses, and the inter-relationship

with sustainable development, at global and regional levels; the long term perspective, i.e., scientific and socio-economic aspects relevant to adaptation and mitigation; and "robust findings," i.e., well-documented conclusions, and key uncertainties.

8. The IPCC's Assessment Reports are initially written by the scientists. Then summaries for policy makers are drafted during a very lengthy negotiation process. Both the scientists and the representatives of all member governments have to sign off on the final versions. These cautious procedures result in conservative reporting.

9. Computer modeling can be used to make projections of possible future climates over a time scale of many centuries but it has two inherent and fundamental limitations: the "scenario uncertainty" and the "model uncertainty." The first refers to the fact that future greenhouse gas emissions cannot be predicted accurately. The second refers to the facts that (a) we do not know, precisely, what the present climate state really is, and (b) no model can give a perfect representation of the real world. (After Hunter, "Estimating Sea-Level Extremes Under Conditions of Uncertain Sea-Level Rise," p. 1.)

10. After Joughin, et al, "Stability of the West Antarctic Ice Sheet in a Warming World," p. 1.

11. National Research Council, "Sea Level Rise and the Coastal Environment," p. 189.

12. Because freshwater is not as dense as saltwater, freshwater actually has a greater volume than an equivalent weight of saltwater. Thus when freshwater melts in the ocean, it contributes a slightly greater volume of melt water than it originally displaced. A paper written in 2007, for example, demonstrated that melt water from sea ice and floating ice shelves could add 2.6% more water to the ocean than the water displaced by the ice, or the equivalent of approximately 1.57 inches (4 centimeters). (Noerdlinger et al, "The Melting of Floating Ice will Raise the Ocean Level.")

13. InterAcademy Council, "InterAcademy Council Report Recommends Fundamental Reform of IPCC Management Structure," p. 1.

14. Ministry of Climate and Energy of Den-

mark, "What Consequences Can We Expect, and What Can We Do?" p. l.

15. Schmidt, "Under and over the ice," p. l.

16. University of New South Wales Climate Change Research Centre, "The Copenhagen Diagnosis," p. 24.

Chapter I

1. After National Research Council, "Climate Stabilization Targets," p. 2.

2. IPCC, "Is Sea Level Rising?"

3. Environmental Protection Agency, "Sea Level Changes," p. l.

4. Environmental Protection Agency, "Greenhouse Gases Threaten Public Health and the Environment," pp. 1–2.

5. After Hoegh-Guldberg and Bruno, "The Impact of Climate Change on the World's Marine Ecosystems," p. 1523.

6. After Archer and Rahmstorf, *The Climate Crisis*, p. 14.

7. An interesting intellectual question is why the concept of global warming can arouse such great hostility among those who deny that it is occurring and that it is largely man-made. Many of these critics seem to believe that any significant moves towards other forms of energy will undermine our relatively inexpensive carbon-based society, will increase the cost of living, and will lead to higher unemployment. And, as Steven Sherwood noted in a prescient 2011 article in *Physics Today* (see bibliography) on "Science controversies past and present," we must recognize in this context "the frailty of human reason and the supremacy of emotional concerns that we humans all share but do not always acknowledge."

8. The U.S. Climate Change Science Program (2002–2009) was a program responsible for coordinating and integrating research on global warming conducted by U.S. Government agencies. It is now known as the U.S. Global Change Research Program.

9. U.S. Climate Change Science Program, "Coastal Elevations and Sensitivity to Sea-Level Rise," p. 2.

10. After Rahmstorf, "A New View on Sea Level Rise," p. l.

11. After Schmidt, "Under and Over the Ice," p. 2, and Rignot, et al, "Acceleration of the Contribution of the Greenland and Antarctic Ice Sheets to Sea Level Rise," p. l.

12. UK Climate Projections, "Marine and coastal projections," section 6.

13. After Lin, "Literature Review for Latest Global Sea Level Rise Projections," p. 13.

14. Nicholls, et al, "Sea-Level Rise and its Possible Impacts Given a 'Beyond 4_C World' in the Twenty-First Century," p. 168.

15. Jevrejeva et al, "Sea Level Projections to AD2500 with a New Generation of Climate Change Scenarios," p. l.

16. After Scheme, et al, "Climate Change Under a Scenario of Near 1.5°C of Global Warming, p. 304.

17. We have borrowed this evocative term (in the context of sea level rise) from Pilkey and Young, "The Rising Sea," pp. 61–79.

18. This section draws from Archer's and Rahmstorf's *The Climate Crisis*, specifically pp. 4, 8, 9, 14, 23, 26–29, and 31–32.

19. Personal communication of 4 August 2010 from Dr. Kevin Trenberth, quoting Trenberth, K.E. et al, "Earth's global energy budget." *Bull. Amer. Meteor. Soc.*, 90, No. 3, pages 311–324, doi: 10.1175/2008BAM2634.1 [PDF].

20. Tyndall (1873) as cited in Weart, *The Discovery of Global Warming*, p. 4.

21. After Dessler and Sherwood, "A Matter of Humidity," p. 2.

22. "Ice Ages and Sea Levels," p. l.

23. Kaser, G. et al., "Mass Balance of Glaciers and Ice Caps," p. l.

24. Steffen, et al, "Cryospheric Contributions to Sea-Level Rise and Variability," p. 211.

25. Ibid, p. 177.

26. After Pollack, *A World Without Ice*, pp. 41–43.

27. "What causes Arctic amplification?" p. l.

28. Both these findings are from Anderegg, et al, "Expert Credibility in Climate Change," p. l.

29. After Yale Project on Climate Change Communication, "Publications and Reports: Global Warming's Six Americas 2010," p. l.

30. Pew Research Center, "Wide Partisan Divide Over Global Warming," p. l.

31. Gallup, "In U.S., Concerns About Global Warming Stable at Lower Levels," p. 2.

32. After Hoeppe, "Trends of Natural Disasters—The Role of Global Warming," pp. 1–17.

33. IPCC, "Key vulnerabilities and hotspots."

Chapter II

1. Some of the points made here are drawn from Wikipedia, "World Ocean," p. l. The quotation is from the *Iliad*, IX, 182 (cited by Wikipedia).

2. After Wikipedia, "Water Cycle," p. 2.

3. Some of the points in this section are drawn from Wikipedia, "Water Cycle," pp. 1–3.

4. Adapted from University of Illinois, "A Summary of the Water Cycle," p. l.

5. After USGS, "The Water Cycle: Summary of the Water Cycle," pp. 1–19.

6. After Wikipedia, "Water cycle," p. 2.

7. After NASA, "Earth Observatory: The Water Cycle," p. 2.

8. After NASA, "Earth Observatory: The Water Cycle," p. 2.

9. After Water Encyclopedia, "Global Warming and the Hydrologic Cycle," p. l.

10. NASA, "Earth Observatory: The Water Cycle," p. 3.

Chapter III

1. After Wikipedia, "The Blue Marble," pp. 1–4, and NASA, "The Blue Marble," p. 1.

2. After the World Resources Institute, "Coastline Length," pp. 1, 5.

3. Karl, et al, "Coastal Areas and Marine Resources," pp. 108 and 113, in *Global Climate Change Impacts in the United States.*

4. Dasgupta, et al, "Exposure of Developing Countries to Sea-Level Rise and Storm Surges," p. 1.

5. After Wikipedia, "Tsunami," p. 1.

6. After Ekman, "The World's Longest Sea Level Series and a Winter Oscillation Index for Northern Europe, 1774–2000," pp. 3–6.

7. Mazina and Kershner, "Nation Under Siege," p. 3.

8. Overpeck and Weiss, "Projections of Future Sea Level Becoming More Dire," p. 1.

9. One vivid if small-scale example of this rebound can be seen on the Gulf of Bothnia coast of northern Sweden. Nineteenth century boat-houses on one island there are now well above present-day sea level as a result of vertical land motion. (Church et al, *Understanding Sea-Level Rise and Variability*, photo and text on p. 13.)

10. After Ruddiman, *Earth's Climate: Past and Future*, p. 162.

11. Church, et al, "Changes in Sea Level," p. 644.

12. After Church, et al, "Ocean Temperature and Salinity Contributions to Global and Regional Sea-Level Change," p. 143.

13. After Nicholls and Cazenave, "Sea-Level Rise and Its Impacts on Coastal Zones," p. 1517.

14. University of New South Wales Climate Change Research Centre, "The Copenhagen Diagnosis," p. 37.

15. After Kargel, et al,, "Greenland's Shrinking Ice Cover: 'Fast Times' but not that Fast," p. 4.

16. Pilkey and Young, *The Rising Sea*, p. 31,

17. Milne, et al, "Identifying the Causes of Sea-Level Change," p. 1.

18. When La Niña is very strong, it evaporates huge amounts of water from the ocean. Most of it falls back into the ocean, but in some years, e.g., 2010–2011, it falls on land. As a result, global sea levels can fall, albeit on a temporary basis. (NASA, "NASA Satellites Detect Pothole on Road to Higher Seas," p. 1.)

19. After Cazenave and Llovel, "Contemporary Sea Level Rise," pp. 163, 168.

20. Milne, et al, "Identifying the causes of sea-level change," p. 1.

21. After "NASA Mission Takes Stock of Earth's Melting Land Ice," p.1.

22. After Edwing, "What the Science Shows Us about How Sea Level Rise and Weather Events Will Affect Ports," p. 10.

23. Leadley, et al, "Biodiversity Scenarios: Projections of 21st Century Change in Biodiversity and Associated Ecosystem Services," p. 103.

24. After CU Sea Level Research Group, "Tide Gauge Sea Level," p. 1.

25. Nicholls, "Impacts of and Responses to Sea-Level Rise," p. 19.

26. After Pirazzoli, et al, "Extreme Sea Levels in Two Northern Mediterranean Areas," p. 10.

27. EPA, "Coastal Zones and Sea Level Rise," p. 1.

28. Permanent Service for Mean Sea Level, "Sea Level," p. 2.

29. Adapted from IPCC, "Climate Change 2007: Working Group II: Impacts, Adaptation and Vulnerability: Executive Summary," p. 1.

30. University of New South Wales Climate Change Research Centre, "The Copenhagen Diagnosis," p. 7.

31. Since the late 1990s, rising sea levels around the Torres Islands (north Vanuatu, southwest Pacific) have caused local and international concern. A 2011 study, however, suggested that the subsidence of the Torres Islands, coupled with large earthquakes there, are responsible for the apparent sea level rise observed on these islands. After Ballu et al, abstract of "Comparing the role of absolute sea-level rise and vertical tectonic motions in coastal flooding, Torres Islands (Vanuatu)."

32. Church was quoted by *Science Daily* in its 11 May 2009 article, "Rising Sea Levels Set To Have Major Impacts Around the World."

33. IPCC, "The Physical Science Basis: Summary for Policy Makers: A Paleoclimatic Perspective," and Kopp et al, "Probabilistic assessment of sea level during the last interglacial stage."

34. After Titus, "Greenhouse Effect, Sea Level Rise, and Land Use," p. 1.

35. Pollack, *A World Without Ice*, p. 126.

36. Inman, "Water in Dams, Reservoirs Preventing Sea-Level Rise," p. 1.

37. See Wada et al, "Global depletion of groundwater resources," p. 4, and Konikow, "Contribution to global groundwater depletion since 1900 to sea-level rise," p. 1.

38. After Cazenave and Llovel, "Contemporary Sea Level Rise," pp. 156, 157.

39. National Research Council, "Advancing the Science of Climate Change," p. 195.

40. Adapted from Nicholls, et al, "Increasing Flood Risk and Wetland Loss Due to Global Sea-Level Rise: Regional and Global Analyses," p. S85 (sic).

41. Nicholls, et al, "Sea-Level Rise and its Possible Impacts Given a "Beyond 4_C World' in the Twenty-First Century," p. 162, and Church, et al, "Ice and Sea-level Change," p. 154.

42. Mandia, "Global Warming: A Sea Change," p. 1.

43. Quoted in Mandia, "Global Warming: A Sea Change," p. 1.

44. Some of these comments were drawn from the IPCC's Fourth Assessment Report (2007), Working Group II, "Impacts, Adaptation and Vulnerability," Section 6.2.2, "Increasing human utilization of the coastal zone," and from the Executive Summary of the IPCC's chapter in this

Report (Chapter 6) on "Coastal systems and low-lying areas."

45. After IPCC, "Coastal Systems and Low-Lying Areas," p. 328.

46. Some of these comments are drawn from Church, et al, "Understanding global sea levels," p. 9.

47. "Mangrove" is a broad term for a diverse group of more than 100 plant species which can tolerate high levels of salt water. Mangroves are only found along warm coasts, e.g., in Asia, Africa, Australia, and the Americas. In the continental United States, mangroves are limited to the Florida peninsula and to isolated growths along the coasts of southern Louisiana and south Texas. Much like salt marshes, mangrove forests form the basis of a rich ecosystem of plants and organisms which can take advantage of the intricate root systems and nutrients available there. Mangrove forests also protect shorelines from hurricanes and other storms. (After Pilkey and Young, *The Rising Sea*, p. 106–108.)

48. Environmental Protection Agency, "Coastal Zones and Sea Level Rise," p. 2.

49. Ibid, 4.

50. Leadley, et al, "Biodiversity Scenarios: Projections of 21st Century Change in Biodiversity and Associated Ecosystem Services," p. 25.

51. After Solentpedia, "Coastal Squeeze," p. 1.

52. After Archer and Rahmstorf, *The Climate Crisis*, p. 174.

53. Lowe et al, "Past and Future Changes in Extreme Sea Levels and Waves," p. 350.

54. Good examples of megadeltas include the Huanghe (Yellow), Changjiang (Yangtze), Pearl, Red, Mekong, Chao Phraya, Irrawaddy, Ganges-Brahmaputra, and Indus.

55. After IPCC, "Coastal systems and low-lying areas," p. 327.

56. The map (from IPCC, "Coastal Systems and Low-Lying Areas," p. 327) categorizes the deltas/megadeltas as follows:
high extreme vulnerability to sea level rise: Ganges-Brahmaputra, Mekong, Nile
vulnerability to sea level rise: Mississippi, Godavari, Changjiang
medium vulnerability to sea level rise: Grijalva, Orinoco, Amazon, Sao Francisco, Rhine, Sebou, Moulouya, Senegal, Volta, Niger, Shatt el Arab, Indus, Mahanadi, Krishna, Red, Zhujiang, Chao Phraya, Mahakam.

57. IPCC, "Coastal systems and low-lying areas," p. 327.

58. Ibid, p. 331.

59. Some of the following points are drawn from Nichols, "Impacts of and Reponses to Sea-Level Rise," pp. 37–40.

60. After IPCC, Synthesis Report, Section 5.3, "Adaptation and mitigation."

61. Dasgupta and Meisner, "Climate Change and Sea Level Rise," p. 1.

62. We have lightly edited this list, which is

drawn from the IPCC, "Coastal Systems and Low-Lying Areas," p. 337.

Chapter IV

1. After Hunter, "A Simple Technique for Estimating an Allowance for Uncertain Sea-Level Rise," p. 2, and a private communication from Dr. Hunter of 30 November 2011.

2. National Hurricane Center, "Storm Surges Overview," p. 1.

3. After Earth Science Australia, "Storm Surges," p. 1.

4. Knutsen, "Tropical Cyclones and Climate Change," p. 1.

5. See Dwyer et al, "Mid-Pliocene Sea Level and Continental Ice Volume Based on Coupled Benthic Mg/Ca Paleotemperatures and Oxygen Isotopes," p. 166.

6. After National Hurricane Center, "Storm Surges Overview," p. 3.

7. Dasgupta, et al, "Exposure of Developing Countries to Sea-Level Rise and Storm Surges," p. 2.

8. Tebaldi, et al, "Characterizing Impact of Local Sea Level Rise through Changes in Extreme Storm Surges along the US Coasts." p. 1.

9. After Chini, "Climate change and sea level rise implication on coastal wave overtopping," pp. 1, 2.

10. After Rayner and MacKenzie, "A First-Order Assessment of the Impact of Long-Term Trends in Extreme Sea Levels on Offshore Structures and Coastal Refineries," pp. 53, 59; and after Nicholls, et al, "Potential Implications of Climate Change and Sea-Level Rise on Coastal Waste Sites," p. 1.

11. After Young, et al., "Global Trends in Wind Speed and Wave Height," pp. 1–3.

12. Chini, et al, "The Impact of Sea Level Rise and Climate Change on Inshore Wind Climate: A Case Study for East Anglia (UK)," p. 1.

13. This example is drawn from Woodworth, "Extreme Sea Levels."

14. After Lowe, et al, "Past and Future Changes in Extreme Sea Levels and Waves," p. 333.

15. After Seung-Ki Min, et al, "Human Contributions to More-Intense Precipitation Extremes," p. 1.

16. Trenberth, "NCAR's Trenberth on the link between global warming and extreme deluges," p. 1.

17. After Lowe, et al, "Past and Future Changes in Extreme Sea Levels and Waves," p. 328, citing two studies by Zhang, et al.

18. After Wilson, et al, "Observing Systems Needed to Address Sea-Level Rise and Variability," p. 398.

19. For information on the GEOSS, see www.earthobservations.org.

20. Rosenthal, "Huff and Puff and Blow Your House Down," p. 3.

21. Quoted by Rosenthal, "Huff and Puff and Blow Your House Down," p. 3.

22. After Shepard, et al, "Assessing Future Risk: Quantifying the Effects of Sea Level Rise on Storm Surge Risk for the Southern Shores of Long Island, New York," p. 1.

Chapter V

1. After Lambeck et al, "Paleoenvironmental Records, Geophysical Modeling, and Reconstruction of Sea-Level Trends and Variability on Centennial and Longer Timescales," p. 83.

2. Adapted from Wikipedia, "Sea Level," p. 61.

3. After Rabineau, et al. "Paleo sea levels reconsidered from direct observation of paleoshoreline during the Glacial Maxima (for the last 500,000 yr.," p. 1.

4. After "Eustatic Sea Level Change Mechanisms," pp. 1–2. As a general proposition, it is clear that the earth's orbit around the sun plays a key role in patterns of glaciation and therefore of changes in sea level. The amount of solar radiation hitting the earth at any latitude or season is determined by three aspects of the position of the earth in its orbit around the sun: (1) the eccentricity of the earth's orbit, (2) the tilt of the earth's axis relative to the orbital plane, and (3) seasonal changes in the time when the earth is nearest to the sun.

5. After Paleoclimates, "Past Climates on Earth," pp. 10–12. See also "Eustatic Sea Level Change Mechanisms," pp. 1–2.

6. Sources used here include German High Advisory Council on Global Change, "The Future Oceans—Warming Up, Rising High, Turning Sour," p. 1; University of California Los Angeles, "The Relationship Between Plate Tectonics and the Carbon Cycle," p. 1; Church et al, "Sea-level rise and Variability—Synthesis and Outlook for the Future," pp. 403–405; and Archer and Rahmstorf, *The Climate Crisis*, pp. 109, 110.

7. After IPCC, "The Physical Science Basis: Summary for Policymakers," p. 9.

8. National Research Council, "Advancing the Science of Climate Change," pp. 184–185.

9. After National Research Council, "Sea Level Rise and the Coastal Environment," p. 185.

10. After Sato and Hansen, "Updating the climate science: What path is the real world following?"

11. After Edwing, "What the Science Shows Us about How Sea Level Rise and Weather Events Will Affect Ports," p. 4.

12. After NOAA, "State of the Climate in 2009," p. S 70.

13. After CSIRO, "Sea Level Rise: Historical Sea Level Changes—Last two decades," p. 1.

14. Rahmstorf, "A new view on sea level rise," p. 1.

15. Vermeer and Rahmstorf, "Global sea level linked to global temperature," p. 1.

16. West German Advisory Council, "The Future Oceans—Warming Up, Rising High, Turning Sour," p. 37; and Overpeck and Weiss, "Projections for future sea level becoming more dire," p. 21462.

17. After Nicholls and Poh Poh Wong, "Coastal Systems and low-lying areas," p. 346.

18. After National Research Council, "Climate Stabilization Targets," p. 14.

Chapter VI

1. Carlson, *The Edge of the Sea*, p. 1. Italics added.

2. See Nicholls, et al, "Coastal systems and low-lying areas," Chapter 6 in the IPCC's 2007 study, *Climate Change 2007: Impacts, Adaptation and Vulnerability*, pp. 315–357; and Environmental Protection Agency, "Coastal zones and sea level rise."

3. Private communication of 16 March 2011 from the Library of Congress, citing "The World's Coastline," edited by Eric C.F. Bird and Maurice L. Schwartz. From a fractal point of view, however, the world's coastline is infinitely long.

4. After IPCC, "Coastal systems and low-lying areas," pp. 318–319.

5. The geology underlying a given place is known as the "geological framework." The very differing characteristics of the Pacific Coast and the Atlantic/Gulf of Mexico Coasts of the United States are good cases in point. Along the Pacific margin of the country, the collision of tectonic plates has led to the creation of a steep coastline, where cliffs overlook much of the shore. In contrast, tectonic activity has been very mild along the Atlantic and Gulf of Mexico coastlines. The geological result there has been that these coasts consist of wide plains, with wide continental shelves extending far offshore. (After Environmental Protection Agency, "Coastal Zones and Sea Level Rise," p. 47.)

6. After Environmental Protection Agency, "Coastal Zones and Sea Level Rise," p. 47.

7. After Environmental Protection Agency, "Coastal Zones and Sea Level Rise," pp. 5, 11.

8. After Anderson, et al, "Coastal Impact Underestimated from Rapid Sea Level Rise," pp. 205–212.

9. After Environmental Protection Agency, "Coastal Zones and Sea Level Rise," p. 27.

10. Carson, *The Edge of the Sea*, p. 125.

11. After Nicholls, et al, "Coastal systems and low-lying areas," pp. 328–329.

12. Environmental Protection Agency, "Coastal Zones and Sea Level Rise," p. 74.

13. After Environmental Protection Agency, "Coastal Zones and Sea Level Rise," p. 81.

14. After Woodworth, et al, "Introduction," in Church *Understanding Sea-Level Rise and Variability*, pp. 1, 3.

15. After Nicholls, "Impacts of and Responses to Sea-Level Rise," in Church, *Understanding Sea-Level Rise and Variability*, p. 34.

16. After IPCC, "Coastal systems and low-lying areas," p. 319.

17. After Griffith, "Potential Impacts of Sea Level Rise on Hilton Head Island, SC," p. 1.

18. After IPCC, "Coastal systems and low-lying areas," pp. 341, 344.

Chapter VII

1. There are many different lists of cities and countries that will be impacted by sea level rise. To use but one example: in 2005 the OECD said that the top 10 cities, in terms of exposed populations, were Mumbai, Guangzhou, Shanghai, Miami, Ho Chi Minh City, Kolkata, Greater New York, Osaka-Kobe, Alexandria, and New Orleans. The top 10 cities, in terms of assets exposed, were Miami, Greater New York, New Orleans, Osaka-Kobe, Tokyo, Amsterdam, Rotterdam, Nagoya, Tampa-St. Petersburg, and Virginia Beach. By the 2070s, the total population exposed could grow to around 150 million people due to the combined effects of climate change (i.e., sea level rise and increased storminess), subsidence, population growth, and urbanization. The asset exposure could grow even more dramatically. (Nicholls et al, "Ranking Port Cities with High Exposure and Vulnerability to Climate Extremes," p. 3.)

2. After Titus and Richman, "Maps of Lands Vulnerable to Sea Level Rise," p. 2.

3. After Insurance Information Institute (2008). "Third year anniversary of Hurricane Katrina — Value of insured coastal property by state."

4. Pilkey and Young, *The Rising Sea*," pp. 141, 143.

5. After IPCC, "Coastal systems and low-lying areas," p. 326.

6. After CoreLogic. "2011 Corelogic storm surge report: Residential exposure estimates of 10 U.S. cities," pp. 18, 22. http://www.corelogic.com/uploadedFiles/Pages/About/Us/ResearchTrends/CL_StormSurgeReport_2011.pdf.

7. King, "Rebuilding New Orleans," p. 3.

8. Blum and Roberts, "Drowning of the Mississippi Delta," p. 1.

9. Ibid.

10. Ibid," pp. 1, 2.

11. The following account is drawn from DeSoto-Duncan, et al, "'The Great Wall of Louisiana': Protecting the Coastline from Extreme Storm Surge and Sea Level Rise," pp. 1–12.

12. After Stanton and Ackerman, "Florida and Climate Change," p. 5.

13. After Pilkey and Young, *The Rising Sea*, p. 51. The emphasis on "minimal" is from their text.

14. See, for example, the City of Miami's Climate Action Plan (listed in the bibliography).

15. "Between the devil and the deep blue sea: Florida's unenviable position with respect to sea level rise," p. 1 of the abstract of the article.

16. Melville, *Moby Dick*, pp. 21–22.

17. After NASA, "NASA Looks at Sea Level Rise, Hurricane Risks to New York City," p. 2.

18. After Gornitz, "Sea Level Rise and Storm Hazards, New York City," p. 16.

19. New York City Panel on Climate Change, "Executive Summary of *Climate Change Adaptation in New York City*," p. 1.

20. After Lin, et al., "Physically based assessment of hurricane surge threat under climate change," p. 1.

21. Drawn from New York Department of Environmental Conservation, "Sea Level Rise Task Force," pp. 1–4, and from the Executive Summary of the Report, pp. 5–6.

22. Katsman, et al, "High-end climate change scenarios for flood protection of the Netherlands," p. 3. This quotation has been lightly edited.

23. Conrad, *Heart of Darkness*, p. 104.

24. Environment Agency, "The Thames Estuary," p. 1.

25. Ibid.

26. After Wikipedia, "Thames Barrier," pp. 1–6.

27. After Tol, et al, "Adaptation to Five Metres of Sea Level Rise," pp. 475–476.

28. Sources on Venice used in this section include Scearce, "Venice and the Environmental Hazards of Coastal Cities," pp. 1–9; Poggioli, "Venice Offers Lessons on Coping with Rising Seas," pp. 1–4; Keahey, "Weighing the Solutions," pp. 1–3; Carbognin, et al, "Global change and relative sea level rise at Venice," p. 1; and Pilkey and Young, *The Rising Sea*, pp. 21–22, 127.

29. Goodreads, "Thomas Mann quotes," p. 2.

30. After Imevbore, "Coastal Erosion in Lagos State," pp. 2–22

31. After Ozor, et al, "Sharing the Lagos Megacity Experience in the Integrated Management of Sea Level Rise and Flooding," p. 1.

32. Wikipedia, "Sea Level Rise," p. 7, citing Klaus Paehler, "Nigeria in the Dilemma of Climate Change."

33. After Fashae, et al, "Impact of Climate Change on Sea Level Rise in Lagos, Nigeria," p. 1.

34. After Nwilo, "Managing the Impacts of Storm Surges on Victoria Island, Lagos," p. 1.

35. After *Dredging Today*, "Nigeria: Lagos Expansion Into Atlantic Ocean," pp. 2–4.

36. Adapted from a private communication of 14 December 2011 from Brent Saddler.

37. After Nicholls, et al, "Regional Issues Raised by Sea-Level Rise and their Policy Implications," p. 12.

38. After International Association for Impact Assessment, "Impact of Sea Level Rise on the Nigerian Coast," p. 3.

39. After Pilkey and Young, *The Rising Sea*, p. 118.

40. After Davis, "Sea Level Rise Threatens Nile Delta Ecosystems and Livelihoods," pp. 1–2, and after Elsharkawy, et al, "Climate Change: The Impacts of Sea Level Rise on Egypt," pp. 1–9.

41. After "Climate Change: Alexandria — Egypt," p. 5.

42. Many of the following comments are drawn from Costa et al, "Vulnerability and impacts related to the rising sea level in the Metropolitan

Center of Recife, Northeast Brazil" or from Boori et al, "A remote sensing and GIS-based approach for climate change and adaptation due to sea-level rise and hazards in Apodi-Mossoro estuary, Northeast Brazil."

43. After Costa, et al, "Vulnerability and Impacts Related to the Rising Sea Level in the Metropolitan Center of Recife, Northeast Brazil," p. 344.

44. Costa, et al, "Vulnerability and Impacts Related to the Rising Sea Level in the Metropolitan Center of Recife, Northeast Brazil," p. 347.

45. After Boori, et al, "A Remote Sensing and GIS-Based Approach for Climate Change and Adaptation Policy Due to Sea Level Rise and Hazards in Apodi-Mossoro Estuary, Northeast Brazil," pp. 22–24.

Chapter VIII

1. Some of the information in this discussion is drawn from Wikipedia, "San Francisco Bay," pp. 1–10, and Wikipedia, "Hydraulic Mining," pp. 1–5.

2. After San Francisco Bay Conservation and Development Commission, "Why BCDC is considering amendments to the San Francisco Bay Plan to address sea level rise," p. 1.

3. San Francisco Bay Conservation and Development Commission, "San Francisco Bay Scenarios for Sea Level Rise Index Map," p. 1.

4. After Weeks, "In San Francisco Bay, A Question Whether to Build or Retreat," pp. 1–3.

5. Sea level rise could severely affect operations at Oakland International Airport. The 2,600 acres on which the airport is located have a maximum elevation of only 9 feet (2.7 meters) above mean sea level. During high tides and winter storms, the three runways of the airport's North Field already experience flooding during high tides and winter storms. The dike protecting the South Field was built in the late 1950s and now requires repairs and upgrading to continue to serve its function. (Pacific Council on International Policy, "Preparing for the Effects of Climate Change — A Strategy for California," p. 18.)

6. Pacific Council on International Policy, "Preparing for the Effects of Climate Change — A Strategy for California," p. 4.

7. After Gleick, "Socioeconomic Impacts of Sea Level Rise in the Bay Area and Addressing Environmental Justice," p. 1.

8. After CNA, "National Security and the Threat of Climate Change," p. 16 (citing Gleick et al, *Assessing the Costs of Adapting to Sea Level Rise: A Case Study of San Francisco Bay.* April 18,1990.)

9. After Kahn, "San Francisco Bay Area Enacts Sea-Level Rise Policy," pp. 1–2.

10. After Heberger, et al, "Potential impacts of increased coastal flooding in California due to sea-level rise," p. 19.

11. After Revell, et al, "A Methodology for Predicting Future Coastal Hazards Due to Sea-Level Rise on the California Coast," p. 22.

12. National Intelligence Council, "China: The Impact of Climate Change to 2030," pp. 1, 2.

13. It should be understood that using a yardstick of 10 meters *does not imply* that sea level will reach this point any time soon. Rather, it is a useful shorthand measurement which can easily be applied to many coasts of the world, no matter what their exact topography.

14. After Balk, et al, "Coastal Demography: Distribution, Composition, and Dynamics," pp. 2–3.

15. After Mee, "Life on the edge: managing our coastal zones," p. 186.

16. Different sources give different figures for the length of the Chinese coast. The figure used here is from the Central Intelligence Agency's *World Factbook.*

17. After Zhongyuan Chen, et al, "Sea-Level Rise on Eastern China's Yangtze Delta," p. 365.

18. National Coordination Committee on Climate Change, "Initial National Communication on Climate Change," pp. 61–62. This quote has been lightly edited.

19. Wang Qian, "Rise in Sea Level Reaches Record High," p. 1.

20. After Lau, "Adaptation to Sea-Level Rise in the People's Republic of China," p. 10. (These losses were calculated at a price level current in 2000.)

21. Quoted by Lao, "Adaptation to Sea-Level Rise in the People's Republic of China," p. 14. The reference to the sword of Damocles evokes a situation of impending doom, when the danger is (or at least should be) visible to any intelligent observer and is very close at hand.

22. Yin, et al, "Multiple Scenario Analyses Forecasting the Confounding Impacts of Sea Level Rise and Tides from Storm-Induced Coastal Flooding in the City of Shanghai, China," p. 6.

23. After Gillet, "Vietnam's Rice Bowl Threatened by Rising Seas," p. 1.

24. After Pilkey and Young, *The Rising Sea,* pp. 132–133.

25. Delta Cities Website, "Ho Chi Minh City," p. 1.

26. Ibid, p. 2.

27. Ibid.

28. Haiphong Portal, 26 September 2010. The Vietnamese statements have been lightly edited.

29. Pham S. Liem, "Vietnam Coastal Cities and Potential Impacts of Sea Level Rise," pp. 1–2.

30. Bangkok State of the Environment 2001, "Land Subsidence," p. 1.

31. Ghosh, "Bangkok Sinking," p. 1.

32. Ibid.

33. After Somboon, "A Sea-Level Rise in the Super-Interglacial Age: Its Geomorphic Impacts on the Low-Lying Areas of Bangkok Metropolis," p. 255.

34. After Dutta, "An Integrated Tool for

Assessment of Flood Vulnerability of Coastal Cities to Sea-level Rise and Potential Socioeconomic Impacts: A Case Study of Bangkok, Thailand," p. 1.

35. After Adger, et al, "Unique and Valued Places," pp. 132–133.

36. "Tuvalu and Global Warming," p. 1.

37. Quoted in Wikipedia, "Kiribati," p. 1.

38. See Chen, et al, "Climate change, sea level rise and rice: global market implications," p. 1.

39. After Nicholls, et al, Executive Summary of "Ranking of the World's Cities Most Exposed to Coastal Flooding Today and in the Future," p. 4.

40. After APEC Virtual Center for Environmental Technology Exchange, p. 2.

41. After IPCC, AR4 WGII, Chapter 11: Australia and New Zealand — 11.ES Executive Summary, p. 1.

42. After Edwards, "Planning for sea-level rise in South Australian Communities," pp. 4, 9–10.

43. After Kuhn, et al, "Visualizing the spatial extent of predicted coastal zone inundation due to sea level rise in south-west Western Australia," p. 1.

44. After Ministry for the Environment, "Adapting to sea-level rise," p. 1.

45. After IPCC, AR4 WGII, Chapter 11: Australia and New Zealand — 11.ES Executive Summary, p. 1.

Chapter IX

1. After Church, et al, "Sea-level Rise and Vulnerable Coastal Populations," p. 1.

2. After Titus, "Greenhouse Effect, Sea Level Rise, and Land Use," p. 12.

3. UNEP/GRID chart.

4. Wikipedia, "Bengal Tiger," p. 3.

5. Wikipedia, "Sundarbans," p. 6.

6. Mohal, et al, "Impact of Sea Level Rise on Coastal River of Bangladesh," p. 1.

7. After Puthucherril, "Operationalising Integrated Coastal Zone Management and Adapting to Sea Level Rise through Coastal Law: Where Does India Stand?," p. 44.

8. Quoted by Kadapa-Bose, "Climate is Changing, But Mumbai is Not," p. 2.

9. After Pavri, "Urban Expansion and Sea-Level Rise Related Flood Vulnerability for Mumbai (Bombay), India Using Remotely Sensed Data," p. 1.

10. After Kumar, "Economic impact of climate change on Mumbai, India," p. 1. Italics added.

11. After Nicholls and Poh Poh Wong, "Coastal Systems and low-lying areas," p. 325.

12. WSF-World Wide Fund for Nature, "Mega-Stress for Mega-Cities," p. 17.

13. Basu, "Sea and storm scare for city," p. 1.

14. IPCC, "Coastal Systems and Low-Lying Areas: Climate and sea-level scenarios," Section 6.3.2.

15. Most of this section is drawn from Wikipedia, "New Moore/South Talpatti," pp. 1–3.

16. BBC, "Disputed Bay of Bengal island 'vanishes,'" pp. 1–2.

17. Quoted in Pilkey and Young, *The Rising Sea*, pp. 20–21.

18. Church, et al, "Sea-level Rise at tropical Pacific and Indian Ocean islands," p. 22.

19. Tirone, "Maldives' disappearing coast prompts appeal to UN space agency," p. 1.

20. In a 2011 report, the IPCC reported that "Small island states in the Pacific, Indian, and Atlantic oceans, often with low elevation, are particularly vulnerable to rising sea levels and impacts such as erosion, inundation, shoreline change, and saltwater intrusion into coastal aquifers. These impacts can result in ecosystem disruption, decreased agricultural productivity, changes in disease patterns, economic losses such as in tourism industries, and population displacement — all of which reinforce vulnerability to extreme weather events." (Source: IPCC, "IPCC SREX Summary for Policymakers," p. 26.)

21. "Maldives Government Holds Underwater Cabinet Meeting," pp. 1–2.

22. After Kwek, "Indonesia Mulls New Capital as Jakarta Sinks," p. 1.

23. Quoted by Kwek, "Indonesia Mulls New Capital as Jakarta Sinks," pp. 1–2.

24. Abidin, et al, "Land Subsidence and Urban Development in Jakarta," p. 16.

25. After Guriro, "Large Portion of Lower Sindh, Including Karachi, Faces Inundation Threat," p. 1.

26. After Inam, et al, "Natural and Man-Made Stresses on the Stability of Indus Deltaic Eco Region," p. 8.

27. After Khan, et al, "Sea Level Variations and Geomorphological Changes in the Coastal Belt of Pakistan," pp. 159–174.

Chapter X

1. After Pilkey and Young, *The Rising Sea*, p. 74.

2. Wikipedia, in its "West Antarctic Ice Sheet" article, sourced this Hansen quote to Jonathan Leake and Jonathan Milne, "Focus: the Climate of Fear," http://www.timesonline.co.uk/tol/news/uk/article732472.ece, *The Sunday Times — Britain*, February 6, 2006.

3. Gomez, et al, "Sea Level as a Stabilizing Factor for Marine-Ice-Sheet Grounding Lines," p. 850. Italics added.

4. After Bamber, et al, "Reassessment of the Potential Sea-Level Rise from a Collapse of the West Antarctic Ice Sheet," p. 901.

5. Some of the information used here regarding the Pine Island Glacier was drawn from Joughin, et al, "Sensitivity of 21st Sea Level to Ocean-Induced Thinning of Pine Island Glacier, Antarctica," pp. 1–5.

6. Private communication of 16 August 2011 from Dr. Robert Bindschadler.

7. Joughin, et al, "Sensitivity of 21st Sea Level

to Ocean-Induced Thinning of Pine Island Glacier, Antarctica," pp. 1, 5.

8. After Jacobs, et al, "Stronger Ocean circulation and Increased Melting Under Pine Island Glacial Ice Shelf," pp. 1–5.

9. See Antarctic Treaty Meeting of Experts, "The Future of the West Antarctic Ice Sheet: Observed and Predicted Changes, Tipping Points, and Policy Considerations."

10. Dr. Jerry X. Mitrovica, et al. made an interesting point in their 2008 article, "The Sea-Level Fingerprint of West Antarctic Collapse," p. 753. They noted: "The rapid melting of ice sheets and glaciers leads to a sea-level change that departs dramatically from the assumption of a uniform redistribution of meltwater. An ice sheet exerts a gravitational attraction on the nearby ocean and thus draws water toward it. If the ice sheet melts, this attraction will be reduced, and water will migrate away from the ice sheet. The net effect, despite the increase in the total volume of the oceans after a melting event, is that the sea level will actually fall within ~2000 km of the collapsing ice sheet and progressively increase as one moves further from this region." This fact means that a WAIS collapse might result in a sea level rise near Washington, D.C. of 4.2 feet (1.3 meters) above what standard sea-level theory predicts. If so, the total rise there could be as much as 20.3 feet (6.3 meters).

11. After Potsdam Institute for Climate Research, "Researchers refine assessment of tipping elements of the climate system," p. 1.

12. In their 2002 study (see bibliography) on "Risk Estimation of Collapse of the West Antarctic Ice Sheet," Vaughan and Spouge listed (on p. 65) 11 estimates, published between 1968 and 1998, on the amount of time needed for a WAIS collapse. These estimates ranged from 50 years to 50,000 years.

13. Much of this section is drawn from the West Antarctic Ice Sheet Divide Ice Core: A Guide for the Media and Public," pp. 1–14.

14. The comments below are taken, nearly verbatim, from Katz and Worster, "Stability of Ice-Sheet Grounding Lines," p. 1597, and from private communications from Dr. Katz.

Chapter XI

1. Some of the following information is drawn from Wikipedia, "Greenland Ice Sheet," pp. 1–8.

2. Wikipedia, "Greenland Ice Sheet," p. 1, citing the IPCC's Third Assessment Report.

3. After Pollack, *A World Without Ice*, p. 237.

4. After Archer and Rahmstorf, *Climate Crisis*, p. 73.

5. After Pollack, *A World Without Ice*, p. 120.

6. After Velicogna, et al, "Increasing Rates of Ice Mass Loss from the Greenland and Antarctic Ice Sheets Revealed by GRACE."

7. Rignot, et al, "Acceleration of the Contribution of the Greenland and Antarctic Ice Sheets to Sea Level Rise," pp. L05502, L05503.

8. After Schmidt, "Under and Over the Ice," p. 2.

9. Steffen, "Cryospheric Contributions to Sea-Level Rise and Variability," p. 212.

10. After Zwallly, "Greenland Ice Sheet Mass Balance," p. 1.

11. After Price, et al, "Committed Sea-Level Rise for the Next Century from Greenland Ice Sheet Dynamics During the Past Decade," p. 5.

Chapter XII

1. Wikipedia, "Cnut the Great," p. 1.

2. This account draws from Wikipedia, "Flood Control in the Netherlands," pp. 1–8; Wikipedia, "Water board (Netherlands)," pp. 1–5; and Deltacommissie, "Working together with water," pp. 1–98.

3. Much of the historical and hydraulic engineering background information used in this chapter is drawn from Janin and van Eil, *Culture Shock: Netherlands*, pp. 4–16.

4. Quoted by Janin and van Eil in *Culture Shock: Netherlands*, p. 4.

5. After Wikipedia, "Flood Control in the Netherlands," and "Water Board (Netherlands)."

6. Some of the following comments in this section are drawn from Schouwenaars, "Adaptation of Polder Systems to Sea Level Rise and Land Subsidence in Fryslan in the Period 1000–2000," p. 1.

7. After Wikipedia, "Delta works," pp. 1–7.

8. Much of the information on the Maeslant Storm Surge Barrier was kindly provided by Emma van den Bosch of the Water Information Center in Hook van Holland in a private communication of 18 October 2011.

9. Deltacommissie, "Working with Water," pp. 12–13.

10. Deltacommissie, "Working together with Water," p. 10. Italics added.

11. U.S. Climate Change Science Program, "Coastal Sensitivity to Sea-Level Rise: A Focus on the Mid-Atlantic Region."

12. Most of the following comments have been drawn from (sometimes nearly verbatim) from the U.S. Climate Change Science Program's 2009 study, "Coastal Sensitivity to Sea-Level Rise," e.g., especially from pp. XIII, 105, 140, 156, 157, 159, 163, 179–180, 179–180, 185.

13. After Titus, "Sea Level Rise," p. 118.

Chapter XIII

1. Some of these following comments are drawn from Vellinga, et al, "Exploring high-end climate change scenarios for flood protection of the Netherlands: International Scientific Assessment," p. 12.

2. After UNEP, "Impact of sea level rise in Bangladesh," p. 1.

3. After Wikipedia, "Mekong Delta," p. 3, citing VietnamNetbrige.

4. After Hoa, et al, "The Combined Impact on the Flooding in Vietnam's Mekong River Delta of Local Man-Made Structures, Sea Level Rise, and Dams Upstream in the River Catchment,," pp. 1, 116.

5. After *The Bridge*, "Environmentally Induced Migration," pp. 1–2.

6. After *The Bridge*, "Environmentally Induced Migration," p. 1.

7. After UNEP, "Potential Impact of Sea Level Rise: Nile Delta," p. 1.

8. After UNEP, "Potential Impact of Sea Level Rise: Nile Delta — Maps and Graphics at UNEP/GRID-Arendal," p. 2.

9. After IPCC Climate Change 2007, "Synthesis Report," pp. 50–52.

10. The following comments are drawn (sometimes verbatim) and edited from Bromirski et al, "Dynamical Suppression of Sea Level Rise Along the Pacific Coast of North America: Indications for Imminent Acceleration," pp. 1–2, 17–18.

11. This section draws heavily from Weiss, et al, "Implications of Recent Sea Level Rise Science for Low-Elevation Areas in Coastal Cities of the Coterminous U.S.A," pp. 1–9.

12. A 2011 study of Washington, D.C. by Dr. Bilal Ayyub et al. (see bibliography) estimated that a sea level rise there of only 3.2 feet (1 meter) would cause damages assessed at $4.2 billion dollars. This estimate does not fully cover damage to coastal improvements and commercial facilities.

13. For these maps, see Weiss, et al, "Implications of Recent Sea Level Rise Science for Low-Elevation Areas in Coastal Cities of the Coterminous U.S.A." pp. 5, 7, 12.

14. Some of the points made in this section are drawn from The National Academies, "Abrupt Climate Change: Inevitable Surprises," pp. 1–4.

15. The National Academies, "Abrupt Climate Change: Inevitable Surprises," pp. 3–4. Italics added.

16. See Katsman, et al, "Exploring High-End Scenarios for Local Sea Level Rise to Develop Flood Protection Strategies for a Low-Lying Delta — the Netherlands as an Example."

17. After Krishnamurthy, "Are We Witnessing the Rise of the Environmental Migrant," p. 5.

18. Wikipedia, "Current sea level rise," p. 7, citing the April 2007 issue of *Environment and Urbanization.*

19. See Wikipedia, "Carteret Islands," pp. 1–4, and Global Greenhouse Warming.com, "Carteret Atoll," pp. 1–3.

20. After a private communication of 2 May 2011 from Krishna Krishnamurthy, a consultant on disaster risk reduction and environmental security.

21. After Curtis, et al, "Understanding the demographic implications of climate change: estimates of localized population predictions under future scenarios of sea-level rise," pp. 1–2.

22. CNA Corporation, "National Security and the Threat of Climate Change," pp. 1, 16, 37.

23. Maybe, et al, "Degrees of Risk: Defining a Risk Management Framework for Climate Security," p. 8.

24. Many of the points made in this section are drawn from Houghton, et al, "Maritime Boundaries in a Rising Sea," pp. 813–816.

25. Houghton et al, "Maritime Boundaries in a Rising Sea," p. 1, citing Caron, D.D., *Ecol. Law Quart.*, 17, 621–653 (1990).

Chapter XIV

1. Personal communication of 9 November 2011 from Dr. Richard Alley.

2. Levitus, S., J. I. Antonov, T. P. Boyer, and C. Stephens (2000), Warming of the world ocean, Science, 287, 2225–2229.

3. Levitus, S., J. Antonov, T. Wang et al. (2001), Anthropogenic warming of Earth's climate system, Science, 292, 267–270.

4. Personal communication of 8 July 2011 from Dr. Peter Wadhams.

5. Personal communication of 11 July 2011 from Dr. Marci Robinson.

6. Personal communication of 9 November 2011 from Dr. Richard Alley.

7. Personal communication of 11 July 2011 from Dr. Marci Robinson.

8. Personal communication of 8 July 2011 from Dr. Peter Wadhams.

9. Personal communication of 9 November 2011 from Dr. Richard Alley.

Chapter XV

1. Some of the points made here are drawn from Wikipedia, "Flood Myth," p. 1.

2. See Rahmstorf, "2000 Years of Sea Level (+ updates)," pp. 1–5.

3. This section is drawn from *Science Daily*, "Fastest Sea-Level Rise in 2,000 Years Linked to Increasing Global Temperatures, p. 1; Kemp, et al, "Climate Related Sea-Level Variations over the Past Two Millennia," pp. 11017–11022; and Rahmstorf, "2000 Years of Sea Level (+updates)," pp. 1–5.

4. After Nicholls, "Planning for the Impacts of Sea Level Rise," p. 149.

5. After Nicolls, et al, "Sea-Level Rise and its Possible Impacts Given a 'Beyond 4_C World' in the Twenty-First Century," pp. 169 ff.

6. After Nicholls, et al, "Sea-Level Rise and its Possible Impacts Given a 'Beyond 4_C World' in the Twenty-First Century," p. 172.

7. After Nicholls, et al, "Sea-Level Rise and its Possible Impacts Given a 'Beyond 4_C World' in the Twenty-First Century," p. 176.

8. Bsyravan and Rajan, "The Ethical Implications of Sea-Level Rise due to Climate Change," p. 239.

9. Adapted from Gardiner, *A Perfect Moral Storm: The Ethical Tragedy of Climate Change.*

10. Some of the points in the following account are drawn from Wikipedia, "Black swan theory," p. 2, and from Taleb, "The Black Swan: The Impact of the Highly Improbable," pp. 1–5.

11. After Taleb, "The Black Swan: The Impact of the Highly Improbable," p. 1.

12. Some of the following points are drawn from Kousky, et al, "Responding to Threats of Climate Change Mega-Catastrophes," pp. 1–5.

13. These comments are drawn from an private communication from Dr. Scambos of 9 September 2011.

14. Nicholls et al. "International Dimensions of Climate Change. R.6:1: The Implications for the UK of the Impacts of Climate Change and Sea-level Rise on Critical Coastal Infrastructure Overseas," pp. 6–7.

15. Quoted in *Science Daily*, "Rising Oceans: Too Late to Turn the Tide?," p. 2.

Chapter XVI

1. After Grannis, "Adaptation Tool Kit: Sea-Level Rise and Coastal Land Use," pp. 1–4.

2. Cazenave, et al. "The Challenge for Measuring Sea Level Rise and Regional and Global Trends," pp. 1–2, 14.

3. Cazenave, et al, "The Challenge for Measuring Sea Level Rise and Regional and Global Trends," p. 2. Italics added.

4. Hallegatte, "SR17: The economic Growth Impact of Sea-Level Rise," p. 16.

5. Hallegatte,, "A Framework to Investigate the Economic Growth Impact of Sea Level Rise," p. 5.

6. Private communication from Dr. John Church of 24 October 2011.

Appendix 1

1. Broder, "Climate Talks End With Modest Deal on Emissions," p. 1.

2. After Broder, "Climate Talks End With Modest Deal on Emissions," p. 2.

3. Broder, "In Glare of Climate Talks, Taking On Too Great a Task," pp. 1–2.

Appendix 2

1. These comments have been drawn from a private communication of 22 February 2011 from Dr. Richard Edwing.

Appendix 3

1. After SimCLIM, "Extreme Event Analysis," pp. 1–2.

Appendix 4

1. Much of the information used in this chapter is drawn from Wikipedia, "Breakwater," and/or from Esteban et al, "Sea Level Rise and the Increase of Rubble Mound Breakwater Damage."

2. Esteban et al, "Sea Level Rise and the Increase in Rubble Mound Breakwater Damage," p. 12.

Appendix 5

1. See Olsthoorn et al, "Neo-Atlantis: Dutch Responses to Five Meter Sea Level Rise," pp. 1–20.

Appendix 6

1. Some of the points made in this appendix are drawn from two studies by Gutierrez et al: "A Bayesian Network to Predict Coastal Vulnerability to Sea Level Rise," and "A Bayesian Network to Predict Vulnerability to Sea-Level Rise: Data Report."

2. After Wikipedia, "Thomas Bayes," pp. 1–2.

3. For a Bayesian network in use, see Kemp, et al, "Climate Related Sea-Level Variations Over the Past Two Millennia," pp. 11017, 11019.

Bibliography

Abidin, Hasanuddin Z., et al. "Land Subsidence and Urban Development in Jakarta (Indonesia)." www.fig.net/pub/vietnam/papers/ts06f/ts06f_abidin_etal_3491.pdf. Accessed 7 November 2010.

Adger, W. Neil, Jon Barnett, and Heidi Ellemor. "Unique and Valued Places." In Schneider, et al. *Climate Change Science and Policy*, 131–138. Washington, D.C.: Island Press, 2010.

"Adjustable adaptation." Editorial in *Nature Geoscience*, 2, 447 (2009). http://www.nature.con/ngeo/journal/v2/n7/full/ngeo 576.html. Accessed 20 June 2010.

Agrawala, Shardul, et al. Executive Summary of "Development and Climate Change in Egypt: Focus on Coastal Resources and the Nile." Environment Directorate, Environment Policy Committee, Working Party of Global and Structural Policies & Working Party on Development Co-operation and Environment, Organisation for Economic Co-operation and Development. Document COM/ENV/DCD/AC(2004)1/FINAL.

Airhart, Marc. "The Future of the West Antarctic Ice Sheet: Exploring Ice Thickness and Global Climate Change." http://geology.com/research/west-antarctic-ice-sheet. html. Accessed 10 December 2010.

Alexander, Kim S., et al. "Managed Retreat of Coastal Communities: Understanding Responses to Projected Sea Level Rise." Socio-Economics and the Environment in Discussion. CSIRO Working Paper Series 2010–06. January 2011. ISSN: 1834–5638.

Ali, A. "Vulnerability of Bangladesh to Climate Change and Sea Level Rise through Tropical Cyclones and Storm Surges." http:www.springerlink.com/content/1842 n0822t6077qO/. Accessed 14 May 2011.

Alley, Richard B. "The Role of Warming in Melting Ice and Sea-Level Rise, and the Possibility of Abrupt Climate Changes." Testimony for the hearing entitled "A Rational Discussion of Climate Change: The Science, the Evidence, the Response," a hearing held by the Subcommittee on Energy and Environment, House Committee on Science and Technology, U.S. House of Representatives, 17 November 2010.

Alley, Richard B., et al. "Ice-Sheet and Sea-Level Changes." *Science*, 21 October 2005, 456–460.

_____. "Understanding Glacier Flow in Changing Times." www.sciencemag.org. Accessed 13 November 2008.

Allison, I., et al. "Ice Sheet Mass Balance and Sea Level." *Antarctic Science* 21 (5), 413–426, (2009).

Anderegg, William R.L., et al. "Expert Credibility in Climate Change." *Proceedings of the National Academy of Sciences*. www.pnas.org/cgi/doi/10.1073/pnas.1003187107. Accessed 1 August 2010.

Anderson, J., et al. "Coastal Impact Underestimated from Rapid Sea Level Rise." *EOS, Transactions of the American Geophysical Union*, vol. 91, no. 23, 8 June 2010, 205–212.

Antarctic and Southern Ocean Coalition [ASOC]. "The Future of the West Antarctic Ice Sheet: Observed and Predicted Changes, Tipping Points, and Policy Considerations." Antarctic Treaty Meeting of Experts, 6–9 April 2010. Svolvaer, Norway. Agenda Item ATME 3, ATME 4, ATME 6. Presented by ASOC. Accessed 14 November 2010.

"Antarctic Circumpolar Current. " In *Introduction of Physical Oceanography*, Chapter 13.4. http://oceanworld.tamu.edu/resources/ocng_textbook/chapter13/chapter13_04.htm. Accessed 18 December 2010.

APEC Virtual Center for Environmental Technology Exchange. "What Results from Global Warming?" http://www.epcc.pref.osaka.jp/apec/eng/earth/global_warming/dounaru.html. Accessed 7 March 2011.

Arcadis, Deltares, Alterra-Wageningen University, and San Francisco Bay Conservation and Development Commission. "San Francisco Bay: Preparing for the Next Level." 21 September 2009.

Archer, David, and Stefan Rahmstorf. *The Climate Crisis: An Introductory Guide to Climate Change.* Cambridge: Cambridge University Press, 2010.

Armstrong, Thomas. "U.S. Climate Change Science Program: Synthesis and Assessment Report 3.4." U.S. Geological Survey, Reston, VA. http://downloads.climatescience.gov/sap/sap3-4/s. Accessed 4 September 2011.

Australian Government Bureau of Meteorology. "Storm Surge Preparedness and Safety." http:www/bom.gov.au/info/cyclone/storm_surge/storm_surge.shtml. Accessed 27 February 2011.

Ayyub, Bilal M., et al. "Prediction and Impact of Sea Level Rise on Properties and Infrastructure of Washington, D.C." *Risk Analysis*, 28 October 2011, doi: 10/1111/j1539-6924.2011.01710. Accessed 1 November 2011.

_____. "Towards the Development of Regional Risk Profiles and Adaptation Measures for Sea Level Rise." *Journal of Risk Analysis and Crisis Response*, vol. 1, no. 1 (July 2011), 75–88. Accessed 9 August 2011.

Balk, Deborah et al. "Coastal Demography: Distribution, Composition, and Dynamics." New York: CUNY Institute for Demographic Research, 27 January 2011.

_____. "Understanding the Impacts of Climate Change: Linking Satellite and Other Spacial Data with Population Data." *Population Dynamics and Climate Change.* United Nations Population Fund: International Institute for Environment and Development, 2009.

Ballu, Valérie, et al. "Comparing the Role of Absolute Sea-level Rise and Vertical Tectonic Motions in Coastal Flooding, Torres Islands (Vanuatu)." http://www.pnas.org/content/early/2022/07/19/11024842108.short. Accessed 2 August 2011.

Bamber, Jonathan L,. et al. "Reassessment of the Potential Sea-level Rise from a Collapse of the West Antarctic Ice Sheet." *Science*, vol. 324, 15 May 2009, 901–903.

Bangkok State of the Environment 2001. "Land Subsidence." www.rrcap.unep.org/reports.../bangkok_land.pdf. Accessed 28 December 2011.

Basu, Jayanta. "Sea and Storm Scare for City." *The Telegraph* (Calcutta), 12 November 2009. http://www.telegraphindia.com/1091112/jsp/calcutta/story_11728531.jsp. Accessed 2 November 2010.

BBC. "Disputed Bay of Bengal Island 'Vanishes.'" http://news.bbc.co.uk/2hi/8584665.stm. Accessed 2 November 2010.

Blum, Michael D., and Harry H. Roberts. "Drowning of the Mississippi Delta Due to Insufficient Sediment Supply and Global Sea-level Rise." www.nature.com/naturegeoscience. Accessed 28 June 2009.

Boori, Mukesh Singh, et al. "A Remote Sensing and GIS-based Approach for Climate Change and Adaptation Due to Sea Level Rise and Hazards in Apodi-Mossoro Estuary, Northeast Brazil." *International Journal of Plant, Animal and Environmental Sciences*, vol. 1, issue 1: March-May 2011, 14–25. www.ijpages.com. Accessed 30 April 2011.

The Bridge [a quarterly review on European integration]. "Environmentally Induced Migration: Sea Level Rise in the Mekong River Delta in Vietnam." http://www.bridge-mag.com/mageazine/index.php?option=com_content&task=Viet&id=516. Accessed 9 May 2011.

Broder, John M. "Climate Talks End with Modest Deal on Emissions." *New York Times.* http://nytimes.com/2010/12/12/science/earth/12climate.html?hp=&pagewanted=print. Accessed 11 December 2010.

_____. "In Glare of Climate Talks, Taking On Too Great a Task." *New York Times.* http://www.nytimes.com/2011/12/11/science/earth/climate-change-expands-far-beyond-a... Accessed 11 December 2011.

Bromirski, Peter D., et al. "Dynamical Suppression of Sea Level Rise Along the Pacific Coast of North America: Indications for Imminent Acceleration." *Journal of Geophysical Research — Oceans*, 2 March 2011. Accessed 5 May 2011.

Burkett, Virginia R., et al. "Sea-level Rise and

Subsidence: Implications for Flooding in New Orleans, Louisiana." www.nwrc. usgs.gov/hurricane/Sea-Level-Rise.pdf. Accessed 10 September 2010.

Byravan, Sujatha, and Sudhir Chella Rajan. "The Ethical Implications of Sea-level Rise Due to Climate Change."

Carbognin, Laura, et al. "Global change and Relative Sea Level Rise at Venice: What Impact in Terms of Flooding?" http://www.springerlink.com/content/f1210 75417614286/. Accessed 6 October 2010.

_____. "Relative Sea Level Rise at Venice, Italy." Geological Society of America. http://gsa.confex.com/gsa/2008AM/final-program/abstract_146406.htm. Accessed 6 October 2010.

Carlson, Rachel. The Edge of the Sea. New York: Mariner Books, 1998.

Carmen, Commander Herbert E., et al. "Broadening Horizons: Climate Change and the U.S. Armed Forces." Washington, D.C.: Center for a New American Security, April 2010.

Carnegie Council for Ethics in International Affairs. Ethics and International Affairs, 24. no. 3 (2010), 239–60.

Carroll, Rebecca. "Mississippi River Delta to 'Drown' by 2100?" http://news.nationalgeographic.com/news/2009/06/090 629-mississippi-river-sea-levels-html. Accessed 11 September 2010.

Cazenave, Anny, et al. "Contemporary Sea Level Rise." Annual Review of Maritime Science. 2:145–73, 2010.

_____. "The Challenge for Measuring Sea Level Rise and Regional and Global Trends." A plenary paper based on community white papers submitted to OceanObs09. Accessed 18 August 2011.

Chand, Pritam, et al. "Shoreline Change and Sea Level Rise Along the Coast of Bhitarkanika Wildlife Sanctuary, Orissa [India]: An Analytical Approach of Remote Sensing and Statistical Techniques." International Journal of Geomatics and Geosciences, vol. 1, no. 3, 2010, 436–455.

Chen, Chi-Chung, et al. "Climate Change, Sea Level Rise and Rice: Global Market Implications." Climate Change. DIO:10.1007/s10584–0ll-0074–0. Accepted for publication 5 April 2011. Accessed 26 April 20ll.

Chen, Zhongyuan, and Daniel Jean Stanley. "Sea-level Rise on Eastern China's Yangtze Delta." Journal of Coastal Research, vol. 14, no. 1, 1998, 360–366. Accessed 24 October 2010.

Chini, Nicolas, et al. Abstract of "The Impact of Sea Level Rise and Climate Change on Inshore Wave Climate: A Case Study for East Anglia (UK)." http:www.science direct.com/science?_ob+ArticleURL&_udi=B6VCX-50JPS3D-1&use." Accessed 27 July 2010.

_____. "Climate Change and Sea Level Implication on Coastal Wave Overtopping." Internal Seminar Series 2011, March 30, 2011. George Begg Building, Room B8, 15:00. School of MACE. University of Manchester. http://cfd.mace.manchester.ac.uk/twkiki/pub/cfd. Accessed 26 March 2011.

Church, John, et al. "Briefing: A Post-IPCC AR4 Update on Sea-level Rise." Antarctic Climate & Ecosystems Cooperative Research Centre. www.acecrc.org.au. Accessed 25 August 2011.

_____. "Changes in Sea Level." http://hdl.handle.net/10013/epic.15081. Accessed 12 February 2011.

_____. "Ice and Sea-level Change." http://www.unep.org/geo/geo_ice/PDF/Geo_C6_6_LowRes_pdf. Accessed 29 October 2011.

_____. "Ocean Temperature and Salinity Contributions to Global and Regional Sea-Level Change." In Understanding Sea-Level Rise and Variability, by John Church, et al., 143–176. Chichester, UK: Wiley-Blackwell, 2010.

_____. "Sea-level Rise and Variability—Synthesis and Outlook for the Future." In Understanding Sea-Level Rise and Variability, by John Church, et al., 402–416. Chichester, UK: Wiley-Blackwell, 2010.

_____. "Sea-level Rise and Vulnerable Coastal Populations." A paper partly funded by the Australian Climate Change Science Program. Accessed 4 March 2011.

_____. "Sea-level Rise at Tropical Pacific and Indian Ocean Islands." Global and Planetary Change. Submitted December 2005.

_____. "Sea-Level Rise from the Late 19th to the Early 21st Century." Surveys in Geophysics, doi: 10.1007/s10712–011–9110–1. Published online 30 March 2011. Accessed 8 August 2011.

_____. "The Changing Oceans." http:www.sciencemag.org/cgi/content/full/328/

5985/1453?ijkey=juCXkL2vilUg&keyty. Accessed 20 June 20, 2010.

_____. "Understanding Global Sea Levels: Past, Present and Future." *Sustainability Science*, 2008, vol. 3, no. 1, 9–22

City of Miami. "City of Miami Climate Action Plan." www.miamigov.com/msi/pages/Climate%20 Action/MiPlan%20 Final%. Accessed 18 September 2010.

"Climate Change: Alexandria — Egypt." Briefing notes, July 5, 2007. www.switch urbanwater.eu.../CALE_BRN_Climate_ca hange_and_water_management_Alexandria.pdf. Accessed 17 October 2010.

Climate Institute. "Oceans & Sea Level Rise." www.climate.org/topics/sea-level/index.html. Accessed 26 March 2011.

CNA Corporation. "National Security and the Threat of Climate Change." Alexandria, Virginia, 2007.

Coastal Wiki. "Effect of Climate Change on Coastline Evolution." www.coastalwiki.org/coastalwiki/Effect_of_climate_change_on_coastline_evolution. Accessed 16 May 2010.

Collilieux, Xavier, and Guy Wöppelmann. "Global Sea-level Rise and its Relation to Terrestrial Reference Frame." Springer-Verlag 2010. Accessed 12 October 2010.

Conrad, Joseph. *Heart of Darkness and Other Tales,* Oxford: Oxford University Press, 1992.

CoreLogic. 2011 CoreLogic storm surge report: "Residential Storm-surge Exposure Estimates for 10 U.S. Cities." http://www.corelogic.cvom/uploadedFiles/Pages/About/Us/ResearchTrends/CL_StormSurgeReport_2011.pdf. Accessed 4 May 2011.

Costa, Mirella B.S.F., et al. "Vulnerability and Impacts Related to the Rising Sea Level in the Metropolitan Center of Recife, Northeast Brazil." In *Pan-American Journal of Aquatic Sciences,* (2010) 5(2): 341–349. Published online January 2011. Accessed 30 April 2011.

CSIRO [Australia's Commonwealth Scientific and Industrial Research Organisation]. "Sea Level Rise: Historical Sea Level Changes — Last Two Decades." http://www.cmar.csiro/au/sealevel/sl_hist_last_15.html. Accessed 14 August 2010.

_____."Sea Level Rise: Sea Level Measurements — Paleo Indicators." www.cmar.csiro.au/sealevel/sl_meas_paleo.html. Accessed 5 August 2010.

CU Sea Level Research Group. "Tide Gauge Sea Level." http://sealevel.colorado.edu/content/tide-gauge-sea-level. Accessed 10 October 2011.

Curtis, Katherine J., and Annemarie Schneider. "Understanding the Demographic Implications of Climate Change: Estimates of Localized Population Predictions Under Future Scenarios of Sea-level Rise." In *Population and Environment,* doi: 10.1007/s1111–011–0136–2. Published online 3 April 2011. Accessed 27 April 2011.

Dasgupta, Susmita, and Craig Meisner. "Climate Change and Sea Level Rise: A Review of the Scientific Evidence." Washington, D.C.: World Bank Environment Department, April 2009.

_____, et al. "Exposure of Developing Countries to Sea-level Rise and Storm Surge." *Climate Change,* doi: 10.1007/s10584–010–9959–6. Springer Science and Business Media B.V., 2010. Published online: 14 December 2010.

_____, et al. "The Impact of Sea Level Rise on Developing Countries: A Comparative Analysis." World Bank Policy Research Working Paper #4136. www.springerlink.com/content/r41021652086775g. Accessed 15 May 2010.

Davis, Crystal. "Sea Level Rise Threatens Nile Delta Ecosystems and Livelihoods." http://earthtrends.wri.org/updates/node/235. Accessed 14 April 2011.

Dawe, Ian. "Sea Level Rise — A New Zealand Context." Greater Wellington Regional Council. www.conferenceworld.com/au/...Ian%20Dawe%20paper%201.pdf. Accessed 3 May 2011.

Delta Cities Website. "Connecting Delta Cities: Ho Chi Minh City." http://www.rotterdamclimateinitiative.nl/delta_cities_website/participatinng_cities/no_c... Accessed 15 October 2010.

Deltacommissie [Delta Commission]. *Working Together with Water: A Living Land Builds for its Future.* Findings of the Deltacommissie 2008. Netherlands, 2008.

Delta Programme Commissioner. "The Delta Programme, New-style Delta Plan." http://www.deltacommisaris.nl/english/topics/. Accessed 27 August 2010.

"Deltas in Times of Climate Change, Rotterdam 2010." Program for the international conference held in Rotterdam, Netherlands, from 29 September to 1 October 2010. Organising Committee, c/o Programme Office Knowledge for Climate/ Climate Change Spatial Planning. Alterra, Wageningen UR, Netherlands. 2010.

DeSoto-Duncan, Angela, et al. "'The Great Wall of Louisiana'": Protecting the Coastline from Extreme Storm Surge and Sea Level Rise." Solutions to Coastal Disasters (PDF). Accessed 11 July 2011.

Dessler, Andrew, and Stephen C. Sherwood. "A Matter of Humidity." *Science*, www. sciencemag.org, 20 February 2009, Vol. 323, 1020–1021.

Domingues, Catia M., et al. "Improved estimates of upper-ocean warming and multi-decadal sea-level rise." *Nature*, vol. 453, 19 June 2008, 1090–1094.

Dudley, Robert W., and Martha G. Nielsen. "Inventory and Protection of Salt Marshes from the Risks of Sea-Level Rise at Acadia National Park, Maine." USGS Fact Sheet 2011–3015, February 2011. http://pubs. usgs.gov/fs/2011/3015. Accessed 13 March 2011.

Dutta, Dushmanta. "An Integrated Tool for Assessment of Flood Vulnerability of Coastal Cities to Sea-level Rise and Potential Socio-economic Impacts: A Case Study of Bangkok, Thailand." *Hydrological Sciences Journal*, vol. 56, no. 5, 2011, 805–823. http://www.tandfonline.com/ doi/abs/10.1080/02626667.20ll.585611. Accessed 20 July 2011.

Dwyer, Gary S., et al. "Mid-Pliocene Sea Level and Continental Ice Volume Based on Coupled Benthic Mg/Ca Paleotemperatures and Oxygen Isotopes." *Philosophical Transactions of the Royal Society A* [sic] (2009), 367, 157–168, doi:10.1098/rsta. 2008.0222. Published on line 14 October 2008.

Earth Science Australia. "Storm Surges." http://earthsci.org/flooding/unit1/ul-06– 00.html. Accessed 27 February 2011.

Edwards, Merinda. "Planning for Sea-level Rise in South Australian Communities." Research project for Town Planning Degree, Urban and Regional Planning, Coastal Protection Branch. No date or publisher. Accessed 4 June 2011.

_____, et al. *International Journal of Climate Change: Impacts and Responses*, vol. 2, no. 1, 233–246.

Edwing, Richard. "What the Science Shows Us about How Sea Level Rise and Weather Events will Affect Ports." NOAA Center for Operational Oceanographic Products and Services. AAPA Climate Change Workshop, January 27, 2011.

Ekman, Martin. "The World's Longest Sea Level Series and a Winter Oscillation Index for Northern Europe 1774–2000." Small Publications in Historical Geophysics, no. 12. Summer Institute for Historical Geophysics, Åland Islands [Finland], 2003.

El-Raey, M., et al. "Adaptation to the Impacts of Sea Level Rise in Egypt." *Climate Research*, vol.12:117–128, 1999. Accessed 17 October 2010.

_____. "Vulnerability Assessment of Sea Level Rise Over Port Said Governorate, Egypt." *Environmental Monitoring and Assessment*, 56: 113–128, 1999. Accessed 17 October 2010.

Elsharkawy H., et al. "Climate Change: The Impacts of Sea Level Rise on Egypt." 45th ISOCARP [International Society of City and Regional Planners] Congress 2009.

Environment Agency. "Findings to Date" [Findings regarding the Thames Estuary]. http://www.environment-agency.gov.uk/ homeandleisure/floods/104697.aspx. Accessed 6 October 2010.

_____. "The Thames Estuary." http://www.-environment-agency.gov.uk/homeand leisure/floods/38351.aspx. Accessed 6 October 2010.

Environmental Defense Fund et al. "Common Ground: A Shared Vision for Restoring the Mississippi River Delta." www.louisianacoast.audubon.org/... Restoration_White_Paper_-_MEDIA_ RELEASE_FINAL.pdf. Accessed 25 March 2011.

Environmental Protection Agency. "Sea Level." http://cfpub.epa.gov/eroe/index. cfm?fuseaction=detail.viewMidImg &lShowInd=0&subtop=315&lv=list.list-ByAlpha&r=216636. Accessed 21 June 2010.

Esteban, M., et al. "Sea Level Rise and the Increase in Rubble Mound Breakwater Damage." UNCDAD Ad Hoc Expert Meeting on Climate Change Impacts and Adaptation: A Challenge for Global Ports, 29–30 September 2011. http://www.unc-tad.org/sections/wcms/docs/AHM2011_ 2_24_Estaban2_en.pdf. Accessed 11 October 2011.

"Eustatic Sea Level Change Mechanisms." http://geology.uprm.edu/Morelock/eustat ic.htm. Accessed 26 November 2011.

Fashae, Olutoyin Adeola, et al. "Impact of Climate Change on Sea Level Rise in Lagos, Nigeria." *International Journal of Remote Sensing.* Published online 19 August 2011, doi: 10.1080/01431161.2011. 581709.http://www.tandfonline.com/doi/ abs/10.1080/01431161.2011.581709. Accessed 30 August 2011.

"Flood Risk Assessment and Management for the Thames Estuary." www.suchenglobal. org/pdf/flood_essay.pdf. Accessed 5 October 2010.

Gallien, T., et al. "Mapping Developed Coastal Flood Zones for Climate Change Adaptation Planning: Accounting for Tides, Waves, Sea Level Rise and Flood Defense Structures." American Geophysical Union, Fall Meeting 2010, abstract #NH21C-1412. http:// adsabs.harvard.edu.abs/2020AGUFMNH 21C1412G. Accessed 27 January 2011.

Gallup. "In U.S., Concerns about Global Warming Stable at Lower Levels." http:// www.gallup.com/pol/146606/Concerns-Global-Warming-Stable-Lower-Levels.aspx. Accessed 20 March 2011.

Gardiner, Stephen M. Oxford University Press review of *A Perfect Moral Storm: The Ethical Tragedy of Climate Change.* Oxford: Oxford University Press, 2011. http:www.oup.com/us/catalog/general/ subject/History/Other/Environmental-History/?view. Accessed 15 August 2011.

Geology.com. "Storm Surge — Storm Tide." http://geology.com.articles/storm-surge. shtml. Accessed 27 February 2011.

German Advisory Council on Global Change. Special Report, 2006. *The Future Oceans — Warming Up, Rising High, Turning Sour.* Accessed 29 July 2010.

Ghosh, Nirmal. "Bangkok Sinking." *Straits Times,* 27 October 2010. http://blogs. straitstimes.com/2010/2/4/bangkok-sinking. Accessed 26 October 2010.

Gleick, Peter. "Socioeconomic Impacts of Sea Level Rise in the Bay Area and Addressing Environmental Justice." Keynote address at Preparing for Sea Level Rise in the Bay Area: A Local Government Forum, Oakland MetroCenter, April 16, 2008.

Gillet, Kit. "Vietnam's Rice Bowl Threatened by Rising Seas." http://www.guardian. co.uk/environment/2011/aug/21/vietnam-rice-bowl-treatening-rising. Accessed 25 August 2011.

Gillett, Nathan P., et al. "Ongoing Climate Change Following a Complete Cessation of Carbon Dioxide Emissions." *Nature Geoscience,* 9 January 2011, doi: 10.1038/ nego 1047.

Gillis, Justin. "As Glaciers Melt, Scientists Seek New Data on Rising Seas." http:// www.nytimes.com/2010/11/14/science/ earth/14ice.html?_r=1&hp. Accessed 14 November 2010.

Global Greenhouse Warming.com. "Carteret Atoll." http://www.global-greenhouse-warming.com/Carteret-Atoll.html. Accessed 30 May 2011.

Goddard Institute for Space Studies. "Sea Level Rise, After the Ice Melted and Today." http://www.giss.nasa.gov/research/ briefs/gornitz_09. Accessed 29 May 2010.

Gomez, Nancy, et al. "Sea Level as a Stabilizing Factor for Marine-ice-sheet Grounding Lines." www.nature.com/naturegeo science. *Nature Geoscience.* vol. 3. December 2010, 850–853.

Goodreads. "Thomas Mann Quotes." http: www.goodreads.com/author/quotes/19405. Thomas_Mann. Accessed 7 October 2010.

Gordon, David G. NOAA Climate Services: "Looking Ahead to Protect Puget Sound." http:www.climatewatch.noaa.gob/2010/ar ticles/time-and-tides-4. Accessed 24 July 2010.

Gornitz, Vivien. "Sea Level Rise and Storm Hazards, New York City." NASA GISS/ CCSR Columbia University. www.stevens. edu/ses/cms/fileadmin/cms/pfd/Vivien_G ornitz. pdf. Accessed 20 September 2010.

Grannis, Jessica. "Adaptation Tool Kit: Sea-Level Rise and Coastal Land Use." Georgetown Climate Center, October 2011. http://www.georgetownclimate.org/sites/ default/files/SLR_Toolkit. pdf. Accessed 22 October 2011.

Gregory, Jonathan. "Projection of Global and Regional Sea Level Change for the 21st Century." Unpublished presentation of graphs, maps, and other data used at the 2010 Deltas in Times of Climate Change Conference in Rotterdam, Netherlands.

Griffith, Adam. "Potential Impacts of Sea Level Rise on Hilton Head Island, SC." 2011 GSA Annual Meeting in Minneapolis (9–12 October 2011), Paper No. 259–5. http://gsa.confex.com/gsa/2011AM/ finalprogram/abstract_196832.htm. Accessed 18 August 2011.

Group on Earth Observations. "GEOSS Online." http://www.earthobservations.org. Accessed 22 February 2010.

Gudrais, Elizabeth. "The Gravity of Glacial Melt." http://harvardmagazine.com/2010/05/gravity-of-glacial-melt. Accessed 30 May 2010.

Guriro, Amar. "Large Portion of Lower Sindh, Including Karachi, Faces Inundation." http?www.dailytimes.com.pk/default.asp?page2010%5C05%5C16%5C6%5Cstory_16-5-2010. Accessed 8 November 2010.

Gutierrez, Benjamin T., et al. "A Bayesian Network to Predict Coastal Vulnerability to Sea Level Rise." *Journal of Geophysical Research*, vol. 116, F02009, 15 pp. 2011. Accessed 26 April 2011.

_____. "A Bayesian Network to Predict Vulnerability to Sea-Level Rise: Data Report." U.S. Geological Survey, Data Series 2011-601. Accessed 2 December 2011.

Haiphong Portal. "Hai Phong High-ranking Officials Learn Experiences in Coping with Climate Changes, Dykes Construction and Management; Hai Phong to Open Wide Doors for Cooperation and Friendship." http://haiphong.gov.vn/Portal/Detail.aspx?/Organization=ubndtp_EN&MenuIC=3292&C. Accessed 25 October 2010.

Hallegatte, Stéphane. "A Framework to Investigate the Economic Impact of Sea Level Rise." Environmental Research Letters, doi: 10.1088/1748-9326/7/1/015604. Accessed 21 January 2012.

_____. "SR17: The Economic Impact of Sea-level Rise." Foresight. www.foresight.gov.uk. Accessed 24 November 2011.

Hansen, H.S. "Modeling the Future Coastal Zone Urban Development as Implied by the IPCC SRES and Assessing the Impact from Sea Level Rise." *Landscape and Urban Planning* (2010), doi: 10.10.16/j.landurbplan.2010.08.018. Accessed 12 October 2010.

Hansen, James E., and Makiko Sato. "Paleoclimate Implications for Human-Made Climate Change." http://arxiv.org/ftp/arxiv/papers/1005/1005.0968.pdf. Accessed 4 January 2012.

Heberger, Matthew, et al. "Potential Impacts of Increased Coastal Flooding in California Due to Sea-level Rise." *Climate Change*, doi: 10.1007/s10584-011-0308-1. Accessed 29 November 2011.

Hoa, Le Thi Viet, et al. "The Combined Impact on the Flooding in Vietnam's Mekong Delta of Local Man-made Structures, Sea Level Rise, and Dams Upstream in the River Catchment." *Estuarine Coastal and Shelf Science*, 71 (2007) 110-116. www.elsevier.com/locate/ecss. Accessed 9 May 2011.

Hoegh-Guldberg, Ove, and John F. Bruno. "The Impact of Climate Change on the World's Marine Ecosystems." *Science*, vol. 328, 18 June 2010, 1523-1528.

Hoeppe, Peter. "Trends of Natural Disasters—The Role of Global Warming." Munich: Munich Reinsurance Company. Accessed 14 February 2011.

Holland, Geoff, and David Pugh, eds. *Troubled Waters: Ocean Science and Government*. Cambridge: Cambridge University Press, 2010.

Houghton, Katherine J., et al. "Maritime boundaries in a Rising Sea." *Nature Geoscience*, Vol. 3, December 2010, 813-816. www.nature.com/naturegeoscience. Accessed 21 October 2011.

Hunter, John. "Estimating Sea-Level Extremes Under Conditions of Uncertain Sea-Level Rise." *Climate Change*, 99:331-350. www.springerlink.com. Accessed 25 April 2011.

_____. "A simple technique for estimating an allowance for uncertain sea-level rise." *Climate Change,* doi: 10.1007/s10584-011-0332-1. Accessed 29 November 2011.

"Ice Ages and Sea Levels." http://www.global-greenhouse-warming.com/ice-ages-and-sea-levels.html. Accessed 29 May 2010.

Imevbore, Victor Ohioze. "Coastal Erosion in Lagos State: Causes and Management." Environmental Resources Managers Ltd., Victoria Island, Lagos, Nigeria.

Inam, A., et al. "Natural and Man-Made Stresses on the Stability of Indus Deltaic Eco Region." www.megadelta.ecnu.edu.cn/main/upload/Asifpaper1.pdf. Accessed 8 November 2010.

Inman, Mason. "Water in Dams, Reservoirs Preventing Sea-Level Rise" in *National Geographic News*, 13 March 2010. http://news.nationalgeographic.com/news/2008/03/080313-dams-water.html. Accessed 11 January 2010.

Insurance Information Institute (2008). "Third Year Anniversary of Hurricane Katrina—Value of Insured Property by

State." http://www.iii.org/media/updates/press.796752/index.html. Accessed 7 June 2010.

InterAcademy Council. "InterAcademy Council Report Recommends Fundamental Reform of IPCC Management Structure." http://mail.aol.com/32447-111/aol-1/fr-fr/mail/PrintMessage.aspx. Accessed 30 August 2010.

Intergovernmental Panel on Climate Change [IPCC]. "AR4 WGII Chapter 11: Australia and New Zealand — 11.ES Executive Summary." http://www.ipcc.ch/publications_and_data/ar4/wg2/en/ch11s11-es.html. Accessed 2 May 2011.

_____. "Assessing Key Vulnerabilities and the Risk from Climate Change." S.H. Schneider, et al, in "Climate Change 2007: Impacts, Adaptation and Vulnerability." Contribution of Working Group II to the Fourth Assessment Report of the IPCC. [M.L. Parry et al. (eds.)], Cambridge. Cambridge University Press, 2007.

_____. "Climate Change 2007: Synthesis Report. An Assessment of the Intergovernmental Panel on Climate Change." IPCC Plenary XXVII (Valencia, Spain, 12–17 November 2007).

_____. Climate Change 2007: Working Group II: Impacts, Adaptation and Vulnerability: Executive Summary." http://www.ipcc/ch/publications_and_data/ar4/wg2/en/ch6s6-es.html. Accessed 5 January 2010.

_____. "Climate Models and their Evaluation" in "Climate Change 2007. Working Group I: The Physical Science Basis." http://www.ipcc.ch/publications_and_data/ar/wg1/en/ch8s8-es.html. Accessed 5 January 2010.

_____. "Commitment to Sea Level Rise: Thermal Expansion." http://www.ipcc.ch/publications_and_data/ar4/weg/1/en/ch10s10-7-4.html. Accessed 3 October 2010.

_____. "How Likely are Major or Abrupt Climate Changes, such as Loss of Ice Sheets or Changes in Global Ocean Circulation?" In "Climate Change 2007: The Physical Science Basis." Contribution of Working Group I to the Fourth Assessment Report of the IPCC. [Solomon, S. et al. (eds.)]. Cambridge: Cambridge University Press, 2007. Accessed 16 May 2010.

_____. "IPCC SREX [Special Report on Managing the Risks of Extreme Events and Disasters to Advance Climate Change Adaptation] Summary for Policymakers." http://www.ipcc.ch/news_and_events/docs/ipcc34/SREX. Accessed 20 November 2011.

_____. "IPCC Workshop on Sea Level Rise and Ice Sheet Instabilities." Kuala Lumpur, Malaysia, 21–24 June 2010. http://www.ipcc-wg1.unibe/ch/publications/supporting material/slw_WorkshopReport.pdf. Accessed 18 August 2011.

_____. "Is Sea Level Rising?" In "Climate Change 2007: The Physical Science Basis." Contribution of Working Group I to the Fourth Assessment Report of the IPCC. [Solomon, S. et al. (eds.)]. Cambridge: Cambridge University Press, 2007. Accessed 16 May 2010.

_____. "6.4.3 Key Vulnerabilities and Hotspots." In "Climate Change 2007: Working Group II: Impacts, Adaptation and Vulnerability." http://www.ipcc.ch/publications_and_data/ar4/wg2/en/ch6s6-4-3.html. Accessed 14 April 2011.

_____. "Summary for Policymakers." In "Climate Change 2007: The Physical Science Basis." Contribution of Working Group I to the Fourth Assessment Report of the IPCC. [Solomon, S. et al. (eds.)]. Cambridge: Cambridge University Press, 2007.

_____. Third Assessment Report. Climate Change 2001. Working Group II: "Impacts, Adaptation and Vulnerability." Section 6.4.1. "Coastal Systems: General Comments." Box 6–3: "Potential Impacts of Climate Change and Sea-Level Rise on Coastal Systems." Cambridge: Cambridge University Press, 2001.

_____. "Towards New Scenarios for Analysis of Emissions, Climate Change, Impacts, and Response Strategies." IPCC Expert Meeting Report, 19–21 September 2007. Noordwijkerhout, Netherlands.

_____. "What Caused the Ice Ages and Other Important Climate Changes Before the Industrial Era?" In "Climate Change 2007," Working Group I: The Physical Science Basis, Frequently Asked Question 6.1. http://www.ipcc.ch/publications_and_data/ar4/wg1/end/faq-6-1.html. Accessed 19 June 2010.

International Association for Impact Assessment. "Impact of Sea Level Rise on the Nigerian Coast." www.iaia.org. Accessed 11 May 2011.

Jacobs, S.S., et al, "Stronger Ocean Circulation and Increased Melting Under Pine

Island Glacier Ice Shelf." *Nature Geoscience*, 2011, 1–5, doi: 10.1038/NEGEO 1188. Accessed 28 June 20ll.

Janjua, Muhammad Yasin. "Presentation on Climate Change and Sea Level Rise." Ministry of Environment, Government of Pakistan. saar-sdmc.nic/in...Pakistan/ Climate%20Changeand%20Sea%20Level%20in%Pakistan. Accessed 8 November 2010.

Janin, Hunt, and Ria van Eil. *Culture Shock! Netherlands: A Survival Guide to Customs and Etiquette*. Tarrytown, NY: Marshall Cavendish, 2008.

Jevrejeva, S., et al. "Sea Level Projections to AD2500 with a New Generation of Climate Change Scenarios." *Global and Planetary Change* (2011), doi: 10.1016/j.gloplacha.20111.09.006. Accessed 17 October 2011.

Johnson, Wm. Robert. "World Ice Inventory." In "What If All the Ice Melts?" www.johnstonsarchives.net/environment/waterworld.html. Accessed 1 May 2010.

Joughin, Ian, et al. "Sensitivity of 21st Century Sea Level to Ocean-Induced Thinning of Pine Island, Antarctica." *Geophysical Research Letters*. Vol. 37, L20502, doi:10.1029/2010GL044819, 2010. Accessed 14 November 2010.

_____. "Stability of the West Antarctic Ice Sheet in a Warmer World." *Nature Geoscience* 4, 506–513 (20011), doi: 10.1038/ngeo1194. Published online 24 July 2011. http://www.nature.com/ngeo/journal/v4/full/nego1194.html. Accessed 23 August 2011.

Kabat, Pavel, et al. "Climate Proofing the Netherlands." *Nature*. Vol. 438, 17 November 2005, 283–284.

_____. "Dutch coasts in transition." *Nature Geoscience* 2, 450–452 (2009). http://www.nature.com/ngeo/journal/v2n/full/ngeo572.html. Accessed 20 June 2010.

Kadapa-Bose, Surekha. "Climate is Changing, But Mumbai is Not." http://www.boloji.com/wfs6/2009/wfs1277.html. Accessed 8 March 9, 2011.

Kahn, Debra. "San Francisco Bay Area Enacts Sea-Level Rise Policy." http://www.scientificamerican.com/article.cfm?id=san-francisco-bay-area-enacts-sea-level. Accessed 7 December 2011.

Kargel, J.A., et al. "Greenland's Shrinking Ice Cover: 'Fast Times' but not that Fast." *The Cryosphere*, www.the-cryosphere.net. http://web.hwr.arizona.edu/~gleonard/20ll_oct27-thecryosphere-greenland-kargeletal_SUBMIT.pdf. Accessed 11 November 2011.

Karl, Thomas R., et al. *Global Climate Impacts in the United States: A State of Knowledge Report from the U.S. Global Change Program.* Cambridge: Cambridge University Press, 2009.

Kaser, G., et al. "Mass Balance of Glaciers and Ice Caps: Consensus Estimates for 1961–2004." In *Geophysical Research Letters*, vol. 33, L19501, doi:101029/2006 GLO27511.

Katsman, Caroline et al. "Exploring High-End Scenarios for Local Sea Level Rise to Develop Flood Protection Strategies for a Low-Lying Delta — the Netherlands as an Example." *Climate Change*, doi: 10.1007/s/10584–011–0037–5. Published online 24 February 2001. Accessed 31 March 2011.

_____. "High-End Climate Change Scenarios for Flood Protection of the Netherlands." Koninklijk Nederlands Meteorologisch Instituut, Ministerie van Infrastrutuur en Milieu. 4 January 2011. http://www.knmi.nl/cms/content/93152-/high-end_climate_change_scenarios_for_flood_prot. Accessed 5 February 20ll.

Katz, Richard F., and W. Grae Worster. "Stability of Ice-Sheet Grounding Lines." *Proceedings of the Royal Society A* [sic], 2010, 466, 1597–1620, published online 13 January 2010, doi:10.1098/rspa.2009.0434. Accessed 12 August 20ll.

Keahey, John. "Weighing the Solutions" NOVA. Sinking City of Venice. PBS. http://www.pbs.org/wgbh/nova/venice/solutions.html. Accessed 7 October 2010.

Kemp, Andrew C., et al. "Climate Related Sea-level variations over the past two millennia" in *Proceedings of the National Academy of Sciences*, July 5, 2011, vol. 108, no. 27, 11017–11022, doi: 10.1073/pnas.101561908. Accessed 9 July 20ll.

Khan, Tariq Masood Ali et al. "Sea Level Variations and Geomorphological Changes in the Coastal Belt of Pakistan." *Marine Geodesy*, 2002, vol. 25, no. 1, 159–174.

King, Hobart. "Rebuilding New Orleans: Subsidence, Sea Level Rise, Global Warming, Faults, Hurricanes." http://geology.com/articles/rebuilding-new-orleans.shtml. Accessed 12 September 2010.

Knutson, T. et al. "Tropical cyclones and climate change." *Nature Geoscience* (3), 157–163, 2010.

Konikow, Leonard F. "Contribution to global groundwater depletion since 1900 to Sea-Level Rise." *Geophysical Research Letters*, 38, L17401, doi: 10.1029/2011GL047604. http://www.agu.org/pubs/crossref/2011/2011GLO048604.shmtl. Accessed 6 September 2011.

Kopp, Robert E., et al. "Probabilistic Assessment of Sea Level during the Last Interglacial Stage." http://www.nature.com/nature/journal/v462/n7275/abs/nature08686.html. Accessed 17 June 2010.

Kousky, Carolyn, et al. "Responding to Threats of Climate Change Mega-Catastrophes." October 19, 2009. (A paper derived by the authors from a background study prepared for the World Bank's Global Facility for Disaster Reduction and Recovery Unit.)

Krauss, Ken W., et al. "Sea-Level Rise and Landscape Change Influence Mangrove Encroachment onto Marsh in the Ten Thousand Islands Region of Florida, USA." *Journal of Coastal Conservation*, doi: 10.1007/zSll852–011–0153–4. Accessed 16 April 20ll.

Krishnamurthy, Krishna. "Are We Witnessing the Rise of the Environmental Migrant?" www.doctorsoftheworld.org.uk/.../105049-arewewitnessingtheriseoftheenvironmenttalkrishnakrishnamurthy.pdf. Accessed 23 May 20ll.

Krosnick, Jon A. "The Climate Majority." http://www.nytimes.com/2010/06/09/opinion/09krosnick.html?pagewanted=print. Accessed 21 June 2010.

Kuhn, M., et al. "Visualizing the spatial extent of predicted coastal zone inundation due to sea level rise in south-west Western Australia." *Ocean & Coastal Management*. volume 54, no. 11, November 2011, 796–806. http:www.sciencedirect.com/science/article/pli/S09645691111001293. Accessed 3 October 2011.

Kumar, Rakesh. "Economic impact of climate change on Mumbai, India. *Regional Health Forum*, volume 12, no. 1, 2008, 38–42.

Kwadijk, Jaap C., et al. "Using Adaptation Tipping Points to Prepare for Climate Change and Sea Level Rise: A Case Study in the Netherlands." http: onlinelibrary.wiley.com/doi/10.1002/wcc.64/full. Accessed 2 September 2010.

Kwek, Glenda. "Indonesia Mulls New Capital as Jakarta Sinks." http://www.google.com.hostednews/afp/article/ALeqM5gHO-eYtWhElo-tDutOelFgr8kn. Accessed 6 November 2010.

Lambeck, Kurt, et al. "Paleoenvironmental Records, Geophysical Modeling, and Reconstruction of Sea-Level Trends and Variability on Centennial and Longer Timescales." In *Understanding Sea-Level Rise and Variability* by John Church, et al., 61–121. Chichester, UK: Wiley-Blackwell, 2010.

_____, and John Chappell. "Sea Level Change Through the Last Glacial Cycle." *Science*, "Paleoclimate," vol. 292, 27 April 2001, 679–686.

Lau, Maren A. "Adaptation to Sea-Level Rise in the People's Republic of China: Assessing the Institutional Dimension of Alternative Organisational Frameworks." Working Paper FNU-94. Research Unit Sustainability and Global Change, Center for Marine and Atmospheric Research, University of Hamburg, Germany. http:www.uni-hamburg.de/Wiss/FB15/Sustainability. Accessed 19 October 2010.

Leadley, P., et al. "Biodiversity Scenarios: Projections of 21st Century Change on Biodiversity and Associated Ecosystems Services: A Technical Report for the Global Diversity Outlook 3." Technical Series No. 50. Montreal: Secretariat of the Convention on Biological Biodiversity, 2010.

Leclercq, P.W., et al. "Estimating the Glacier Contribution to Sea-Level Rise for the Period 1800–2005." *Surveys in Geophysics*, doi: 10,1007/s10712–011–9121–7. Accessed 28 May 2011.

Leiserowitz, Anthony, and Nicholas Smith. "Knowledge of Climate Change across Global Warming's Six Americas." Yale University. New Haven, CT: Yale Project on Climate Change Communication, 2010. http:environment.yale.edu/climate. Accessed 18 April 2011.

Lemonick, Michael D. "The Secret of Sea Level Rise: It Will Vary Greatly by Region." *Yale Environment 360*. 22 March 2010. e360.yale.edu/feature/the_secret_of_sea_level_rise_it/2255. Accessed 13 January 2011.

Lettenmaier, Dennis P., and P.C.D. Milly. "Land Waters and Sea Level." *Nature Geoscience* 2, 452–454 (2009). http://www, nature.com/ngeo/journan/vn2/n7/full/ngeo567.html. Accessed 20 June 2010.

Lewis, Joanna I., et al. "Understanding Climate Change in China." In *Climate Change Science and Policy* by Stephen H. Schneider, et al. Washington, D.C.: Island Press, 2010, 296–316.

Lieberman, Bruce. "Continuing Concerns over Implications of Climate Change for National Security." November 2, 2010. http://www.yaleclimatemediaforum.org/2010/11/climate-change-for-national-security. Accessed 3 November 2010.

Lin, Ning, et al., "Physically Based Assessment of Hurricane Surge Threat Under Climate Change." *Nature Climate Change*, 1–6 (2012). Accessed 14 February 2012.

Lin, Ting. "Literature Review for Latest Global Sea Level Rise Projections." Stanford: Stanford Civil and Environmental Engineering, Winter 2010.

Loáiciga, Hugo A., et al. Abstract of "Sea Water Intrusion by Sea-Level Rise: Scenarios for the 21st Century." http://online library.wiley.com/doi/10.1111/j.1745–6584.2011.00800.x/full. Accessed 3 March 2011.

Lovelock, Catherine E., et al. "The Role of Surface and Subsurface Processes in Keeping Pace with Sea Level Rise in Intertidal Wetlands of Moreton Bay, Queensland, Australia." *Ecosystems*, doi: 10.1007/s10021-011-9443-9. http://www.springer-link.com/content/r807256260083321. Accessed 17 May 2011.

Lowe, Jason A., et al. "Past and Future Changes in Extreme Sea Levels and Waves." In *Understanding Sea-Level Rise and Variability*, by John Church, et al., 326–375. Chichester, UK: Wiley-Blackwell, 2010.

Mabey, Nick, et al. "Degrees of Risk: Defining a Risk Management Framework for Climate Security." London: Third Generation Environmentalism, February 2011.

"Maldives Government Holds Underwater Cabinet Meeting." http://www.telegraph.co.uk/news/newstopics/howaboutthat/6356036/Maldives-government. Accessed 7 November 2010.

Mandia, Scott. "Global Warming: A Sea Change?" http://profmandia.wordpress.com/2020/06/21/global-warming-a-sea-change. Accessed 21 June 2010.

Maury, M.F. "The Physical Geography of the Sea." New York: Harper, 1855. http://docs.lib.NOAA.gov/rescue/oceanheritage/GC11M451sted1855.pdf. Accessed 15 October 2011.

Mazira, Edward, and Kristina Kershner. "Nation under Siege: Sea Level Rise at Our Doorstep." September 2007. www.architecture2030.org/current_situation/cutting_edge.html. Accessed 15 May 2010.

McGranahan, Gordon, et al. "The Rising Tide: Assessing the Risks of Climate Change and Human Settlements in Low Elevation Coastal Zones." In *Environment and Urbanization*, International Institute for Environment and Development, 2007, 19:17. http://eau.sagepub.com/content/19/1/17. Accessed 3 May 2011.

McKay, Nicolas P., et al. "The Role of Ocean Thermal Expansion in Last Interglacial Sea Level Rise." *Geophysical Research Letters*, 2011, doi:10.1029/2011GL048280. Accessed 23 July 2011.

McKinney, Vanessa. "Sea Level Rise and the Future of the Netherlands." ICE Case studies, no. 212, May 2007. www1.american.edu/ted/ice/dutch-sea.html. Accessed 13 January 2011.

Mee, Lawrence. "Life on the Edge: Managing our Coastal Zones." In *Troubled Waters: Ocean Science and Governance* by Geoff Holland and David Pugh. Cambridge: Cambridge University Press, 2010, 185–199.

Melville, Herman. *Moby Dick*. New York: New American Library, 1961.

Metropolitan Transportation Commission. "Shoreline Areas Vulnerable to Sea Level Rise: 2040–2060." Research and Demographic Unit, and Geographic Information Systems Unit. Map of the Month: June 2009.

Miller, Kenneth G., "Sea Level Change, Last 250 Million Years." www.springer.com/978–1–4020–4551–6_Sea+Level+Change,+Last+250+Million+Years_Miller_web.PDF. Accessed 17 June 2010.

Milliman, John D., et al. "Environmental and Economic Implications of Rising Sea Level and Subsiding Deltas: The Nile and Bengal Examples." *Ambio*, vol. 18, no. 6 (1989), 340–345. http://www.jstor.org/pss/4313605. Accessed 14 May 2011.

Milne, Glenn A., et al. "Identifying the Causes of Sea-Level Change." *Nature Geoscience* 4, 471–478 (2009). Published online 14 June 2009. http://nature.com/ngeo/journal/V2n7/full/ngeo544.html. Accessed 20 June 2010.

Ministry for the Environment. "Adapting to Sea-Level rise." November 2010. http://www.mfe.govt.nz/issues/climate/adaptation/sea-level-rise.html. Accessed 2 May 2011.

Ministry of Climate and Energy of Denmark. "What Consequences Can We Expect, and What Can We Do?" http://en.cop15.di/climate+facts/what+consequences+can+we+expect. Accessed 5 December 2009.

"Mississippi River Delta Basin." http://la coast.gov/landchange/basins/mr. Accessed 12 September 2010.

Mitra, A., and K. Bannerjee. "Pigments of *Heritiera formes* [Mangrove] Seedlings under Different Salinity Conditions: Perspective Sea Level Rise." *Mesopotamian Journal of Marine Science*, 2010 (1), 1–10.

Mitrovica, Jerry X., et al. "The Sea-Level Fingerprint of West Antarctic Collapse." *Science*, vol. 323, 6 February 2009, www.sciencemag.org. Accessed 13 November 2010.

Mohal, Nasreen, et al. "Impact of Sea Level Rise on Coastal Rivers of Bangladesh." www.riversymposium.com/2006/index.php?element. Accessed 31 October 2010.

Mondal, Muhammad Abdul Matin. "Sea Level Rise along the Coast of Bangladesh. www.gloss_sealevel.org/publications.../bangladesh_2001.pdf. Accessed 31 October 2010.

Morelock, J. "Sea Level Changes Text Summary." http://geology.uprm/Morelock/summary3.htm. Accessed 17 June 2010.

Myers, Norman. "Environmental Refugees: An Emergent Security Issue." 13th Economic Forum. Prague, Session III — Environment and Migration, 23–27 May 2005, 1–5.

National Academies. "Abrupt Climate Change: Inevitable Surprises." Committee on Abrupt Climate Change. National Academies Press, Washington, D.C., 2004.

National Hurricane Center. "Storm Surge Overview." http://www.nhc.noaa.gov/ssurge_overview.shtml. Accessed 26 February 2011.

National Intelligence Council. "China: The Impact of Climate Change to 2030." A Commissioned Research Report prepared by the Joint Global Change Research Institute and Battelle Memorial Institute, Pacific Northwest Division. NIC 2009–02D, April 2009. http://www.dni.gov/nic/PDF-GIF_otherprod/climate_change/climate2030_china.pdf. Accessed 12 October 2011.

NASA. "Antarctica Overview Map." http://lima.nasa.gov/pdf/A3_overview.pdf. Accessed 16 January 2012.

_____. "The Blue Marble." http://visibleearth.nasa.gov/view_rec.php?id=2429. Accessed 1 February 2010.

_____. "Collapse of the Larsen-B Ice Shelf." http://earthobservatory.nasa.gov/Features/WorldOfChange/larsenb.php. Accessed 16 January 2012.

_____. "Earth Observatory: The Water Cycle." http://earthobservatory.nasa.gov/Features/Water/page2.php. Accessed 7 May 2011.

_____. "NASA Looks at Sea Level Rise, Hurricane Risks to New York City." http://www.nasa.gov/mission_pages/hurricanes/archives/2006/sealevel_nyc_prt.html. Accessed 19 September 2010.

_____. "NASA Mission Takes Stock of Earth's Melting Land Ice." http://www.jpl.nasa.gov/news/news.cfm?release=2012–036. Accessed 10 February 2012.

_____. "NASA Research Finds 2010 Tied for Warmest Year on Record." *http://www.giss.nasa.gov/research/news/20110112/*. Accessed 23 June 2011.

_____. "NSAS Satellites Detect Pothole on Road to Higher Seas. Global Sea Level Drops 6 mm in 2010." http://www.jpl.nasa.gov/news/cfm?releast=2011–262. Accessed 26 August 20ll.

National Coordination Committee [of the People's Republic of China] on Climate Change. "Initial National Communication on Climate Change. Beijing. 2004." Unfccc.int/resource/docs/natc/chnnclexsum.pdf. Accessed 24 October 2010.

National Hurricane Center. "Storm Surges." http://www.nhc.noaa.gov/HAW2/english/storm_surges.shtml. Accessed 10 September 2010.

National Research Council of the National Academies. *Advancing the Science of Climate Change*. Washington, D.C.: National Academies Press, 2010.

_____. "Climate Stabilization Targets: Emissions, Concentrations, and Impacts over Decades to Millennia." Washington, D.C.: National Academies Press, 2010.

_____. "Sea Level Rise and the Coastal Environment." *Advancing the Science of Climate Change*, 184–199, http:www.nap.edu/openbook.php?record_id=12782&page+R1. Accessed 21 June 2010.

National Snow and Ice Data Center. "Thawing Permafrost Will Accelerate Global Warming." *http://mail.aol.com/33222-111/aol-6/fr/mail/PrintMessage.aspx. Accessed 16 February 2011.*

New York City Panel on Climate Change. Executive Summary of *Climate Change Adaptation in New York City: Building a Risk Management Response.* http://online libary.wiley.com/doi/10.1111/j.1749–6632.2009.05398.x/full. Accessed 21 September 2010.

New York State Department of Environmental Conservation. "Sea Level Rise Task Force." http://www.dec.ny/gov/energy/45202.html. Accessed 11 February 2011.

Nicholls, Robert J., et al. "Coastal Systems and Low-Lying Areas." In IPCC "Climate Change 2007: Impacts, Adaptation and Vulnerability." Cambridge: Cambridge University Press, 2007.

_____. "Impacts of and Responses to Sea-Level Rise." In *Understanding Sea-Level Rise and Variability* by John Church, et al., 17–51. Chichester, UK: Wiley-Blackwell, 2010.

_____, et al. "Increasing Flood Risk and Wetland Loses Due to Global Sea-Level Rise: Regional and Global Analyses." *Global Environmental Change* (9, S69-S87). www.elsevier.cm/locate/gloencha. Accessed 13 January 2011.

_____. "International Dimensions of Climate Change. R 6.1: The Implications on the UK of the Impacts of Climate Change and Sea-Level Rise on Critical Coastal Infrastructure Overseas, 2010 to 2100." A report submitted to the UK Government's Foresight Project on the International Dimensions of Climate Change, Government Office for Science, July 2010. Accessed 19 July 2011.

_____, et al. "Potential Implications of Climate Change and Sea-Level Rise on Coastal Waste Sites." *Geophysical Research Abstracts.* Vol. 13, EGU2011–12535, EGU General Assembly 2011.

_____. "Planning for the Impacts of Sea Level Rise." *Oceanography*, vol. 24, no. 2, June 2011, 144–157, doi:10.5670/oceanog.2011.34. Accessed 10 July 2011.

_____. "Ranking of the World's Cities Most Exposed to Coastal Flooding Today and in the Future." Paris: OECD Environment Working Paper No. 1 (ENV/WKP(2007)1), 2007.

_____, ct al. "Ranking Port Cities with High Exposure and Vulnerability to Climate Extremes: Exposure Estimates." Organisation for Economic Co-operation and Development. Environment Directorate. ENV/WKP(2007)1, 19 November 2008.

_____. "Regional issues raised by Sea-Level rise and their policy implications." *Climate Research*. Vol. 11:5–18, 17 December 1998.

_____. "Sea-Level Rise and its Impact on Coastal Zones." *Science*, vol. 328, 18 June 2010, 1517–1520. Accessed 20 June 2010.

_____. "Sea-Level Rise and its Possible Impacts Given a 'Beyond 4_C World' in the Twenty-first Century." In Royal Society of London, *Philosophical Transactions*, Biological Sciences, vol. 369, no. 1934, 161–181. nl.wurpubs%2F401076. Accessed 4 June 2011.

"Nigeria: Lagos Expansion into Atlantic Ocean." *Dredging Today*. http:www.dredgingtoday.com/2010/09/20/nigeria-lagos-expansion-into-atlantic-ocean/. Accessed 12 October 2010.

NOAA. "Sea Levels Online." http://tidesandcurrents.noaa.gov/sltrends/sltrends.shtml. Accessed 2 March 2011l.

_____. "State of the Climate in 2009." Arndt, D.S., M.O. Baringer, and M.R. Johnson (eds.) in *Bulletin of the American Meteorological Society*, 91 (6), S1-S224.

_____. "Storm Surge Overview." http://www.nhc.noaa.gov/surge/. Accessed 23 June 2011.

_____.. "The Water Cycle." *http://www.srh.noaa.gov/jetstream/downloads/hydro2010.pdf*. Accessed 23 June 2011.

NOAA Northwest Region: "Special Project: Climate Assessment and Proactive Response Initiative (CAPRI)." http://www.darrp.noaa.gov/northwest/puget_sound/index.html. Accessed 24 July 2010.

NOAA Satellite and Information Service. NOAA Paleoclimatology: Climate Science — Beyond 100,000 Years." http://www.ncdc.noaa.gov/paleo/ctl/cliscibeyond.html. Accessed 7 August 2010.

Noerdlinger, P.D., et al. "The Melting of Floating Ice Raises the Ocean Level." *Geophysical Journal International*, 170: 145–150, doi: 10.1111/j.1365–246X.2007.03472.v. Accessed 7 May 2011.

Noses, Reed F. "Between the Devil and the Deep Blue Sea: Florida's Unenviable Position with Respect to Sea Level Rise." *Climatic Change*, accepted 13 May 2011, doi: 10.1007/s10584=011–0109–6. Accessed 7 June 2011.

Nossiter, Adam. "Riches in Nigeria Lost after Arrival." http://www.nytime.com/2011/02/09/world/africa/09nigeria.

html?ref=global-home&pagew. Accessed 9 February 2011.

Notz, Dirk. "The Future of Ice Sheets and Sea Ice: Between Reversible Retreat and Unstoppable Loss." December 8, 2009. www.pnas.org/cgi/doi/10.1073/pnas.0902356106.

Novoa, David Corderi, et al. "An Economic Analysis of Water Infrastructure Investments, Agricultural Productivity and Climate Change in the Mekong Delta: Adapting to Increased Salinity and Sea Level Rise." No. 103875, 2011 Annual Meeting, July 24–26,2011, Pittsburgh, Pennsylvania, Agricultural and Applied Economics Association. http://econpapers.repec.org/paper/agsaaea11/103875.htm. Accessed 17 May 2011.

Nwilo, Peter Chigozie. "Managing the Impact of Storm Surges on Victoria Island, Lagos, Nigeria." In *Destructive Water: Water-Caused Natural Disasters, their Abatement and Control.* Proceedings of the Conference held at Anaheim, California, June 1996. IAHS Pub. No. 239, 1997, 325–330.

Okusipe, Obademi McArthur. "Lagos Lagoon Coastal Profile: Information Database for Planning Theory." Department of Urban and Regional Planning, University of Lagos, Lagos, Nigeria.

Olsthoorn, Xander, et al. "Neo-Atlantis: Dutch Reponses to Five Meter Sea Level Rise." Institute for Environmental Studies. Vrije Universiteit, Amsterdam, Netherlands, 2005. Accessed 20 April 2011.

Omokhomion, Catherine. "National Report on Sea Level Status in Nigeria." Nigerian Institute for Oceanography and Marine Research, Victoria Island, Lagos, Nigeria.

Organisation for Economic Development and Co-operation [OECD]. Environmental Directorate. Environmental Policy Committee. Working Party on Global and Structural Policies. "Metrics for Assessing the Economic Benefits of Climate Change Policies: Sea Level Rise." Paris, 26 July 2006.

Ouroussoff, Nicolai. "Imagining a More Watery New York." http://www.nytimes.com/2010/03/26/arts/design/26rising.html. Accessed 22 September 2010.

Overpeck, Jonathan T., et al. "Paleoclimatic Evidence for Future Ice-Sheet Instability and Rapid Sea-Level Rise." *Science.* Vol. 311, 24 March 2006. www/sciencemag.org. Accessed 10 August 2011.

_____. "Projections of Future Sea Level Becoming More Dire." *Proceedings of the National Academy of Sciences.* December 22, 2009, vol. 106, no. 51, 21461–21462.

Ozor, Nicholas, et al. "Sharing the Lagos Megacity Experience in the Integrated Management of Sea Level Rise and Flooding" in *Resilient Cities,* Local Sustainability, 2011, vol. 1, pt. 4, 319–327. Accessed 24 May 2011.

Pacific Council on International Policy. "Preparing for the Effects of Climate Change — A Strategy for California." A Report by the California Adaptation Advisory Panel to the State of California, 2010. Full report at www/pacificcouncil.org. Accessed 3 March 4, 2011.

Paleoclimates. "Past Climates on Earth." http://www.globalchange.umich/edu/globalchange/current/lectures/kling/paleoclimate/ind. Accessed 10 March 2011.

Parris, Adam, et al. "Sea Level Rise in the San Francisco Bay — Considering Morphology in Adapting Management." *Vignettes: Key Concepts in Geomorphology,* http:serc.carleton.edu/48726. Accessed 11 April 20ll.

Parry, M.L., O.F. Canziani, J.P. Palutikof, P.J. van der Linden and C.E. Hanson, eds. "Contribution of Working Group II to the Fourth Assessment Report of the Intergovernmental Panel on Climate Change," Cambridge University Press, Cambridge, UK, p. 327.

Parthemore, Christine. "Climate Change and the Maritime Services." In "Broadening Horizons: Climate Change and the U.S. Armed Forces" by Carmen, et al. Washington, D.C.: Center for a New American Security, April 2010, 25–34.

Pavri, Firooza. Abstract: "Urban Expansion and Sea-Level Rise Related Flood Vulnerability for Mumbai (Bombay), India Using Remotely Sensed Data." http://www.springerlink.com/content/q0kt48617153p40x. Accessed 8 March 9, 2011.

Permanent Service for Mean Sea Level. "Sea Level: Frequently Asked Questions and Answers." http://www.psmsl.org/train_and_info?faqs. Accessed 26 July 2010.

Pew Research Center. "Wide Partisan Divide Over Global Warming." http://pewresearch.org.pubs/1780/poll-global-warming-scientists-energy-policies-offshor. Accessed 10 28 October 2010.

Pew Research Center for the People and the Press. Public opinion poll of 25 January

2010: "Public's Priorities for 2010: Economy, Jobs, Terrorism." http://people-press.org/report/584/policy-priorities-2010. Accessed 9 April 2010.

Pham Si Liem. "Vietnam Coastal Cities and Potential Impacts of Sea Level Rise." http://www.vncold.vn/EN/Web/Content.aspx?distid=466. Accessed 25 October 2010.

PhysicalGeography.net. "Introduction to the Hydrosphere: The Hydrologic Cycle." http://www.physicalgeography.net/fundamentals/8b.html. Accessed 7 May 2011.

Pilkey, Orrin H., and Rob Young. *The Rising Sea.* Washington, D.C.: Island Press, 2009.

Pirazzoli, Palo Antonio, et al. "Extreme Sea Levels in Two Northern Mediterranean Areas." *Méditerranée: Journal of Mediterranean Geography*, 108, 2007, 1–16. http:///mediterranee.revues.org/index 170.html. Accessed 12 February 2011.

Poggioli, Sylvia. "Venice Offers Lessons on Coping with Rising Seas." http://www.npr.org/templates/story/story.php?Id =17910734. Accessed 7 October 2010.

Pollack, Henry. *A World Without Ice.* New York: Avery, 2009.

Polling Report, Inc. "Polling Results on Environmental Issues." http://www.pollingreport.com/enviro.htm. Accessed 2 September 2010.

Potsdam Institute for Climate Impact Research. "Researchers Refine Assessment of Tipping Elements of the Climate System." http://www.pik.potsdam.de/news-/press-releases/kipp-elemente-im-klimasystem-forscher.v. Accessed 19 August 2011.

_____. "Sea Level." http://www.pik-potsdam.de/sealevel. Accessed 25 July 2011.

Price, Stephen F., et al. "Committed Sea-Level Rise for the Next Century from Greenland Ice Sheet Dynamics During the Past Decade." *Proceedings of the National Academy of Sciences* [PNAS], PNAS Early Edition, April 19, 2011. www.pnas.org/cgi/doi/10.1073/pnas.1017313108. Accessed 24 May 2011.

Pugh, David. *Changing Sea Levels: Effects of Tides, Weather and Climate.* Chapter 8 — "Extreme Sea Levels." Cambridge University Press, 2004, published on-line February 2011. www.cup.es/resources/0521532183/317_0521825326C08,_p.180–188. pdf. Accessed 12 February 2011.

Puthucherril, Tony George. "Operationalising Integrated Coastal Zone Management and Adapting to Sea Level Rise through Coastal Law: Where Does India Stand?" *The International Journal of Coastal and Maritime Law.* 26, 20ll, 1–44, doi: 10.1163/157180811X593407. Accessed 2 November 2011.

Rabineau, M., et al. "Paleo Sea Levels Reconsidered from Direct Observations of Paleoshoreline Position During Glacial Maxima (For The Last 500,000 yr.)" *Earth and Planetary Science Letters*, Vol. 252, Issues 1–2, 30 Nov. 2006, Pages 119–137. http://dx.doi/10.1016/j.epsl.2006.09.033. Accessed 5 August 2010.

Rahmstorf, Stefan. "A New View on Sea Level Rise." http://www.nature.com/climate/2010/1004/full/climate.2010.29.html. Accessed 16 May 2010.

_____. "2000 Years of Sea-Level (+ updates)." *Realclimate.* http://www.realclimate.org/index/php/archives/2011/06/2000-years-of-sea-level. Accessed 16 October 2011.

_____, and Martin Vermeer. "Discussion of: Houston, J.R. and Dean, R.G., 2011. Sea-Level Acceleration Based on U.S. Tide Gauges and Extensions of Previous Global-Gauge Analyses." *Journal of Coastal Research*, 27(3), 409–417. Accessed 14 July 2011.

Ranasinghe, Roshanka, et al. "Estimating Coastal Recession Due to Sea Level Rise: Beyond the Bruun Rule [this rule predicts a landward and upward displacement of the cross-shore sea bed profile in response to rising sea levels]." *Climate Change,* doi: 10.1007/s10584–011–0107–8. Springer-link.com. Accessed 10 July 2011.

Rayner, Ralph, and Bev MacKenzie. "A First-Order Assessment of the Impact of Long-Term Trends in Extreme Sea Levels on Offshore Structures and Coastal Refineries." In *Understanding Sea-Level Rise and Variability*, by John Church,, et al., 52–60. Chichester, UK: Wiley-Blackwell, 2010.

RealClimate. "Going to Extremes." http://www.realclimate.org/index.php/archives/2011/01/going-to-extremes. Accessed 21 February 2011.

Rekacewicz, P., and Simonett, O., "Impact of Sea Level Rise on the Nile Delta." http://maps.grida.no/go/graphic/impact-of-sea-level-rise-on-the-nile-delta. Accessed 02 February 2012.

Rekacewicz, P., and UNEP/GRID-Arendal, "Potential Impact of Sea-Level Rise on Bangladesh." http://maps.grida.no/go/graphic/potential-impact-of-sea-level-rise-on-bangladesh. Accessed 19 December 2011.

Ren Jia Wen, et al. "Initial Estimate of the Contribution of Cryospheric Change in China to Sea Level Rise" in *Chinese Science Bulletin*, June 2011, vol. 56, no. 16: 1661–1664. csb.sichina.com. Accessed 28 May 2011.

Revell, David L., et al. "A Methodology for Predicting Future Coastal Hazards Due to Sea-Level Rise on the California Coast." *Climate Change*, doi: 10.1007/S10584–011–0315–2, 21 September 2011. Accessed 12 December 2011.

Revkin, Andrew C. "Global Warming: Overview." http://topics.nytimes.com/top/news/science/topics/global warming/index.html?inline+nyt-cl. Accessed 4 December 2009.

Rice University. "18,000 Years Ago the Ice Sheets Covered Large Areas of Land." http://earth.rice.edu/mtpe/cryo/cryosphere/topics/ice_age.html. accessed 30 May 2010.

Riché, Pierre, and Jacques Verger. *Des nains sur des épaules de géants*. Tallandier, 2006.

Rick, U.K., et al. "Effective Media Reporting of Sea Level Rise Perceptions: 1989–2009." *Environmental Research Letters* 6 (2011) 014004 (5 pp.).

Rignot, E. "Acceleration of the Contribution of the Greenland and Antarctic Ice Sheets to Sea Level Rise." *Geophysical Research Letters*, vol. 38, L05503, doi: 10.1029/2011 GL046583, 2011. Accessed 10 March 10, 2011.

Rogers, Will, and Jay Gulledge. "Lost in Translation: Closing the Gap Between Climate Science and National Security Policy." Center for a New American Security. www.cnas.org/node/4391. Accessed 22 April 2011.

Rosenthal, Elisabeth. "Climate Fears Turn to Doubts Among Britons." http://www.nytimes.com/2010/05/25/science/earth/25climate.html?ref=global-home. Accessed 25 May 2010.

_____. "Huff and Puff and Blow Your House Down." *New York Times*, Sunday edition, 13 February 2011. Environment section, 3.

Ruddiman, William F. *Earth's Climate: Past and Future*. 2nd ed. New York: Freeman, 2008.

San Francisco Bay Conservation and Development Commission. "Climate Change." www.bcdc.ca.gov/planning/climate_change/climate_change.shtml. Accessed 16 May 2010.

_____."The San Francisco Bay Estuary." http://www.bcdc.ca.gov/bay_estuary.shtml. Accessed 4 March 2011.

_____."Shoreline Areas Vulnerable to Sea Level Rise, San Francisco Bay Area." http://www.bcda.ca.gov/planning/climate_change/index_map.shtml. Accessed 4 March 2011.

_____."Why BCDC is Considering Amendments to the San Francisco Bay Plan to Address Sea Level Rise." http://www.bcdc.ca.gov/proposed_bay_plan/fqs.shtml. Accessed 4 March 2011.

Sato, M., and J. Hansen. "Updating the Climate Science: What Path is the Real World Following?" http://www.columbia.edu/~mhs119/SeaLevel. Accessed 15 November 2011.

Scearce, Carolyn. "Venice and the Environmental Hazards of Coastal Cities." CSA Discovery Guides. http://www.csa.com/discoveryguides/discoveryguides-main.php. Released January 2007. Accessed 6 October 2010.

Schewe, J., et al. "Climate Change Under a Scenario Near 1.5 °C of Global Warming: Monsoon Intensification, Ocean Warming and Steric Sea Level Rise." *Earth System Dynamics Discussions*, 1, 297–324, 2010. www.earth-syst-dynam-discuss.net/1/297/2010. Accessed 19 October 2010.

Schmidt, Gavin A. "Under and Over the Ice." *RealClimate*. http://realclimate.org/index.php/archives/2011/03/under-and-over-the-ice. Accessed 10 March 2011.

Schneider, Stephen H. *Science as a Contact Sport*. Washington, D.C.: National Geographic, 2009.

_____, Armin Rosencranz, Michael D. Mastrandrea, and Kristin Kuntz-Duriseti. *Climate Change: Science and Policy*. Washington, D.C.: Island Press, 2010.

_____. "How Much Will Sea Levels Rise in the 21st Century?" www.skepticalscience.com/sea-level-rise-predictions.html. Accessed 16 May 2010.

Schouwenaars, J.M. "Adaptation of Polder Systems to Sea Level Rise and Land Subsidence in Fryslan in the Period 1000–

2000." A paper published by the Wetterskip Fryslan Regional Water Board, Leeuwarden, Netherlands. Accessed 28 May 2011.

Schrope, Mark. "Unarrested Development." *Nature*, published online 6 April 2010. http://www.nature.com/climate/2010/1044/full/climate.2010.27.html. Accessed 15 September 2010.

Science Daily. "Rising Oceans: Too Late to Turn the Tide?" http://www.sciencedaily.com/releases/2011/07/110718092220.htm. Accessed 23 July 2011.

_____. "Rising Sea Levels Set To Have Major Impacts around the World." http://www.sciencedaily/com/releases/2009/03/090310104742.htm. Accessed 4 December 2009.

_____. "Sea Level Rise Due to Global Warming Poses Threat to New York City." http://www.sciencedaily.com/releases/2009/03/090315155112.htm. Accessed 19 September 2010.Scientific Committee on Antarctic Research. (John Turner, et al. eds.) "Antarctic Climate Change and the Environment." Cambridge: Victoire Press, 2009.

_____. "Sea Level Rise: Case Study for Venice." http://www.columbia.edu/~gms2141/affecting.html. Accessed 6 October 2010.

Sea Level Rise Maps Gallery. "Gallery of Regions Vulnerable to Sea Level Rise." http://www.globalwarmingart.com/wiki/Sea_Level_Rise_Maps_Gallery. Accessed 4 March 2011.

Seung-Ki Min, et al. "Human Contribution to More-Intense Precipitation Extremes." 378, *Nature*, vol. 470, 17 February 2011. Accessed 31 March 2011.

Shepard, Christine C., et al. "Assessing Future Risk: Quantifying the Effects of Sea Level Rise on Storm Surge Risk for the Southern Shores of Long Island, New York." *Natural Hazards*, doi: 10.1007/S11069–011–0046–8. 8 November 2011. Accessed 10 December 2011.

Shepard, Katherine A. "Can Tidal Marshes Keep Up with Sea-Level Rise? Productivity and Decomposition of a Brackish Marsh in a Changing Environment." MS thesis, Villanova University, 2011, 80 pp., 1491803. http:gradworks.umi.com/14/91/1491803.html. Accessed 9 June 2011.

Sherwood, Steven. "Science Controversies Past and Present." *Physics Today*, vol. 64, no. 10. http://www.physicstoday.org/

resource1/phtoad/v64/i10/p39_s1? bypassSSO=1. Accessed 13 October 2011.

Shuman, Christopher A., et al. "2001–2009 Elevation and Mass Losses in the Larsen A and B Embayments, Antarctic Peninsula." *Journal of Glaciology*, 57 (204), 2011.

Siddall, M., et al. "Sea-Level Fluctuations During the Last Glacial Cycle." *Nature*, 423:853–858, 2003.

SimClim. "Extreme Event Analysis." http://www.climsystems.com/sunclim/eea.php. Accessed 18 February 2011.

Skeptical Science. "Greenland is Rising Faster as Ice Loss Accelerates." http://webmail.aol.com/31793–111/aol-1/fr-fr/mail/PrintMessage.aspx. Accessed 24 May 2010.

Socioeconomic Data and Applications Center, "Bangledesh Population Density and Low Elevation Coastal Zones." http://sedac.ciesin.columbia.edu/gpw/maps/lecz/Bangladesh_population_density_and_lecz.pdf. Accessed 16 January 2012.

Sokolov, A.P., et al. "Probabilistic Forecast for 21st Century Climate Based on Uncertainties in Emissions (without Policy) and Climate Parameters." MIT Joint Program on the Science and Policy of Global Change. Report No. 169, January 2009.

Solentpedia. "Coastal Squeeze." http://www.solentpedia.info/our_changing_coast/coastal_squeeze. Accessed 30 April 2011.

Somboon, J.R.P., et al. "A Sea-Level Rise in the Super-Interglacial Age: Its Geomorphic Impacts on the Low-Lying Areas of Bangkok Metropolis." *Development Geology for Thailand into the Year 2000*. Session III: Quaternary Geology, Clay Mineralogy and Miscellaneous. Chulalongkorn University, Department of Mineral Resources, Bangkok, Thailand, 13–14 December 1990.

Stanton, Elizabeth A., and Frank Ackerman. "Florida and Climate Change: The Costs of Inaction." Medford: Tufts University, 2007.

State of California. "State of California Sea-Level Rise Interim Guidance Document." October 2010. http: www. slr.ca.gov/Sea_Level_Rise/SLR_Guidance_Document_SAT_Re. Accessed 3 October 2011.

Steffen, Konrad,, et al. "Cryospheric Contributions to Sea-Level Rise and Variability." In *Understanding Sea-Level Rise and Vari-*

ability, by John Church, et al., 177–225. Chichester, UK: Wiley-Blackwell, 2010.

_____. "Rapid Changes in Glaciers and Ice Sheets and their Impacts on Sea Level." Chapter 2 of the U.S. Geological Survey's Synthesis and Assessment Product 3.4 Report by the U.S. Climate Change Science Program and the Subcommittee on Global Change Research. December 2008.

Sterman, David. "Climate Change in Egypt: Rising Sea Level, Dwindling Water Supplies." *Climate Institute*. http://www.climate.org/topics/international-action/egypt.html. Accessed 17 October 2010.

Stocker, Thomas, et al. "IPCC Workshop on Sea Level Rise and Ice Sheet Instabilities." Kuala Lumpur, Malaysia, 21–24 June 2010. Accessed 25 April 2011.

Tebaldi, C. "An Adaptation Strategy to Address Sea Level Rise Along Coastal Developments. American Geophysical Union, Fall Meeting 2010, abstract #NH11D-06. Accessed 27 January 2011.

_____, et al. "Characterizing Impact of Local Sea Level Rise through Changes in Extreme Storm Surges along the US Coasts." American Geophysical Union, Fall Meeting 2010, abstract #GC52C-02. http://adsabs.harvard.edu/abs/2010AGUF MGC52C.02T. Accessed 14 April 2011.

_____. "Modelling Sea Level Rise Impacts on Storm Surges along US Coasts." A paper submitted to *Environmental Research Letters* in 2011. Accessed 30 August 2011.

Taleb, Nassim Nicholas. "The Black Swan: The Impact of the Highly Improbable." *New York Times*, 22 April 2007. http://www.nytimes.com/2007/04/22/boo ks/chapters/0422-1st-tale.html?page wanted=print. Accessed 10 August 2011.

Tirone, Jonathan. "Maldives' Disappearing Coast Prompts Appeal to UN Space Agency." http://sealevelrise.blogspot. com/2009/06/maldives-disappearing-coast-prompts.html. Accessed 5 November 2010.

Titus, James G. "Greenhouse Effect, Sea Level Rise, and Land Use." *Land Use Policy*, April 1990, vol. 7, no. 2; 138–53 [page numbers in the on-line edition run 1–15.] Accessed 14 April 2011.

_____. "Sea Level Rise." In Environmental Protection Agency, "The Potential Effects of Global Climate Change in the United States," 1989, Chapter 7. http://epa.gov/ climatechange/effects/downloads. Accessed 16 October 2011.

_____, and Charlie Richman. "Maps of Lands Vulnerable to Sea Level Rise." http://www.epa.gov/climatechange/ effects/coastal/slmaps_vulnerable.html. Accessed 4 March 2011.

Tol, Richard S.J., et al. "Adaptation to Five Metres of Sea Level Rise." *Journal of Risk Research*, vol. 9, no. 5, 467–482, July 2006.

_____. "The Double Trade-Off between Adaptation and Mitigation for Sea Level Rise: an Application of FUND [Framework for Uncertainty, Negotiation and Distribution]." *Mitigation and Adaptation Strategies for Global Change*, 2007, 12:741–753, 9 May 2007.

Trail, Lochran W., et al. "Managing for Change: Wetland Transitions under Sea-Level Rise and Outcomes for Threatened Species." http://onlinelibray.wiley.com/ doi/10.1111/j.1472–4642.2011,00807.x/full. Accessed 23 July 2011.

Trenberth, Kevin. "Exclusive Interview: NCAR's Trenberth on the Link between Global Warming and Extreme Deluges." Interview of June 14, 2010, in *Climate Progress*, http://climateprogress.org/2010/ 06/14/ncar-trenberth-global-warming-extreme-weather-rain-deluge. Accessed 1 May 2011.

"Tuvalu and Global Warming." http:// tuvaluislands.com/warming.htm. Accessed 1 November 2010.

UK Climate Projections. "Marine and Coastal Projections." http://ukclimate projections.defra.gov.uk/content/view/110 2/500. Accessed 10 November 10, 2010.

_____. "Reports & Guidance: Marine % Coastal Sea Level Rise Projections." Section 6. http:://ukclimateprojections.defra. gov.uk/content/view/1102/500. Accessed 10 November 2010.

Union of Concerned Scientists. "Mississippi Delta — Controlling a River: The Mississippi River Deltaic Plain." http://www. ucsusa.org/gulf/gcplacesmis.html. Accessed 11 September 2010.

_____. "Sea-Level Change." http://www.ucs usa.org/gulf/gcimpactsea.html. Accessed 11 September 2010.

United Nations Environment Programme [UNEP]. Computer-Generated Chart of Sea Level by UNEP/GRID, Geneva. Accessed 31 October 2010.

_____. "Impact of Sea Level Rise in

Bangladesh." http://maps.grida.no/gp/graphic/impact-of-Sea-Level-rise-in-bangladesh. Accessed 14 May 2011.

_____. "Potential Impact of Sea Level Rise: Nile Delta." http://www.inforse.dk/europe/dieret/Climate/climate%20graphics/34.htm. Accessed 12 May 2011.

_____. "Potential Impact of Sea Level Rise: Nile Delta — Maps and Graphics at UNEP-/GRID-Arendal." http://maps.grida.no/go/graphic-Potential-impact-of-sea-level-rise-nile-delta. Accessed 12 May 2011.

U.S. Climate Change Science Program. "Coastal Sensitivity to Sea-Level Rise: A Focus on the Mid-Atlantic Region." Synthesis and Assessment Product 4.1. January 2009. Washington: U.S. Environmental Protection Agency.

U.S. Environmental Protection Agency. "Coastal Zones and Sea Level Rise." www.epa.gov/climatechange/effects/coastal/index.html. Accessed 15 May 2010.

_____. "Future Sea Level Changes." www.epa.gov/climatechange/science/futureslc.html. Accessed 18 August 2010.

_____. "Greenhouse Gases Threaten Public Health and the Environment." http://yosemite.epa.gov/admpress.nfs/0/08D11A451131BCA58527685005BF. Accessed 8 December 2009.

_____. "Sea Level." http://cfpub.epa.gov/eroe/index.cfm?fuseaction=detail.viewInd&lv=list.listByAlha&r=18. Accessed 18 June 2010.

_____. "Sea Level Changes." http://www.epa.gov/climatchange/science/recentslc.html. Accessed 18 August 2010.

U.S. Geological Survey [USGS]. "Sea Level and Climate." http://pubs.usgs.gov/fs/fs2–00/. Accessed 2 October 2010.

_____. "Sea-Level Change." http://marine.usgs.gov/cgi-bin/locator?selected_topic=29&selected_region=n&selected_co. Accessed 19 January 2010.

_____. "Summary of the Water Cycle." http://ga.water.usgs.gov/edu/watercyclesummary.html. Accessed 7 May 2011.

_____. "Where is Earth's Water Located?" http://ga.water.usgs.gov/edu/earthwherewater.html. Accessed 19 August 2010.

University of California Los Angeles. "The Relationship between Plate Tectonics and the Carbon Cycle." http://dilu.bol.ucla.edu. Accessed 31 July 2010.

University of California San Diego. "Climate Change, Past and Future, The Ice Ages: General Overview of the Ice Ages." http://earthguide.ucsd.edu/virtualmuseum/climatechange2/01_1.shtml. Accessed 29 May 2010.

University of Illinois. "A Summary of the Hydrologic Cycle: Bringing All the Pieces Together." http://www2010.atmos.uiuc.edu/%28Gh%29/guides/mtr/hyd/smry.rxml. Accessed 2 June 2011.

University of New South Wales Climate Change Research Centre. "The Copenhagen Diagnosis, 2009: Updating the World on the Latest Climate Science." Sydney: 2009.

Unnikrishnan, A.S., et al. "Sea Changes along the Indian Coast: Observations and Projections." *Current Science*, Special Section: "Climate Change and India." Vol. 90, No. 3, 10 February 2006,

Van, Trinh Cong. "Identification of Sea Level Rise Impacts on the Mekong Delta and Orientation of Adaptation Activities." Vietnam: Hydraulic Engineering Consultant Corp. Accessed 9 May 2011.

Vaughan, David G. "West Antarctic Ice Sheet Collapse — the Fall and Rise of a Paradigm." http://nora.nerc.ac.uk/769. Accessed 12 November 2010.

_____, and John Spouge. "Risk Estimation of Collapse of the West Antarctic Ice Sheet." *Climatic Change*. 52, 65–91, 2002. Accessed 19 November 2010.

Velicogna, I., et al. "Increasing Rates of Ice Mass loss from the Greenland and Antarctic Ice Sheets Revealed by GRACE." *Geophysical Research Letters*, vol. 36, L19503, 4 pp., doi:10.1029/2009GLO40222. Accessed 20 July 2010.

Vellinga, Pier, et al. "Exploring High-End Climate Change Scenarios for Flood Protection of the Netherlands: International Scientific Assessment." Carried out at request of the Delta Committee, The Netherlands, September 2008. Accessed 18 May 2011.

Verchick, Robert R.M. *Facing Catastrophe: Environmental Action for a Post-Katrina World.* Cambridge, MA: Harvard University Press, 2010.

Vermeer, Martin, and Stefan Rahmstorf. "Global Sea Level Linked to Global Temperature." www.pnas.org/cgi/doi/10.1073/pnas.0907765106. Accessed 22 December 2009.

Visionlearning. "The Hydrologic Cycle: Water's Journey through Time." http://www.visionlearning.com/library/

module_viewer.php?mid=99. Accessed 7 May 2011.

Wada, Yoshide,, et al. "Global Depletion of Groundwater Resources." *Geophysical Research Letters*, vol. 37, L20402, 26 October 2010. http:/tanaya.ed/~tdas/data/review_iitkgp/2010gl044571.pdf. Accessed 14 January 2011.

WAIS [West Antarctic Ice Sheet] Divide Science Coordination Office. "West Antarctic Ice Sheet Divide Ice Core: Climate, Ice Sheet History, Cryobiology: A Guide for the Media and Public." Field Session 2010–2011. www.waisdivide.unh.edu. Accessed 3 January 2011.

Wang Qian. "Rise in Sea Level Reaches Record High." http://www.chinadaily.com/cn/China/2010-01/28/content_9388096. Accessed 21 October 2010.

Warrick, R., and J. Orelemanns. "Sea Level Rise." http://www/ipccreports/far/wg_I/ipcc. Accessed 22 March 2010.

Wassman, Reiner, et al. "Sea Level Rise Affecting the Vietnamese Mekong Delta: Water Elevation in the Flood Season and Implications for Rice Production" in *Earth and Environmental Science: Climatic Change.* Volume 66, Numbers 1–2, 89–107. Accessed 9 May 2011.

Water Encyclopedia. "Global Warming and the Hydrologic Cycle." http://www.waterencyclopedia.com/Ge-Hy/Global-Warming-and-the-Hydrologic-Cycle.html. Accessed 9 May 2011.

Waterland [Dutch water information network]. "Maeslant Storm Surge Barrier (The Netherlands)." http:www.waterland.net/index/cfm.site/Water%20in%20the%20Netherlands/pageid/5A2. Accessed 27 September 2010.

Weart, Spencer R. *The Discovery of Global Warming*, Cambridge, MA: Harvard University Press, 2008.

Weeks, Jennifer. "In San Francisco Bay, A Question Whether to Build or Retreat?" http://www.climatecentral.org/breaking/news/in_san_francisco_bay_a_question_whether_to. Accessed 23 September 2010.

Weiss, Jeremy L., et al. "Implications of Recent Sea Level Rise Science for Low-Elevation Areas in Coastal Cities of the Conterminous U.S.A." *Climatic Change.* Springer doi: 10.1007/s10584–011–0024-x. Accessed 10 March 2011.

"What Causes Arctic Amplification?" Subscriber email of 2 May 2010 from the Skeptical Science website.

Wikipedia. "Alexandria." http://en.wikipedia.org/wiki/Alexandria. Accessed 14 October 2010.

_____. "Antarctic Ice Sheet." http://en.wikipedia.org.wiki/Antarctic_ice_sheet. Accessed 24 May 2010.

_____. "Bengal Tiger." http://en.wikipedia.org/w/index.php?title=Bengal_tiger&printable=yes. Accessed 28 December 2011.

_____. "Black Swan Theory." http://en.wikipedia.org/w/index.php?title=Black_swan_theory&printable= yes. Accessed 15 July 2011.

_____. "Blue Marble." http://en.wikipedia.org/w/index.php?title=The_Blue_Marble&printable=yes. Accessed 1 February 2010.

_____. "Breakwater (Structure)." http://en.wikikpedka.org/w/index/php?title=Breakwater_(structure)&printable=yes. Accessed 11 October 2011.

_____. "Cryosphere." http://en.wikipedia.org/w/index.php?title=Cryospere&printable=yes. Accessed 2 June 2010.

_____. "Carteret Islands." http://en.wikipedia.org/w/inde.php?title=Carteret_Islands&printable=yes. Accessed 30 May 2011.

_____. "Cnut the Great." http://en/wikipedia.org/wiki/Cnut_the_Great. Accessed 22 January 2011.

_____. "Current Sea Level Rise." http://en.wikipedia.org/w/index.php?title=Current_sea_level_rise&printable=yes. Accessed 5 May 2011.

_____. "Delta Works." http:en.wikipedia.org/wiki/Delta_Works. Accessed 23 January 2011.

_____. "Ecology of the San Francisco Estuary." http://en.wikipedia.org.w/index.php?title=Ecology_of_the_San_Francisco_Estuary&printable. Accessed 5 March 2011.

_____. "The Edge of the Sea." http://en.wikipedia.org/w/index.php?title=The_Edge_of_the_Sea_&printable=yes. Accessed 23 March 2011.

_____. "Effects of Global Warming." http://en.wikipedia.org/wiki/Effects_of_global_warming. Accessed 22 May 2010.

_____. "Environnemental Migrant." http://en.wikipedia.org/w/index.php?title=Environmental_migrant&printabe=yes. Accessed 1 May 2011.

_____. "Flood Control in the Netherlands."

http:en.wikipedia.org.wiki/Flood_con trol_in_the_Netherlands. Accessed 24 January 2011.

_____. "Flood Myth." http://en.wikipe dia.org/w/index.php?title=Flood_myth& printable=yes. Accessed 14 July 201.

_____. "Future Sea Level." http://en.wiki pedia.org/w/index.php?title=Future_ sea_level&printable=yes. Accessed 24 February 2011.

_____. "Ganges Delta." http://en.wiki pedia.org/w/index.php?title=Ganges _Delta&printable=yes. Accessed 21 April 2011.

_____. "Global Earth Observation Systems of Systems." http://en.wikipedia.org/w/index. php?title=Global_Earth_Observation_ System_of_Systems. Accessed 22 February 2011.

_____. "Greenland Ice Sheet." http://en. wikipedia/org/w/index.php?title=Green land_ice_sheet&printable=yes. Accessed 27 March 2010.

_____. "Hydraulic Mining." http://en. wikipedia.org/w/index.php?title=Hydrau lic_mining&printable=yes. Accessed 5 March 2011.

_____. "Ice Age." http:en.wikipedia. org/wiki/Ice_age. Accessed 29 May 2010.

_____. "Intergovernmental Panel on Climate Change." http://en.wikipedia.org/wiki/ Internationalgovernmental_Panel_on_ Climate_Change. Accessed 16 May 2010.

_____. "IPCC Fifth Assessment Report." http://en.wikipedia.org/w/index.php?title =IPCC_Fifth_Assessment_Report &printable=yes. Accessed 23 February 2011.

_____. "Kiribati." http://en.wikipedia.org/ wiki.Kiribati. Accessed 27 October 2010.

_____. "Kobe." http:en.wikipedia.org/w/ index.php?title=Kobe&printable=yes. Accessed 8 March 2011.

_____. "Lagos." http://en.wikipedia.org/w/ index.php?title=Lagos&printable= yes. Accessed 10 October 2010.

_____. "List of Countries by Length of Coastline." http://en.wikipedia.org/w/ index.php?title=List_of_countries_by_ length_of_coastline&print. Accessed 25 February 2011.

_____. "Maeslantkering" [Maeslant Storm Surge Barrier]. http://en.wikipedia.org/ wiki/Maeslantkering. Accessed 2 March 2011.

_____. "Mekong Delta." http://en.wikipe dia.org/w/index.php?title=Mekong_Delta &printable=yes. Accessed 21 April 2011.

_____. "Mumbai." http://en.wikipedia. org/w/index.php?title=Mumbai&print able=yes. Accessed 8 March 2011.

_____. "New Moore/South Talpatti." http:// news.bbc.co.uk/2/hi/8584665.stm. Accessed 4 November 2010.

_____. "Nile Delta." http://en.wikipedia. org/w/index.php?title=Nile_Delta& printagle=yes. Accessed 21 April 2011.

_____. "Ocean." http://en.wikipedia.org/ wiki/Ocean. Accessed 7 May 2011.

_____. "Osaka." http://en.wikipedia.org/ w/index.php?title=Osaka&printable= yes. Accessed 8 March 2011.

_____. "Radiative Forcing." http://en.wiki pedia.org/wiki/Radiative_forcing. Accessed 31 May 2010.

_____. "San Francisco Bay." http://en.wiki pedia.org/w/index.php?title=San_ Francisco_Bay&printable=yes. Accessed 5 May 2011.

_____. "San Francisco Bay Conservation and Development Commission." http:en.wiki pedia.org/wiki/San_Francisco_Bay_ Conservation_and_Development_Com mission. Accessed 4 March 2011.

_____. "Sea Level." http://en.wikipedia. org/w/index.php?title=Sea_level&print able=yes. Accessed 24 February 2011.

_____. . "Sequence Stratigraphy." http://en wikipedia.org/wiki/Sequence_strati graphy. Accessed 29 August 2010.

_____. "Sundarbans." http://en.wikipedia. org/w/index.php?title=Sundarbans&print able=yes. Accessed 1 November 2010.

_____. "Storm Surges." http://en.wikipedia. org/w/index.php?title=Storm_surges& printable=yes. Accessed 26 February 2011.

_____. "Thames Barrier." http://en.wikipe dia.org/wiki/Thames_Barrier. Accessed 3 October 2010.

_____. "Thomas Bayes." http://en.wikipe dia.org/w/index.php?=Thomas_Bayes &printable=yes. Accessed 25 May 2011.

_____. "Tsunami." http://en.wikipedia.org/ wiki/Tsunami. Accessed 13 March 2011.

_____. "2005 Levee Failures in Greater New Orleans." http://en.wikipedia.org/wiki/ 2005_levee_failures_in_Greater_New_ Orleans. Accessed 9 September 2010.

_____. "Water board (Netherlands)." http://en.wikipedia.org/Water_board (Netherlands). Accessed 24 January 2011.

_____. "Water Cycle." http:en.wikipedia.

org/w/index.php?title=Water_cycle&print able=yes. Accessed 7 May 2011.

_____. "West Antarctic Ice Sheet." http://wn. wikipedia.org/w/index.php?title=West_ Antarctic_Ice_Sheet&printable=yes. Accessed 15 November 2010.

_____. "World Ocean." http://en.wikipe dia.org/w/index.php?title=World_Ocean &printable=yes. Accessed 8 May 2011.

Wilson, W. Stanley, et al. "Observing Systems Need to Address Sea-Level Rise and Variability." In *Understanding Sea-Level Rise and Variability* by John Church, et al., 376–401. Chichester, UK: Wiley-Blackwell, 2010.

Wong, W.T., et al. "Long Term Sea Level Change in Hong Kong." Reprint 556. Hong Kong Meteorological Society Bulletin, vol. 13, nos. 1–2, 2003, 24–40. Accessed 20 October 2010.

Woodward, Colin. "The Sinking City: Venice's $3 Billion Plan to Stop a Rising Sea Gets Mixed Review." *The Environmental Magazine*, March-April 2003. http://findarticles.com/p/articles/mi_m1594/ is_2_14/ai_98469933/. Accessed 7 October 2010.

Woodworth, Philip L. "Extreme Sea Levels." www.psmsl.org/train_and_info/training/ ...chile/PW_chile-extreme. PPT. Accessed 12 February 2011.

World Delta Database. "Ganges-Brahmaputra Delta, India, Asia." http: www.geo.lsu.edu/WDD/ASIAN/Ganges-Brahmaputra/ganga.htm. Accessed 21 April 2011.

World Resources Institute. "Coastline length." http://earthtrends.wri.org/text /coastal-marine/variable-61.html. Accessed 23 July 2010.

WWF-World Wide Fund for Nature. "Mega-Stress for Mega-Cities: A Climate Vulnerability Ranking of Major Coastal Cities in Asia." 2009. assets.panda.org/downloads/ mega_cities_report.pdf. Accessed 4 November 2010.

Yale Project on Communication Change. "Publications and Reports: Global Warming's Six Americas 2010." http://environment.yale.edu/climate/publications/globa l-warmings-six-americas-jan-20. Accessed 18 April 2011.

Yin, Jianjung, et al. "Spatial Variability of Sea Level Rise in Twenty-First Century Projections." American Meteorological Society, 2010.

Yin, Jie, et al. "Multiple Scenario Analyses Forecasting the Confounding Impacts of Sea Level Rise and Tides from Storm-Induced Coastal Flooding in the City of Shanghai, China." *Earth and Environmental Science*, 1 October 2010. Accessed 30 October 2010.

Yoskowitz, David W., James Gibeaut, and Ali McKensie. "The Socio-Economic Impact of Sea Level Rise in the Galveston Bay Region: Executive Summary." Harte Research Institute for Gulf of Mexico Studies, Texas A&M University — Corpus Christi, June 2009.

Young, I.R., et al. "Global Trends in Wind Speed and Wave Height." *Sciencexpress*, www.sciencesxpress.org, 24 March 2011, p. 1/10.1126/science.1197219. Accessed 31 March 2011.

Young, Rob, and Orrin Pilkey. "How High Will Seas Rise? Great Ready for Seven Feet." *Yale Environment 360.* 14 January 2010. e360.yale.edu/content/feature. ms?id=2230. Accessed 13 January 2011.

Zwally, H. Jay, et al. "Greenland Ice Sheet Mass Balance: Distribution of Increased Mass Loss with Climate Warming; 2003–07 versus 1992–2002." *Journal of Glaciology*, Vol. 57. No. 201, 2111. Accessed 30 March 2011.

_____. "Mass Changes of the Greenland and Antarctic Ice Sheets and Shelves and Contributions to Sea-Level Rise: 1992–2002." *Journal of Glaciology*, vol. 51, no. 175, 2005. http://icesat.gsfc.nasa.gov/icesat/publications. Accessed 29 March 20ll.

Index